Windows® INTERNET EXPLORER®

INTRODUCTORY

D0165213

Gary B. Shelly

Steven M. Freund

COURSE TECHNOLOGY
CENGAGE Learning®

Australia • Brazil • Japan • Korea • Mexico • Singapore • Spain • United Kingdom • United States

COURSE TECHNOLOGY
CENGAGE Learning

Windows® Internet Explorer® 9: Introductory
Gary B. Shelly
Steven M. Freund

Vice President, Publisher: Nicole Pinard

Executive Editor: Kathleen McMahon

Product Manager: Nada Jovanovic

Associate Product Manager: Caitlin Womersley

Editorial Assistant: Angela Giannopoulos

Director of Marketing: Elisa Roberts

Senior Marketing Manager: Tristen Kendall

Marketing Coordinator: Adrienne Fung

Production Director: Patty Stephan

Senior Content Project Manager: Jill Braiewa

Art Director: Marissa Falco

Print Buyer: Julio Esperas

Developmental Editor: Karen Stevens

Text Designer: Joel Sadagursky

Cover Designer: Lisa Kuhn, Curio Press, LLC

Cover Photo: Tom Kates Photography

Copyeditor: Karen Annett

Proofreader: Suzanne Huizenga

Indexer: Alexandra Nickerson

Compositor: GEX Publishing Services

© 2012 Course Technology, Cengage Learning

ALL RIGHTS RESERVED. No part of this work covered by the copyright herein may be reproduced, transmitted, stored or used in any form or by any means graphic, electronic, or mechanical, including but not limited to photocopying, recording, scanning, digitizing, taping, Web distribution, information networks, or information storage and retrieval systems, except as permitted under Section 107 or 108 of the 1976 United States Copyright Act, without the prior written permission of the publisher.

For product information and technology assistance, contact us at
Cengage Learning Customer & Sales Support, 1-800-354-9706

For permission to use material from this text or product, submit all requests online at **cengage.com/permissions**
Further permissions questions can be emailed to
permissionrequest@cengage.com

Library of Congress Control Number: 2011936166

ISBN-13: 978-0-538-48239-4

ISBN-10: 0-538-48239-7

Course Technology
20 Channel Center Street
Boston, Massachusetts 02210
USA

Microsoft, Windows, and the Internet Explorer logo are either registered trademarks or trademarks of Microsoft Corporation in the United States and/or other countries. Course Technology, a part of Cesngage Learning, is an independent entity from the Microsoft Corporation, and not affiliated with Microsoft in any manner.

Cengage Learning is a leading provider of customized learning solutions with office locations around the globe, including Singapore, the United Kingdom, Australia, Mexico, Brazil, and Japan. Locate your local office at:
www.cengage.com/global

Cengage Learning products are represented in Canada by Nelson Education, Ltd.

To learn more about Course Technology, visit **www.cengage.com/coursetechnology**

To learn more about Cengage Learning, visit **www.cengage.com**

Purchase any of our products at your local college bookstore or at our preferred online store **www.cengagebrain.com**

d in the United States of America
5 6 7 17 16 15 14 13 12 11

Windows
INTERNET EXPLORER® 9
INTRODUCTORY

Contents

Appendices

Preface

The Shelly Cashman Series® offers the finest textbooks in computer education. We are proud of the fact that the previous editions of this textbook have been so well received by computer educators. With each new edition, we have made significant improvements based on the software and comments made by instructors and students. *Windows Internet Explorer 9* continues with the innovation, quality, and reliability that you have come to expect from the Shelly Cashman Series.

In the short time since its birth, the World Wide Web has grown beyond all expectations. During this time, Web usage has increased from a limited number of users to billions of users worldwide, accessing Web pages on any topic you can imagine. Individuals, schools, businesses, and government agencies are all taking advantage of this innovative way of accessing the Internet to provide information, products, services, and education electronically. *Windows Internet Explorer 9* provides the novice as well as the experienced user a window with which to look into the Web and tap an abundance of resources.

Objectives of This Textbook

Windows Internet Explorer 9: Introductory is intended for use in a one-credit, three- to five-week course, or in combination with other books in an introductory computer concepts or applications course. The objectives of this book are:

- To teach students how to use Internet Explorer 9, including features like Accelerators, Web Slices, tabbed browsing, and RSS Feeds, as well as its redesigned interface

- To expose students to various resources on the Internet

- To acquaint students with popular search engines

- To show students how to evaluate Web pages and do research using the World Wide Web

- To teach students how to communicate via the Internet, including e-mail, online social networking, and instant messaging

The Shelly Cashman Approach

A Proven Pedagogy with an Emphasis on Project Planning

Each chapter presents a practical problem to be solved, within a project planning framework. The project orientation is strengthened by the use of Plan Ahead boxes, that encourage critical thinking about how to proceed at various points in the project. Step-by-step instructions with supporting screens guide students through the steps. Instructional steps are supported by the Q&A, Experimental Step, and BTW features.

A Visually Engaging Book that Maintains Student Interest

The step-by-step tasks, with supporting figures, provide a rich visual experience for the student. Call-outs on the screens that present both explanatory and navigational information provide students with information they need when they need to know it.

Supporting Reference Materials (Quick Reference, Appendices)

The appendices provide additional information about the Application at hand, such as the Help Feature and customizing the application. With the Quick Reference, students can quickly look up information about a single task, such as keyboard shortcuts, and find page references of where in the book the task is illustrated.

Integration of the World Wide Web

The World Wide Web is integrated into the Internet Explorer 9 learning experience by (1) BTW annotations; (2) a Quick Reference Summary Web page; and (3) the Learn It Online section for each chapter.

End-of-Chapter Student Activities

Extensive end-of-chapter activities provide a variety of reinforcement opportunities for students where they can apply and expand their skills through individual and group work.

Instructor Resources

The Instructor Resources include both teaching and testing aids and can be accessed via CD-ROM or at login.cengage.com.

Instructor's Manual Includes lecture notes summarizing the chapter sections, figures and boxed elements found in every chapter, teacher tips, classroom activities, lab activities, and quick quizzes in Microsoft Word files.

Syllabus Easily customizable sample syllabi that cover policies, assignments, exams, and other course information.

Figure Files Illustrations for every figure in the textbook in electronic form.

Powerpoint Presentations A multimedia lecture presentation system that provides slides for each chapter. Presentations are based on chapter objectives.

Solutions To Exercises Includes solutions for all chapter reinforcement exercises.

Test Bank & Test Engine Test Banks include 112 questions for every chapter, featuring objective-based and critical thinking question types, and including page number references and figure references, when appropriate. Also included is the test engine, ExamView, the ultimate tool for your objective-based testing needs.

Additional Activities For Students Consists of Chapter Reinforcement Exercises, which are true/false, multiple-choice, and short answer questions that help students gain confidence in the material learned.

Online Companion at CengageBrain.com

The Online Companion includes Learn It Online exercises for each chapter, as well as BTWs, Q&As, and The Great Outdoors Web site. To access these course materials, please visit **www.cengagebrain.com**. At the CengageBrain.com home page, search for *Windows Internet Explorer 9: Introductory* using the search box at the top of the page. This will take you to the product page where you can click the Access Now button below the Study Tools heading.

SAM: Skills Assessment Manager

SAM 2010 is designed to help bring students from the classroom to the real world. It allows students to train on and test important computer skills in an active, hands-on environment.

SAM's easy-to-use system includes powerful interactive exams, training, and projects on the most commonly used Microsoft Office applications. SAM simulates the Microsoft Office 2010 application environment, allowing students to demonstrate their knowledge and think through the skills by performing real-world tasks such as bolding word text or setting up slide transitions. Add in live-in-the-application projects, and students are on their way to truly learning and applying skills to business-centric documents.

Designed to be used with the Shelly Cashman Series, SAM includes handy page references so that students can print helpful study guides that match the Shelly Cashman textbooks used in class. For instructors, SAM also includes robust scheduling and reporting features.

Content for Online Learning

Course Technology has partnered with the leading distance learning solution providers and class-management platforms today. To access this material, instructors will visit our password-protected instructor resources available at login.cengage.com Instructor resources include the following: additional case projects, sample syllabi, PowerPoint presentations per chapter, and more. For additional information or for an instructor user name and password, please contact your sales representative. For students to access this material, they must have purchased a WebTutor PIN-code specific to this title and your campus platform. The resources for students may include (based on instructor preferences), but are not limited to: topic review, review questions, and practice tests.

CourseNotes

Course Technology's CourseNotes are six-panel quick reference cards that reinforce the most important and widely used features of a software application or technology concept in a visual and user-friendly format. CourseNotes serve as a great reference tool for students, both during and after the course.

CourseNotes are available for Google Apps: Recharged, Web 2.0: Recharged, Buyer's Guide: Tips for Purchasing a New Computer, Best Practices in Social Networking, Hot Topics in Technology and many more. Visit **www.cengagebrain.com** to learn more!

A Guided Tour

Add excitement and interactivity to your classroom with "*A Guided Tour*" product line. Play one of the brief mini-movies to spice up your lecture and spark classroom discussion. Or, assign a movie for homework and ask students to complete the correlated assignment that accompanies each topic. "*A Guided Tour*" product line takes the prep work out of providing your students with information about new technologies and applications and helps keep students engaged with content relevant to their lives; all in under an hour!

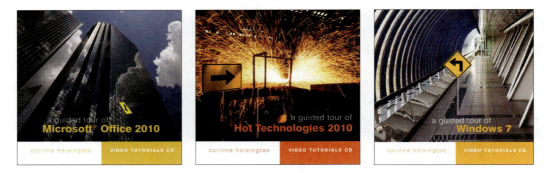

About Our Covers

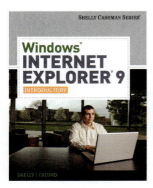

The Shelly Cashman Series is continually updating our approach and content to reflect the way today's students learn and experience new technology. This focus on student success is reflected on our covers, which feature real students from Bryant University using the Shelly Cashman Series in their courses, and reflect the varied ages and backgrounds of the students learning with our books. When you use the Shelly Cashman Series, you can be assured that you are learning computer skills using the most effective courseware available.

Textbook Walk-Through

The Shelly Cashman Series Pedagogy: Project-Based — Step-by-Step — Variety of Assessments

Plan Ahead boxes prepare students to create successful projects by encouraging them to think strategically about what they are trying to accomplish before they begin working.

Step-by-step instructions now provide a context beyond the point-and-click. Each step provides information on why students are performing each task, or what will occur as a result.

Introduction to Internet Explorer

Introduction

The Internet is one of the most popular and fastest growing areas in computing today. Using the Internet, you can do research for a class, send and receive files, obtain a loan, shop for services and merchandise, search for a job, buy and sell stocks, display weather maps, obtain medical advice, watch movies, listen to high-quality music, and converse with people worldwide.

Although a complex system of hardware and software forms the Internet, it is accessible to the general public because personal computers with user-friendly tools have reduced its complexity. The Internet, with its millions of connected computers, continues to grow with thousands of new users coming online each day. Schools, businesses, newspapers, television stations, and government agencies all can be found on the Internet. All around the world, service providers offer access to the Internet free of charge or for minimal cost.

Overview

As you read this chapter, you will learn how to browse the Web and use Internet Explorer by performing these general tasks:

- Start Internet Explorer
- Enter a Web address in the Address bar
- Browse a Web page by clicking links and using the Back and Forward buttons
- Navigate to previously viewed Web pages by using the History list and the Favorites Center
- Save a picture from a Web page
- Save a Web page
- Print a Web page

Plan Ahead

Internet Usage Guidelines
Internet usage involves navigating to, viewing, and interacting with the various resources on the Internet. Preparations you make before using the Internet will determine the effectiveness of your experience. Before using the Internet, you should follow these general guidelines:

1. **Determine whether your computer has the proper hardware and software necessary to connect to the Internet.** Connecting to the Internet requires your computer to communicate with other computers. Special hardware and software, discussed later in this chapter, are designed to facilitate this communication. If you are unsure of whether your computer is capable of connecting to the Internet, a technician from a company that provides Internet access will be able to help.

(continued)

IE 2

BTW

Clearing the History List
If the list of Web sites you have visited has become too large to be meaningful, you might want to clear the History list. You can clear the History list by clicking the Tools button on the toolbar, pointing to Safety, clicking 'Delete browsing history' on the Safety submenu, verifying that a check mark appears in the History check box, and then clicking the Delete button (Delete Browsing History dialog box). Clearing the History list also clears the Address bar Autocomplete list.

Using the History List to Displa

Internet Explorer maintains another list o
History list. The History list is a list of Web pag
(over many sessions). You can use this list to dis
time. Clicking the 'View favorites, feeds, and his
History tab, and then clicking Today displays th

To find a recently visited Web page using
History list, select the order in which you want
desired Web page title. The Web page titles can
or order visited today. In addition, you are able
Web site.

If you are browsing the World Wide Web
might not want Internet Explorer to save any in
visited. **InPrivate Browsing** is a feature that all
Web browser recording any information. For ex
using InPrivate Browsing, Internet Explorer wi
will it save any cookies or other temporary Inte
InPrivate Browsing, click the Tools button on t
InPrivate Browsing on the Safety submenu. Inte
with an InPrivate icon in the Address bar. Whe
mode, simply close the window.

To Display a Web Page Using the History List

If you have a small list of pages you have visited, or the Web page you want to view is only one or two pages away, using the Back and Forward buttons to traverse the lists will likely be faster than displaying the Recent Pages list and selecting the correct title. If you have visited a large number of pages, however, you will need to step forward or back through many pages, and it might be easier to use the Address bar Autocomplete list or the History list to select the exact page. To display a recently visited Web page without having to click the Back button multiple times, perform the following steps to display the Web page using the History list.

1
- Click the 'View favorites, feeds, and history' button on the toolbar to display the Favorites Center.
- Click the Pin the Favorites Center button to pin the Favorites Center to the Internet Explorer window (Figure 1–24).

Q&A
Why did the Favorites Center move?

When the Favorites Center is pinned, it

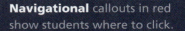

Figure 1–24

appears on the left side of the display area. When the Favorites Center is not pinned, it appears on the right side of the display area.

BTW

Screen Shots
Callouts in screen shots give students information they need, when they need to know it. The Series has always used plenty of callouts to ensure that students don't get lost. Now color is used to distinguish the content in the callouts to make them more meaningful.

Navigational callouts in red show students where to click.

Explanatory callouts summarize what is happening on screen.

Textbook Walk-Through

Q&A boxes offer questions students may have when working through the steps and provide additional information about what they are doing right where they need it.

Experiment Steps within our step-by-step instructions encourage students to explore, experiment, and take advantage of new software features. These steps are not necessary to complete the projects, but are designed to increase the confidence with the software and build problem-solving skills.

To Browse the Web by Entering a Web Address

To navigate to the home page for the Great Outdoors Travel Web site, you will need to enter the Web address in the Address bar.

1
• Click the Address bar to highlight the Web address (Figure 1–9).

Figure 1–9

2
• Type `www.scsite.com/ie9/greatoutdoors` in the Address bar to enter the new Web address (Figure 1–10).

Q&A Why is it unnecessary to type http:// at the beginning of each Web address?

Depending on how the Web server is configured, it might not require you to type http:// or www. at the beginning of the Web address. In the case of this Web site, you can type `scsite.com/ie9/greatoutdoors` or `www.scsite.com/ie9/greatoutdoors` as the Web address.

Q&A What if I typed the wrong Web address?

If you type the wrong letter and notice the error before pressing the ENTER key, use the BACKSPACE key to erase all the characters back to and including the one that is wrong. If the error is easier to retype than correct, click the Web address in the Address bar and retype it correctly.

Figure 1–10

3
• Click the Add button (Add a Favorite dialog box) to add the Great Outdoors Travel Web page to the Favorites Center.

• Click the 'View favorites, feeds, and history' button on the toolbar, and then click the Favorites tab, if necessary, to display the Favorites Center and verify the new favorite is add

• Close the Favorites Center.

Experiment

• After you add the favorite, check the Favorites menu to verify that your new favorite appears in the list. Press the ALT key to display the menu bar, press A, verify that the favorite appears, and then press the ESC key twice to close the Favorites menu and hide the menu bar.

Other Ways
1. Press the ALT key, click Favorites on menu bar, and then click 'Add to favorites'
2. Press CTRL+D, press ENTER
3. Press ALT+A, press A, press ENTER

BTW

Importing and Exporting Favorites
If you already have favorite Web sites set up on another computer or Web browser, or want to transfer your favorite Web sites to another computer, you can use Internet Explorer's Import/Export Wizard to preserve your favorites. Click the 'View favorites, feeds, and history' button on the toolbar, click the 'Add to favorites' list arrow in the Favorites Center, and then click 'Import and export' to start the Import/Export Wizard. Follow the steps in the wizard to import or export your favorites.

If you plan to store many favorites on your computer, you might choose to give your favorite Web sites meaningful names by renaming them and storing them in folders. In the Add a Favorite dialog box shown in Figure 1–30, clicking the New folder button displays the Create a Folder dialog box. Next, you can name the folder by typing an appropriate name in the Folder Name text box, and then clicking the Create button. After renaming the folder, you can drag an existing favorite to the folder to store the favorite in that folder. You also can change the name of a folder or favorite in the Favorites Center by clicking a folder or favorite in the Organize Favorites dialog box, clicking Rename, typing the new name, and then pressing the ENTER key. For example, if you frequently visit many Web sites to read the news, you might choose to store the Web addresses of these sites as favorites in a News folder. If you are a student, for example, you might store school-related Web sites in an Academics folder.

Other Ways boxes that follow many of the step sequences explain the other ways to complete the task presented.

To Quit Internet Explorer

The following step quits Internet Explorer.

1
- Click the Close button in the upper-right corner of the Internet Explorer window to close the window (Figure 1–63).

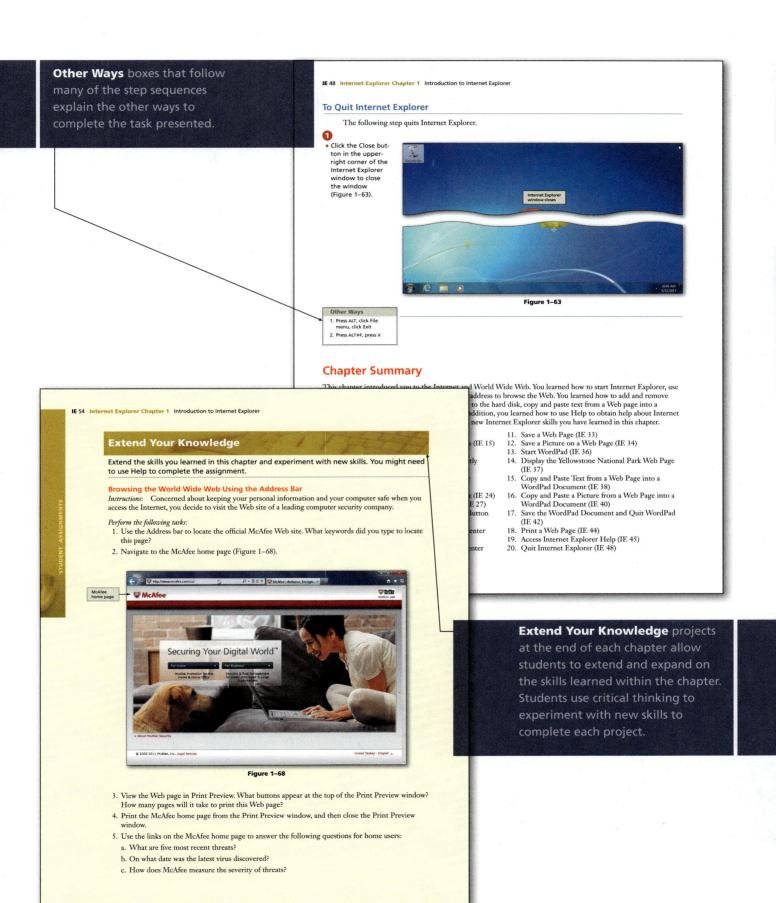

Internet Explorer window closes

Figure 1–63

Other Ways
1. Press ALT, click File menu, click Exit
2. Press ALT+F, press X

Chapter Summary

This chapter introduced you to the Internet and World Wide Web. You learned how to start Internet Explorer, use address to browse the Web. You learned how to add and remove to the hard disk, copy and paste text from a Web page into a addition, you learned how to use Help to obtain help about Internet new Internet Explorer skills you have learned in this chapter.

11. Save a Web Page (IE 33)
s (IE 15)   12. Save a Picture on a Web Page (IE 34)
13. Start WordPad (IE 36)
tly   14. Display the Yellowstone National Park Web Page (IE 37)
15. Copy and Paste Text from a Web Page into a WordPad Document (IE 38)
(IE 24)   16. Copy and Paste a Picture from a Web Page into a
E 27)   WordPad Document (IE 40)
Button   17. Save the WordPad Document and Quit WordPad (IE 42)
enter   18. Print a Web Page (IE 44)
19. Access Internet Explorer Help (IE 45)
enter   20. Quit Internet Explorer (IE 48)

STUDENT ASSIGNMENTS

Extend Your Knowledge

Extend the skills you learned in this chapter and experiment with new skills. You might need to use Help to complete the assignment.

Browsing the World Wide Web Using the Address Bar
Instructions: Concerned about keeping your personal information and your computer safe when you access the Internet, you decide to visit the Web site of a leading computer security company.

Perform the following tasks:
1. Use the Address bar to locate the official McAfee Web site. What keywords did you type to locate this page?
2. Navigate to the McAfee home page (Figure 1–68).

McAfee home page

Securing Your Digital World™

Figure 1–68

3. View the Web page in Print Preview. What buttons appear at the top of the Print Preview window? How many pages will it take to print this Web page?
4. Print the McAfee home page from the Print Preview window, and then close the Print Preview window.
5. Use the links on the McAfee home page to answer the following questions for home users:
   a. What are five most recent threats?
   b. On what date was the latest virus discovered?
   c. How does McAfee measure the severity of threats?

Extend Your Knowledge projects at the end of each chapter allow students to extend and expand on the skills learned within the chapter. Students use critical thinking to experiment with new skills to complete each project.

Textbook Walk-Through

In the Lab

Lab 2: Adding, Viewing, Printing, and Removing Your Favorites

Instructions: Your instructor would like you to practice browsing the Internet and adding Web sites to the Favorites Center. As proof of completing this assignment, print out the first page of each Web site you visit.

Perform the following tasks:
Part 1: Create a Folder in the Favorites Center
1. Click the 'View favorites, feeds, and history' button on the toolbar, click the 'Add to favorites' list arrow, and then click Organize favorites to display the Organize Favorites dialog box (Figure 1–71).

Figure 1–71

2. Click the New Folder button in the Organize Favorites dialog
   folder, type your first and last name as the folder name, and the
3. Click the Close button to close the Organize Favorites dialog b

Part 2: Add Favorites to Your Folder
1. Click the Address bar, type **www.defense.gov** to enter th
   ENTER key to display U.S. Department of Defense home page.
2. Add a U.S. Department of Defense favorite to the folder identi
   'View favorites, feeds, and history' button on the toolbar, and th
   button (Figure 1–72). Click the Create in drop-down list butto

The in-depth **In the Lab** assignments require students to utilize the chapter concepts and techniques to solve problems on a computer.

---

2. Type **InPrivate Browsing** in the Search Help text box, press the ENTER key, and browse the topics necessary to answer the following questions.
   a. What is InPrivate Browsing?
   b. What is InPrivate Filtering?
3. Select the text in the Search box, type **SmartScreen Filter**, press the ENTER key, and browse the search results to answer the following questions.
   a. What is the SmartScreen Filter?
   b. How do you report a phishing Web site?
4. Select the text in the Search box, type **Tracking Protection**, press the ENTER key, and browse the search results to answer the following questions.
   a. What is tracking protection?
   b. How do you turn on tracking protection?
5. Select the text in the Search box, type **Download Manager**, press the ENTER key, and browse the search results to answer the following question.
   a. What is the Download Manager?
   b. How can you choose where downloads are stored?
6. Select the text in the Search box, type **keyboard shortcuts**, press the ENTER key, and browse the search results to answer the following questions.
   a. What is the keyboard shortcut to select the text in the Address bar?
   b. What is the keyboard shortcut to open an InPrivate Browsing window?
   c. What is the keyboard shortcut to delete the browsing history?
7. Close the Windows Help and Support window.
8. Close the Internet Explorer window.
9. Submit the answers to the questions to your instructor.

Cases and Places

Apply your creative thinking and problem-solving skills to browse for information.

1: Browsing the Web for Stock Information

Academic

Your assignment in your finance class is to find fundamental stock information about three companies of your choice—for example, Microsoft Corporation (MSFT), Google Inc. (GOOG), or Apple Inc. (AAPL). Use the Yahoo! Finance Web site (finance.yahoo.com) to obtain today's stock price, dividend rate (look for Div value), daily volume, 52-week range, and the P/E (price earnings ratio). To display this information, enter the stock symbol and then click the Get Quotes button to display the information. Print the detailed results for each stock. In addition, click the first article under the Headlines heading for the stock of your choice and then print the page.

Continued >

The **Cases & Places** exercises call on students to apply creative thinking and problem-solving skills.

Windows®
INTERNET
EXPLORER® 9

INTRODUCTORY

1 | Introduction to Internet Explorer

Objectives

You will have mastered the material in this chapter when you can:

- Define the Internet and the World Wide Web
- Discuss security concerns on the Internet
- Explain a link, a Web address, and Hypertext Markup Language (HTML)
- Describe Internet Explorer features
- Enter a Web address
- Use the History list and the Favorites Center

- Use buttons on the toolbar
- Add and remove a favorite
- Save a picture or text from a Web page or an entire Web page
- Copy and paste text or pictures from a Web page into WordPad
- Print a WordPad document and Web page
- Use Internet Explorer Help

Introduction to Internet Explorer

Introduction

The Internet is one of the most popular and fastest growing areas in computing today. Using the Internet, you can do research for a class, send and receive files, obtain a loan, shop for services and merchandise, search for a job, buy and sell stocks, display weather maps, obtain medical advice, watch movies, listen to high-quality music, and converse with people worldwide.

Although a complex system of hardware and software forms the Internet, it is accessible to the general public because personal computers with user-friendly tools have reduced its complexity. The Internet, with its millions of connected devices, continues to grow with thousands of new users coming online each day. Schools, businesses, newspapers, television stations, and government agencies all can be found on the Internet. All around the world, service providers offer access to the Internet free of charge or for minimal cost.

Overview

As you read this chapter, you will learn how to browse the Web and use Internet Explorer by performing these general tasks:

- Start Internet Explorer
- Enter a Web address in the Address bar
- Browse a Web page by clicking links and using the Back and Forward buttons
- Navigate to previously viewed Web pages by using the History list and the Favorites Center
- Save a picture from a Web page
- Save a Web page
- Print a Web page

Plan Ahead

Internet Usage Guidelines
Internet usage involves navigating to, viewing, and interacting with the various resources on the Internet. Preparations you make before using the Internet will determine the effectiveness of your experience. Before using the Internet, you should follow these general guidelines:

1. **Determine whether your computer has the proper hardware and software necessary to connect to the Internet.** Connecting to the Internet requires your computer to communicate with other computers. Special hardware and software, discussed later in this chapter, are designed to facilitate this communication. If you are unsure of whether your computer is capable of connecting to the Internet, a technician from a company that provides Internet access will be able to help.

(continued)

(continued)

2. **Choose an appropriate method to connect to the Internet.** The quality and speed of your Internet connection plays an important role in your overall experience. Various Internet connection options are available, and it is important to choose one that not only allows you to quickly and easily access the information that you desire but also falls within your price range.

3. **Determine whether your computer is protected properly from threats on the Internet.** The Internet can be a breeding ground for software that can do harm to your computer. You should not connect to the Internet unless you have the proper software installed on your computer that will protect you from these various threats.

4. **Determine why you are using the Internet.** People connect to the Internet for many reasons. If you are connecting to the Internet to accomplish a specific task, be clear about what you want to accomplish and then identify which resources might prove useful. Many people find it easy to become distracted from the task at hand when they are online.

5. **Determine how much time you want to spend on the Internet.** For some people, the Internet can be an extremely addictive environment. In fact, many companies that provide Internet access to their employees have strict policies in place that outline what they consider to be acceptable Internet usage while on the job. The Internet has the potential to significantly lower an employee's productivity, thus costing the employer money. Similarly, parents should be concerned that their children have a safe experience online. Parents can guide children to age-appropriate content and teach their children to keep personal information private.

Using the Internet not only can be addicting, it also can be costly. Depending upon the method you use to connect to the Internet, the amount that you are charged to connect can directly relate to the amount of data you transfer while connected. Some Internet connection plans allow unlimited usage, while others might only allow you to transfer a certain amount of data before charging an additional fee.

The Internet

The **Internet** is a worldwide collection of networks (Figure 1–1 on the next page), each of which is composed of a collection of smaller networks. A **network** is composed of several computers connected together to share resources and data. For example, on a college campus, the network in the student computer lab can connect to the faculty computer network, which is connected to the administration network, and they all can connect to the Internet.

BTW

The Internet
The Internet started as a government experiment for the United States military. The military wanted the ability to connect to and communicate via different computers running different operating systems. From this experiment, a communication technique originated called Transmission Control Protocol/Internet Protocol, or TCP/IP.

Figure 1–1

Networks are connected with high-, medium-, and low-speed data lines that allow data to move from one computer to another (Figure 1–2). The Internet has high-speed data lines that connect major computers located around the world, which form the Internet backbone. Other, less-powerful computers, such as those used by local ISPs (Internet service providers), often attach to the Internet backbone using medium-speed data lines. Finally, the connection between your computer at home and your local ISP, often called the last mile, employs low-speed data lines such as telephone lines, cable television lines, and fiber-optic cable. In some cases today, fixed wireless access is replacing wires over the last mile, which significantly improves access to the Internet.

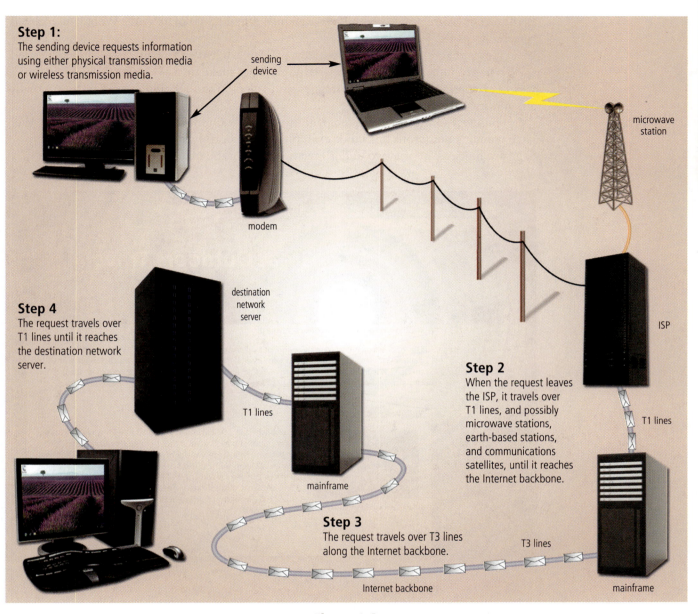

Step 1:
The sending device requests information using either physical transmission media or wireless transmission media.

sending device

microwave station

modem

Step 4
The request travels over T1 lines until it reaches the destination network server.

destination network server

T1 lines

mainframe

ISP

Step 2
When the request leaves the ISP, it travels over T1 lines, and possibly microwave stations, earth-based stations, and communications satellites, until it reaches the Internet backbone.

T1 lines

mainframe

Step 3
The request travels over T3 lines along the Internet backbone.

T3 lines

Internet backbone

Figure 1–2

The World Wide Web

Modern computers and many digital devices have the capability of delivering information in a variety of ways, using images, sound, video, animation, virtual reality, and, of course, regular text. This multimedia capability is known as **hypermedia**, which is the combination of text, images, audio, video, and interactivity, delivered over the Internet.

You access hypermedia by clicking a **hyperlink**, or simply a **link**, which points to the location of the computer on which the hypermedia is stored and to the hypermedia itself. A link, which can be in the form of text or an image, can point to hypermedia on any computer connected to the Internet that is configured as a Web server. A **Web server**, which runs Web server software, provides resources such as text, images, files, and links to other computers on the Internet. Thus, clicking a link on a computer in New York City could display hypermedia located in San Diego. All of the resources and links found throughout

BTW

Web Sites
An organization can have more than one Web site. Separate departments might have their own Web servers, allowing faster response to requests for Web pages and local control over the Web pages stored at that Web site.

the Internet create an interconnected network called the **World Wide Web**, which also is referred to as the **Web**, or WWW.

Text, images, and other hypermedia available at a Web site are stored in a file called a **Web page**, and a collection of related Web pages make up a **Web site**. When you are viewing hypermedia such as text, images, and video on the World Wide Web, you actually are viewing a Web page.

Figure 1–3 illustrates a Web page at the Great Outdoors Travel Web site. This Web page contains numerous links. For example, the six buttons on the left side of the Web page are links, as are the two underlined headings in the main text.

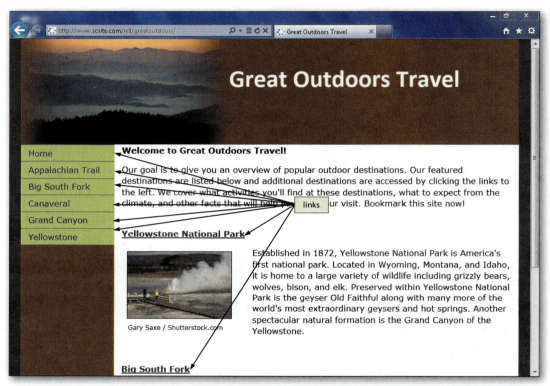

Figure 1–3

Security Concerns on the Internet

BTW

Microsoft Security Essentials
Microsoft Security Essentials is a program that provides virus, spyware, and other malicious software protection, free of charge to Windows users. To download Microsoft Security Essentials, navigate to Microsoft's Web site (microsoft.com) and search for Microsoft Security Essentials.

Although there are many advantages to accessing and using the Internet, consider some of the disadvantages to Internet access. When your computer connects to the Internet, other computers can see your computer and possibly connect to it. Computer-savvy individuals with malicious intentions sometimes take advantage of Internet users who do not take the proper security precautions—by deleting, modifying, or even stealing their data, often without their knowledge. A person or Web site could install spyware on your computer. **Spyware** is a program that tracks the actions you take on your computer, such as which Web sites you visit, what products you purchase online, and your credit card information, and sends them to a third party. Spyware can decrease your computer's performance, as well as compromise any secure information you have stored on your computer. Another type of malicious software that can be installed on your computer without your knowledge is adware. **Adware** randomly displays advertisements and other messages while you use your computer. Adware and spyware could be installed by someone who connects to an unsecure computer, or by downloading and running a program or file from the Internet. To avoid downloading harmful files and programs, it is important to learn how to tell the difference between legitimate and fraudulent Web sites, files, and programs on the Internet.

In addition to adware and spyware, your computer also could be infected by a computer **virus** if you download an infected file from a Web page or open an infected e-mail attachment. Your computer also can be infected by a virus if someone exploits a security vulnerability, or bug, in a program that is installed on your computer.

Adware, spyware, and viruses are not the only problems that exist on the Internet. **Phishing scams**, or attempts by individuals to obtain confidential information from you, often via the Internet, are growing in popularity. A phishing scam works by falsifying one's identity in an attempt to convince an unsuspecting victim to disclose information such as credit card numbers, bank account information, and Social Security number. A **phisher** might falsify his or her identity by sending an e-mail that appears to come from someone else, or by creating a Web site that appears to be that of a legitimate company. The worst part about a phishing scam is that the victim often does not know that someone else took advantage of him or her until it is too late. Victims of phishing scams also can be exposed to identity theft and financial loss.

To lower the risk of being victimized by a malicious Web site or a phishing scam, Internet Explorer 9 includes a SmartScreen Filter. The **SmartScreen Filter** is designed to identify malicious and fraudulent Web sites, and will inform you by displaying an appropriate warning. While the SmartScreen Filter might not detect all malicious and fraudulent Web sites, it greatly reduces your chances of visiting a malicious Web site or becoming a victim of a phishing scam.

Because of these security threats, it is important for everyone to practice safe browsing techniques while connected to the Internet. Before connecting your computer to the Internet, you should make sure that you have antivirus software installed. **Antivirus software** will inform you if it detects a virus on your computer. Antivirus software manufacturers release virus definition updates that "teach" the software how to detect newly created viruses. In addition to installing antivirus software, you should install a software firewall on your computer. A software **firewall** blocks unauthorized connections to and from your computer. When using your computer on the Internet, it is important to regularly scan your computer for adware and spyware. Some adware and spyware scanners are available online for free or for a fee, and some are available in retail stores that sell computer software.

To combat security vulnerabilities that are present in programs installed on your computer, software manufacturers often release updates, also known as patches or service packs, which correct these vulnerabilities. It is good practice to install these updates as soon as they become available. The Automatic Update feature in Windows, for example, can be configured to automatically download and install security updates as they become available. Finally, be selective with the Web sites you visit. Millions of Web sites exist on the Internet today, and it is easy to arrive inadvertently at a site other than the one you intended to visit. In addition, you should take extra precaution while visiting Web sites that are hosted by unknown individuals or obscure companies. Avoid downloading anything from these sites or entering any personal information. If you are unsure of whether a Web site is legitimate, it is better to be cautious and simply navigate to another site.

Web Addresses

Each Web page has a unique address, called a **Web address**, usually referred to as a **Uniform Resource Locator** (**URL**), which distinguishes it from all other pages on the Internet. The Web address in Figure 1–3 is http://www.scsite.com/ie9/greatoutdoors.

A Web address is composed of multiple parts (Figure 1–4 on the next page). The first part is the protocol. A **protocol** is a set of rules. Most Web pages use the Hypertext

BTW

Online Security
Because of the importance of protecting yourself and your computer while you are connected to the Internet, the government and other organizations have developed Web sites that offer advice and guidelines for ensuring a safe online experience. For more information, visit onguardonline.gov or staysafeonline.org.

BTW

Children and the Internet
The Internet can be a great source of entertainment and education for children, but there also is the potential for children to encounter inappropriate content or behavior. While there are many ongoing efforts to make the Internet safer for children, children still should be properly supervised and educated about Internet threats. For more information, visit enough.org.

BTW

HTTPS
You might notice that when browsing the Web, some Web sites use the https protocol, instead of http. The https protocol is a more secure version of the http protocol. The https protocol is designed to make it difficult for others to see the data being transferred between your computer and the Web server.

Transfer Protocol. **Hypertext Transfer Protocol (HTTP)** describes the rules used to transmit Web pages electronically over the Internet. You enter the protocol in lowercase as http followed by a colon and two forward slashes (http://). If you do not begin a Web address with a protocol, Internet Explorer will assume it is http, and automatically will append http:// to the front of the Web address.

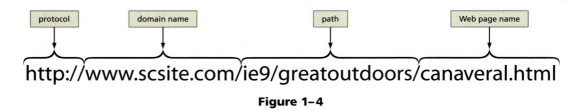

Figure 1–4

The second part of a Web address is the domain name. The **domain name** is the Internet address of the computer where the Web page is located. Each computer on the Internet has a unique address, called an **Internet Protocol address**, or **IP address**. The domain name identifies where to forward a request for the Web page referenced by the Web address. The domain name in the Web address in Figure 1–4 is www.scsite.com. The last part of the domain name (.com in Figure 1–4) is called an extension and indicates the type of organization that owns the Web site. For example, the extension .com indicates a commercial organization, usually a business or corporation. Countries throughout the world also have their own domain name extensions. For example, Germany's domain name extension is .de, and China's domain name extension is .cn. Table 1–1 shows some types of organizations and their extensions.

Table 1–1 Organizations and Their Domain Name Extensions	
Types of Organizations	**Original Domain Name Extensions**
Commercial organizations, businesses, and companies, but now can be registered by anyone	.com
Postsecondary educational institutions	.edu
United States government agencies	.gov
United States military	.mil
Originally available only to network providers, but now can be registered by anyone	.net
Nonprofit organizations	.org
Types of Organizations	**Additional Domain Name Extensions**
Accredited museums	.museum
Aviation community members	.aero
Business cooperatives such as credit unions and rural electric co-ops	.coop
Businesses of all sizes	.biz
Businesses, organizations, or individuals providing general information	.info
Certified professionals such as doctors, lawyers, and accountants	.pro
Individuals or families	.name
Web sites offering media and other broadband content	.tv

The optional third part of a Web address is the file specification of the Web page. The **file specification** includes the file name and possibly a directory or folder name. This information is called the path. If no file specification of a Web page is specified in the

Web address, a default Web page appears. This means you can display a Web page even though you do not know its file specification.

You can find Web addresses that identify Web sites in magazines or newspapers, on television, from friends, or even from just browsing the Web. Web addresses of well-known companies and organizations usually contain the company or organization name. For example, cengage.com is the Web address for Cengage Learning, and the Web address for Dell Inc. is dell.com.

Hypertext Markup Language

Web page authors use a special language called **Hypertext Markup Language** (**HTML**) to create Web pages. Behind all the formatted text and eye-catching graphics is plain text. Special HTML formatting codes and functions that control attributes of a page, such as font size, colors, and text alignment, surround the text and picture references. Figure 1–5 shows part of the Hypertext Markup Language used to create the Web page shown in Figure 1–3 on page IE 6.

BTW

Web Page Authoring
Many Web page authoring programs make it easy to create Web pages without learning HTML syntax. Editing programs include Expression Web, Adobe Dreamweaver, and CoffeeCup.

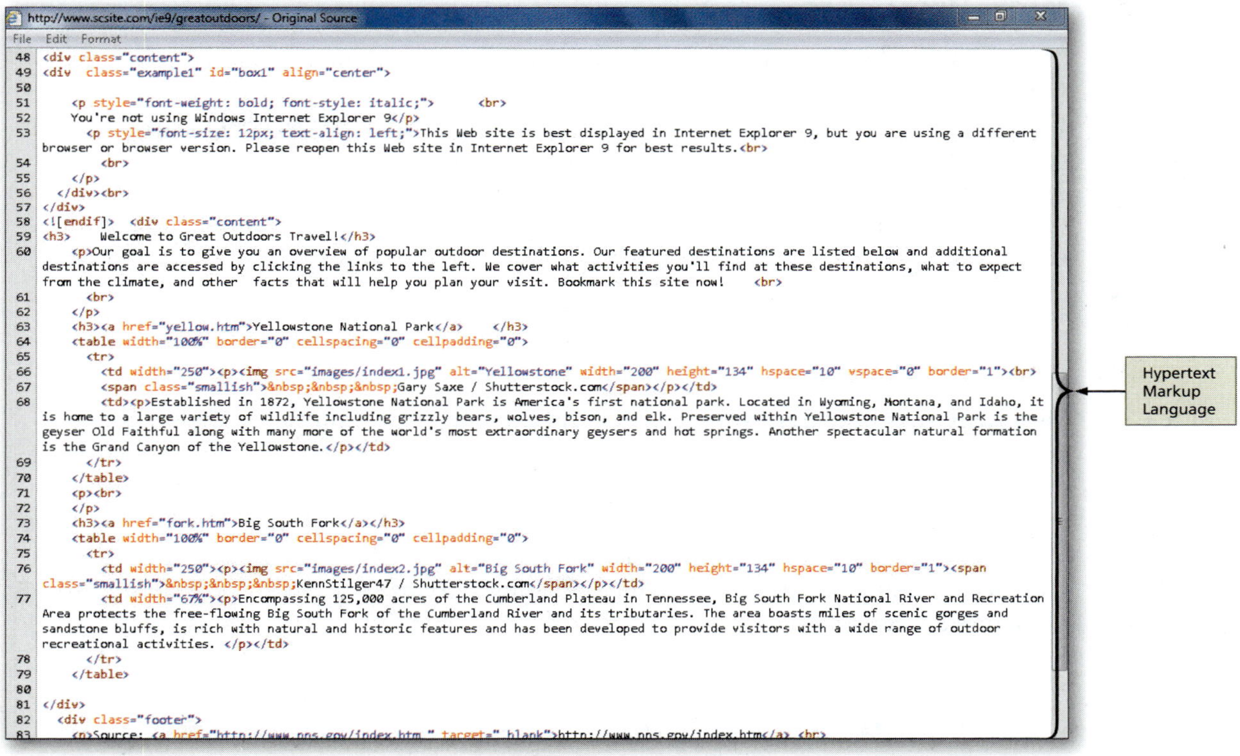

Figure 1–5

HTML is considered a markup language. A **markup language** contains text as well as information about the text. This information can include how the text is formatted and how it is positioned on a page. Using HTML, you can create your own Web pages and place them on the Web for others to see. New versions of HTML are released periodically to allow Web developers to take advantage of new and exciting technologies that can be delivered over the World Wide Web. As new versions of HTML are released, browser software on your computer must be updated to support new and updated features.

Home Pages

No main menus or particular starting points exist in the World Wide Web, but most people start a visit to the Web via specially designated Web pages called home pages. A **home page** is the introductory page for a Web site. All other Web pages for that site usually are accessible from the home page via links. When you enter a domain name with no file specification, such as disneyland.com or nbc.com, the home page is the page that is displayed.

Because the home page is the starting point for most Web sites, Web designers try to make a good first impression. These pages often display attractive, eye-catching images, specially formatted text, and a variety of links to other pages at the Web site as well as to other related Web sites.

A home page also can refer to the Web page or the multiple Web pages that first appear when you start your Web browser. For example, if you normally read the news online when you connect to the Internet, you might set your browser's home page to your favorite news Web site.

Web Browsers

Graphical user interfaces (GUIs) such as Microsoft Windows simplify working with a computer by using a point-and-click method. Similarly, a browser such as Internet Explorer makes using the World Wide Web easier by removing the complexity of having to remember the syntax, or rules, of commands used to reference Web pages at Web sites. A **Web browser** takes the Web address associated with a link or the Web address entered by a user, locates the computer containing the associated Web page, and then reads the returned HTML to display a Web page.

What Is Internet Explorer 9?

Windows Internet Explorer 9, also known as Internet Explorer, is Web browsing software that allows you to search for and view Web pages, save links for future use, maintain a list of the pages you visit, obtain information from various sources, listen to radio stations, and watch videos. The Internet Explorer 9 program is available free of charge to Windows users on Microsoft's Web site (microsoft.com). To install Internet Explorer 9, you must be using one of the following operating systems: Windows 7, Windows Vista, or Windows Server 2008.

Starting Internet Explorer

If you are stepping through this chapter on a computer and want your screen to match the figures in this book, your monitor's resolution should be set to 1024×768. For more information about how to change the resolution on your computer, contact your instructor.

BTW

The Internet Explorer Icon
If Internet Explorer is installed, the Internet Explorer icon and name are displayed in the All Programs list and may be displayed as the first entry on the Start menu. The Internet Explorer icon also might appear on the taskbar.

BTW

Customize Your Home Page
You can change the home page that appears when you start Internet Explorer by clicking the Tools button, clicking the Internet options command, and in the General sheet clicking the Use current, Use default, or Use blank button, or typing your desired Web address in the Home page text box.

To Start Internet Explorer

The following step, which assumes Windows is running, starts Internet Explorer based on a typical installation. You might need to ask your instructor how to start Internet Explorer on your computer.

1

- Click the Internet Explorer button on the Windows taskbar to start Internet Explorer and open the MSN.com – Windows Internet Explorer window (Figure 1–6).

- If the Internet Explorer window is not maximized, double-click its title bar to maximize it.

Q&A
Why does my browser display a different home page?

The home page that appears when you start the browser can change depending on the browser settings.

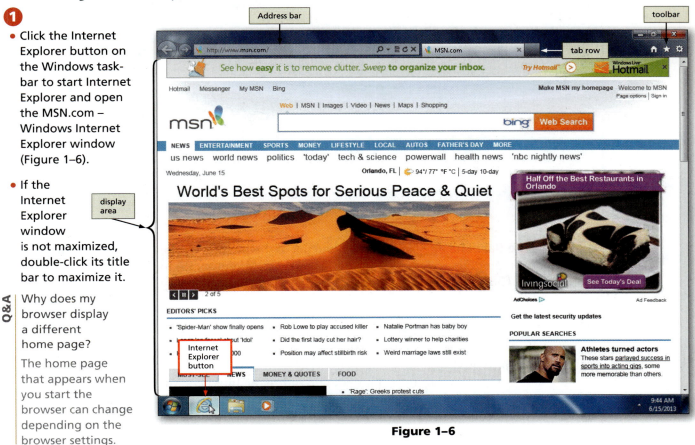

Figure 1–6

Figure 1–7 on the next page illustrates the Internet Explorer window with all bars displayed.

The Internet Explorer Window

The Internet Explorer window (Figure 1–6) consists of a range of features that make browsing the Internet easy. By default, the Internet Explorer window will display navigation buttons, the Address bar, the tab row, and a toolbar. However, you also can configure Internet Explorer to display additional bars to enhance your browsing experience. These bars include the menu bar, Command bar, status bar, and Favorites bar. The display area is the portion of the Internet Explorer window that displays the Web pages you visit, and scroll bars might be available if the entire Web page does not fit in the display area at one time. Figure 1–7 on the next page illustrates the Internet Explorer window with all bars displayed. You can add additional bars in Internet Explorer by right-clicking on the title bar and clicking the desired bar to display.

Other Ways

1. Click Start button on Windows taskbar, click Internet Explorer icon on Start menu
2. Click Start button on Windows taskbar, click All Programs, click Internet Explorer
3. Double-click Internet Explorer icon on desktop
4. Press CTRL+ESC, press I, press ENTER

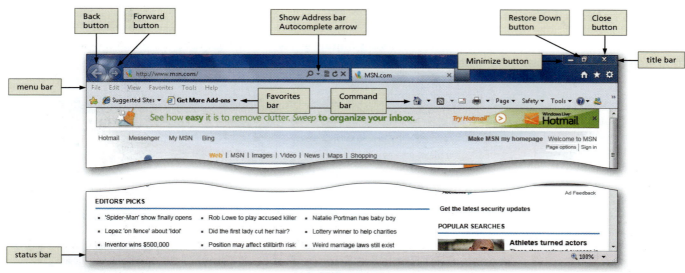

Figure 1–7

Title Bar The title bar appears at the top of the Internet Explorer window. As shown at the top of Figure 1–7, the title bar includes the Minimize, Restore Down (or Maximize), and Close buttons on the right. Click the Minimize button to minimize the Internet Explorer window. When you minimize the window, it still is open but it no longer appears on the desktop and the Internet Explorer button on the taskbar becomes inactive (a lighter color). After minimizing, clicking the button with the Internet Explorer icon on the Windows taskbar displays the Internet Explorer window in the previous position it occupied on the desktop and changes the button to an active state (a darker color).

Click the Maximize button to maximize the Internet Explorer window so that it expands to fill the entire desktop. When the window is maximized, the Restore Down button replaces the Maximize button on the title bar. Click the Restore Down button to return the window to the size and position it occupied before being maximized. The Restore Down button changes to the Maximize button when the Internet Explorer window is in a restored state.

You also can double-click the title bar or drag the title bar to the top of the Windows 7 desktop to restore and maximize the Internet Explorer window. If the window is in a restored state, you can drag the title bar to move the window around the desktop.

Navigation Buttons The navigation buttons in Internet Explorer include the Back button and the Forward button. Clicking the Back button retrieves the previous page. To retrieve a page you visited before the previous one, click and hold the Back button, and then click a Web page title in the list. The Forward button retrieves the page you visited after the one you are currently viewing. To navigate more than one page that you have previously viewed after the one you are currently viewing, click and hold the Forward button, and then click a Web page title in the list. The Forward button only is available after you have clicked the Back button one or more times to return to a previous page.

Address Bar The Address bar contains the Web address for the page currently shown in the display area. The Address bar also can be used to search for information on the World Wide Web.

The Web address updates automatically as you browse from page to page. If you know the Web address of a Web page you want to visit, click the Web address in the Address bar to highlight it, type the new Web address, and then press the ENTER key to display the corresponding page. As you type a Web address in the Address bar, Internet Explorer will display a list of suggestions, including AutoComplete suggestions and previously visited Web pages, files, and feeds. In addition, you can click the Show Address bar Autocomplete arrow at the right end of the Address bar to display a list of previously displayed Web pages. Clicking a Web address in the Address list displays the corresponding Web page.

The Address bar also includes a security feature known as domain highlighting. Domain highlighting displays the top-level domain in a black font, while the remainder of the Web address is displayed in a gray font (Figure 1–8). This helps to protect the user from phishing scams by allowing the user easily to identify whether the Web site currently displayed in the window is the Web site he or she intended to visit.

BTW

The Address Bar
To move the insertion point to the Address bar when the box is empty, or to highlight the Web address in the Address bar, press ALT+D.

Figure 1–8

Tab Row   The tab row, shown in Figure 1–6 on page IE 11, is located adjacent to the Address bar. The tab row enables you to keep multiple Web pages open simultaneously in one browser window. After clicking the New Tab button in the tab row, you can type the Web address of the Web page in the Address bar and it will be displayed in the new tab. The tab row also allows you to switch between tabs, reorder tabs, and close single tabs. Although you can open multiple Internet Explorer windows to display multiple Web pages, it is recommended that you open new Web pages in tabs. Opening multiple browser windows consumes additional system resources, which can decrease your computer's performance. While a Web page loads in the display area, the Internet Explorer icon in the corresponding tab changes to an animated circle. When the Web page finishes loading, the Web page icon or the Internet Explorer icon is displayed on the tab.

Display Area   Only a portion of many Web pages will be visible on the screen. You view the portion of the page displayed on the screen in the display area (Figure 1–6 on page IE 11). To the right of the display area is a vertical scroll bar, scroll arrows, and a scroll box, which you can use to move the text in the display area up and down and reveal other parts of the page. Occasionally a Web page might be wider than the display area can show, and a horizontal scroll bar will appear at the bottom of the display area.

Notice the links on the Internet Explorer home page shown in Figure 1–3 on page IE 6. When you position the mouse pointer on one of these links, the mouse pointer changes to a pointing hand. This change in the shape of the mouse pointer identifies these elements as links. Clicking a link retrieves the Web page associated with the link and displays it in the display area.

Menu Bar   When displayed, as in Figure 1–7, the menu bar is located below the Address bar. Because the most common Internet Explorer commands are accessible from other areas of the Internet Explorer window, Internet Explorer hides the menu bar by default. To display the menu bar, press the ALT key. Each menu name on the menu bar represents a list of commands you can use to perform actions such as saving Web pages, copying and pasting, using the 'Find on this page' command, sending a page as an e-mail message,

BTW

Full Screen Mode
If you would like Internet Explorer to display Web pages in full screen mode (without the title bar, toolbars, or other components of the window), you can either press the F11 key on the keyboard or press the ALT key to display the menu bar and then select the Full screen command on the View menu.

setting Internet Explorer options, and exiting Internet Explorer. To display a menu when the menu bar is displayed, click the menu name on the menu bar. To select a command on a menu, click the command name or press the keyboard shortcut shown to the right of some of the commands on the menu.

Favorites Bar The Favorites bar (Figure 1–7 on page IE 12), which does not display by default, contains a button that allows you to add a Web site to your Favorites bar. As you add to your favorites (discussed later in this chapter), more buttons can appear on this bar.

BTW

The Command Bar
To display text labels for the buttons on the Command bar, right-click the Command bar, point to Customize on the shortcut menu, and then click 'Show all text labels'.

Command Bar The Command bar, when displayed, provides easy access to most Internet Explorer functions. The buttons on the Command bar allow you to change your home page options, access your e-mail account, print the current Web page and access printing options, access Internet Explorer tools, explore safety and Web page options and more. You can customize the tools that appear on the Command bar by right-clicking the Command bar, pointing to Customize on the shortcut menu, and then clicking 'Add or remove commands'. Depending on the size of the Command bar in your Internet Explorer window, it is possible that not all commands will be displayed. If a small double caret appears to the right of the Command bar, it indicates additional Command bar options are available. The options on your Command bar might be different, depending on the software installed on your computer and your computer's configuration. Table 1–2 identifies the default commands on the Command bar and briefly describes the function of each command.

Table 1–2 Commands on the Command Bar

Command	Function
🏠	Displays the home page, and includes options to add, change, or remove the home page
📶 📗	When active, these buttons allow you to view the RSS feeds or Web Slices on the current Web page
✉	Starts your default e-mail program
🖨	Prints the current Web page, or displays a menu providing access to various printing options
Page ▾	Displays a menu containing selected popular commands from the File, Edit, and View menus on the menu bar
Safety ▾	Displays a menu containing commands that allow you to configure safety and security options
Tools ▾	Displays commonly used commands that are also accessible on the View and Tools menus on the menu bar
❓▾	Displays the Help menu, which is also accessible via the menu bar

BTW

The Great Outdoors Travel Web Site
Notice that the Web address you enter for the Great Outdoors Travel page contains a domain name (scsite.com) that belongs to the publishing company. The Great Outdoors Travel Web site has been developed exclusively for use with this chapter.

Browsing the World Wide Web

The most common way to browse the World Wide Web is to obtain the Web address of a Web page you want to visit and then enter it into the Address bar. By visiting various Web sites, you can begin to understand the enormous appeal of the Web. The following steps show how to visit the Web page titled Great Outdoors Travel, which contains information and photographs of five popular outdoor destinations in the United States. The Web address for the Great Outdoors Travel Web site is www.scsite.com/ie9/greatoutdoors.

To Browse the Web by Entering a Web Address

To navigate to the home page for the Great Outdoors Travel Web site, you will need to enter the Web address in the Address bar.

- Click the Address bar to highlight the Web address (Figure 1–9).

Figure 1–9

- Type **www. scsite. com/ie9/ greatoutdoors** in the Address bar to enter the new Web address (Figure 1–10).

Q&A Why is it unnecessary to type http:// at the beginning of each Web address?

Depending on how the Web server is configured, it might not require you to type http:// or www. at the beginning of the Web address. In the case of this Web site, you can type `scsite.com/ie9/greatoutdoors` or `www.scsite.com/ie9/greatoutdoors` as the Web address.

Figure 1–10

Q&A What if I type the wrong Web address?

If you type the wrong letter and notice the error before pressing the ENTER key, use the BACKSPACE key to erase all the characters back to and including the one that is wrong. If the error is easier to retype than correct, click the Web address in the Address bar and retype it correctly.

3

● Press the ENTER key to load the Great Outdoors Travel Web page (Figure 1–11).

Q&A

What happens if a Web page is not displayed correctly?

Internet Explorer 9 follows a more strict interpretation of HTML, and as a result some Web pages might not display as expected. If you encounter a Web page that is not displayed correctly, you might be able to correct the problem by displaying the Web page in Compatibility View. To display a Web page in Compatibility View, click the Compatibility View button on the Address bar.

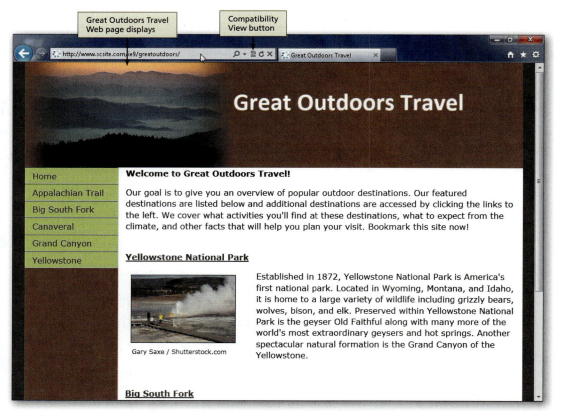

Figure 1–11

4

● Click the Yellowstone link to display the Yellowstone National Park Web page (Figure 1–12).

Q&A

What should I do if I see a warning regarding playing media?

Because this Web site is from a trusted source (the publisher of this textbook), click the Allow button to permit the video to play.

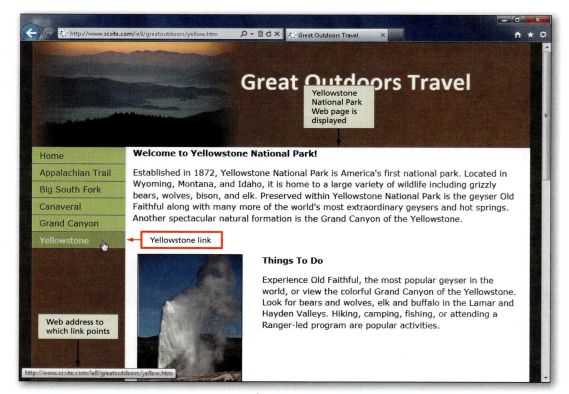

Figure 1–12

5

• Scroll through the display area using the vertical scroll bar to display the photo gallery link (Figure 1–13).

Q&A

Why is the text, photo gallery, underlined?

Usually, links to other Web pages and Web sites are underlined. Typically, Web site designers and developers do not underline text unless the text will act as a hyperlink.

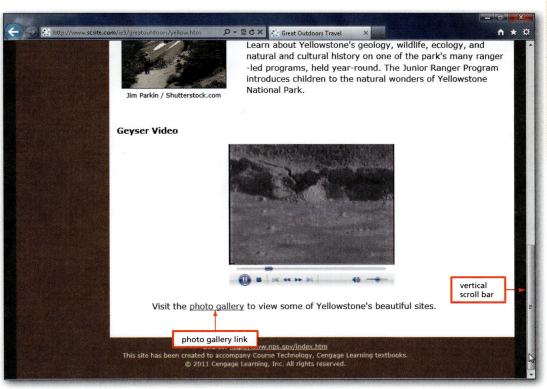

Figure 1–13

6

• Click the photo gallery link to display the Yellowstone National Park Photo Gallery Web page (Figure 1–14).

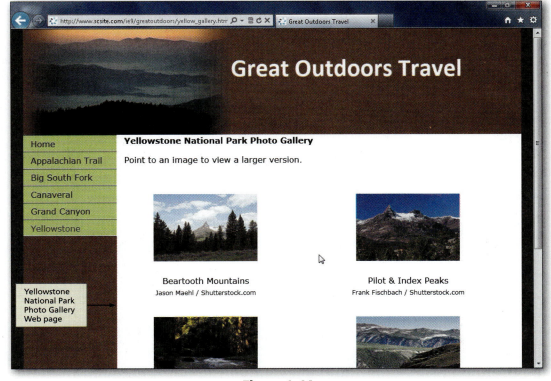

Figure 1–14

7

• If necessary, scroll through the display area to view the four pictures.

• Point to the Eagle Creek picture to display a larger version of the Eagle Creek picture (Figure 1–15).

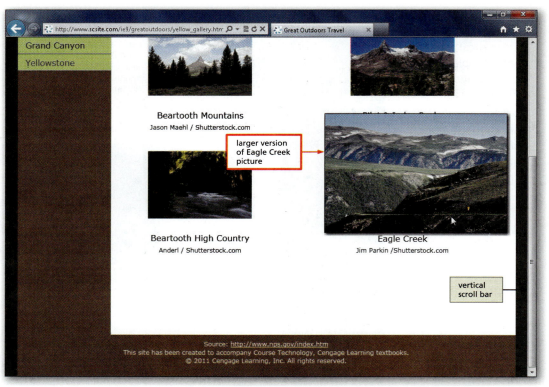

Figure 1–15

Other Ways

1. On File menu, click Open, type Web address in Open box, click OK

2. Press CTRL+O, type Web address in Open box, press ENTER

3. Press ALT+F, press O, type Web address in Open box, press ENTER

Understanding Alternate Text

Pointing to an image on a Web page might display alternate text in a small pop-up box (Figure 1–16). Alternate text is text that is displayed in place of the image if a user configures his or her Web browser not to display images. In addition, visually impaired users typically have special software installed on their computers that reads the contents of their screens through the computers' speakers. Because this software cannot read an image, it reads the alternate text instead. Web page authors typically write alternate text that briefly describes the image it represents. Poorly written alternate text can make it difficult for visually impaired users to understand what is on the Web page.

Figure 1–16

Stopping the Transfer of a Page

If a Web page you are trying to view is taking too long to transfer or if you have clicked the wrong link, you might decide not to wait for the page to finish transferring. The Stop button on the Address bar (Figure 1–17 on the next page) allows you to stop the transfer of a page while the transfer is in progress. You will know that the transfer still is in progress if the icon on the current tab is in motion. Stopping the transfer of a Web page will leave a partially transferred Web page in the display area. Pictures or text displayed before the Stop button is clicked remain visible in the display area and any links can be clicked to display the associated Web pages. Because high-speed Internet connections are increasingly common, Web pages load quickly and the need for the Stop button is decreasing. People who connect to the Internet with a slower Internet connection, such as dial-up access, however, might have a greater need to use the Stop button.

Refreshing a Web Page

One of the great features of the Internet is how quickly content on Web pages can be updated or changed. As you display different Web pages, Internet Explorer keeps track of the pages you visit, so that you can find those pages quickly in the future. Internet Explorer stores the Web pages you visit in a folder on the hard disk. When you display a previously viewed Web page, the page is displayed quickly because Internet Explorer is able to retrieve the page from the folder on the hard disk instead of from a Web server on the Internet. For this reason, the Web page you are viewing might not be the most up-to-date version. Web pages containing stock quotes, weather, and news are updated frequently to reflect the most current information. If you are unsure of whether the content you are viewing on a Web page is current, you should refresh the Web page. You also should refresh a Web page if you think the Web page has loaded incorrectly. You can refresh the Web page by using the Refresh button on the Address bar (Figure 1–17).

To Refresh a Web Page

The following step refreshes the contents of the Web page to ensure that you are viewing the most recent version of the page.

1

- Click the Refresh button on the Address bar to cause Internet Explorer to initiate a new transfer of the Web page from the Web server to your computer (Figure 1–17).

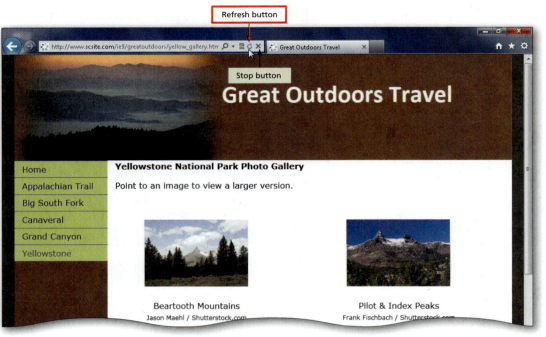

Figure 1–17

Other Ways

1. Click Web address in Address bar, press ENTER key
2. Press ALT, click View, click Refresh
3. Press ALT+V, press R
4. Press F5

Finding a Previously Displayed Web Page

One method to find a previously displayed Web page is to use the Back button and the Recent Pages list. Each time a Web page appears in the display area, the title of the Web page is added to the Recent Pages list. You can redisplay a previously viewed page by clicking and holding the Back button and selecting the desired Web page from the Recent Pages list (Figure 1–18a). The Forward button activates only after you click the Back button to return to a recent page. Each time you end an Internet session by quitting Internet Explorer, the entries on the Recent Pages list are cleared.

Another method for retrieving previously viewed pages is the Go to list, which contains the titles of all Web pages in the order they were displayed during the current session (Figure 1–18b). A check mark preceding a name in the list identifies the page currently displayed. To view the Go to list, press the ALT key to display the menu bar, click View on the menu bar, and then point to Go to on the View menu. Clicking a title in the Go to list displays the associated Web page in the display area.

A third method uses the Show Address bar Autocomplete button to display previously viewed Web pages. Clicking the Show Address bar Autocomplete button displays a list of Web addresses that you have previously typed into the Address bar (Figure 1–18c).

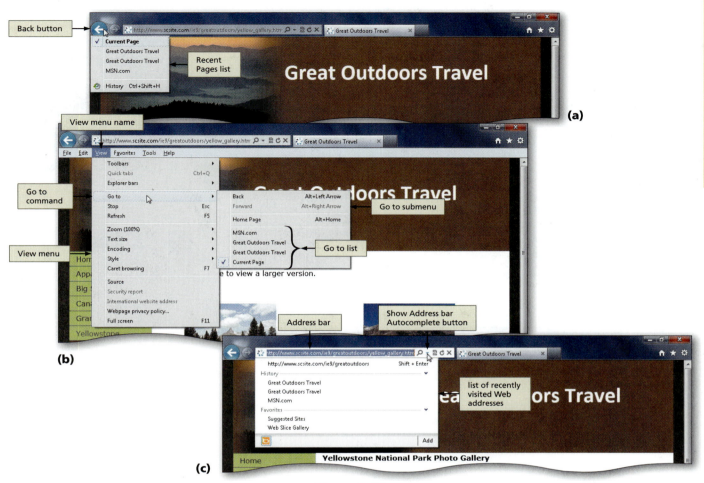

Figure 1–18

To Use the Navigation Buttons to Find Recently Displayed Web Pages

The Back and Forward buttons often are used when you want to revisit a Web page you recently have visited since you last opened Internet Explorer. The following steps use the Back and Forward buttons.

1

• Click the Back button on the toolbar to display the Yellowstone National Park Web page (Figure 1–19).

Q&A

How far back can I navigate?

You can continue to page backward until you reach the beginning of the Recent Pages list. At that time, the Back button becomes inactive, which indicates that the list contains no additional pages to which you can move back.

Figure 1–19

2
- Click the Forward button on the toolbar to display the Yellowstone National Park Photo Gallery Web page (Figure 1–20).

Figure 1–20

Other Ways

1. Click and hold Back button, click Web page title

2. Press ALT, click View, point to Go to, click Web page title on Go to submenu (or Back or Forward)

3. Back: press ALT+LEFT ARROW; forward: press ALT+RIGHT ARROW

To Display a Web Page Using the Address Bar Autocomplete List

It is possible to jump to any previously visited page by clicking its title in the Address bar Autocomplete list. In this way, you can find a recently visited page without displaying an intermediate page. The following steps illustrate how to navigate quickly and easily to a recently visited page without having to click the Back button multiple times to reach the page.

1
- Click the Show Address bar Autocomplete button on the Address bar to display a list of recently visited Web addresses (Figure 1–21).

Q&A

Why does my list look different?

If Internet Explorer was running before beginning this chapter, your list might contain additional pages.

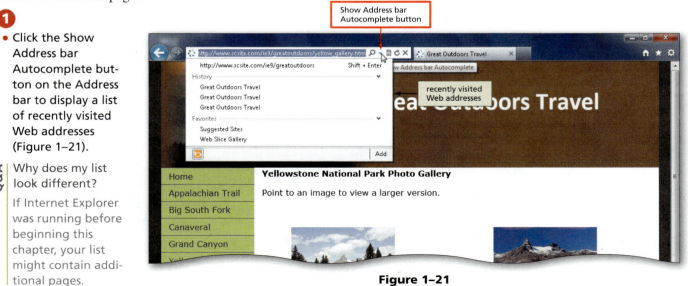

Figure 1–21

2

● Point to the second Great Outdoors Travel listing under the History heading to display information about the Web page (Figure 1–22).

Q&A Why do multiple entries say Great Outdoors Travel?

If multiple Web pages have the same title, they will appear the same in the list of Web addresses. Pointing to each entry will display additional identifying information about each Web page.

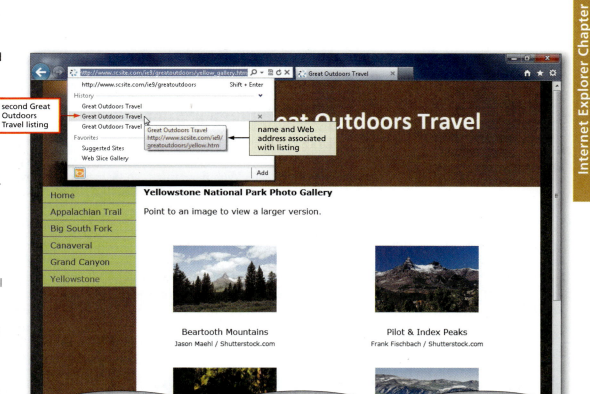

Figure 1–22

3

● Click the second Great Outdoors Travel listing to display the Yellowstone National Park Web page (Figure 1–23).

Figure 1–23

Welcome to Yellowstone National Park!

Established in 1872, Yellowstone National Park is America's first national park. Located in Wyoming, Montana, and Idaho, it is home to a large variety of wildlife including grizzly bears, wolves, bison, and elk. Preserved within Yellowstone National Park is the geyser Old Faithful along with many more of the world's most extraordinary geysers and hot springs. Another spectacular natural formation is the Grand Canyon of the Yellowstone.

Things To Do

Experience Old Faithful, the most popular geyser in the world, or view the colorful Grand Canyon of the Yellowstone. Look for bears and wolves, elk and buffalo in the Lamar and Hayden Valleys. Hiking, camping, fishing, or attending a Ranger-led program are popular activities.

Other Ways

1. Press ALT, click View, point to Go to, click Back on Go to submenu
2. Press ALT+LEFT ARROW

Using the History List to Display Web Pages

BTW

Clearing the History List

If the list of Web sites you have visited has become too large to be meaningful, you might want to clear the History list. You can clear the History list by clicking the Tools button on the toolbar, pointing to Safety, clicking 'Delete browsing history' on the Safety submenu, verifying that a check mark appears in the History check box, and then clicking the Delete button (Delete Browsing History dialog box). Clearing the History list also clears the Address bar Autocomplete list.

Internet Explorer maintains another list of previously visited Web pages in the History list. The History list is a list of Web pages visited over a period of days or weeks (over many sessions). You can use this list to display Web pages you accessed during that time. Clicking the 'View favorites, feeds, and history' button on the toolbar, clicking the History tab, and then clicking Today displays the History list for the current day.

To find a recently visited Web page using the History list, first display the entire History list, select the order in which you want to view the history, and then click the desired Web page title. The Web page titles can be categorized by date, site, most visited, or order visited today. In addition, you are able to search this History list for a particular Web site.

If you are browsing the World Wide Web from a public or shared computer, you might not want Internet Explorer to save any information about the Web sites you have visited. **InPrivate Browsing** is a feature that allows you to visit Web pages without the Web browser recording any information. For example, if you visit your bank's Web site using InPrivate Browsing, Internet Explorer will not save the site in your History list, nor will it save any cookies or other temporary Internet files from the Web site. To enable InPrivate Browsing, click the Tools button on the toolbar, point to Safety, and then click InPrivate Browsing on the Safety submenu. Internet Explorer will open a new window with an InPrivate icon in the Address bar. When you want to exit InPrivate Browsing mode, simply close the window.

To Display a Web Page Using the History List

If you have a small list of pages you have visited, or the Web page you want to view is only one or two pages away, using the Back and Forward buttons to traverse the lists will likely be faster than displaying the Recent Pages list and selecting the correct title. If you have visited a large number of pages, however, you will need to step forward or back through many pages, and it might be easier to use the Address bar Autocomplete list or the History list to select the exact page. To display a recently visited Web page without having to click the Back button multiple times, perform the following steps to display the Web page using the History list.

1

- Click the 'View favorites, feeds, and history' button on the toolbar to display the Favorites Center.

- Click the Pin the Favorites Center button to pin the Favorites Center to the Internet Explorer window (Figure 1–24).

Q&A

Why did the Favorites Center move?

When the Favorites Center is pinned, it appears on the left side of the display area. When the Favorites Center is not pinned, it appears on the right side of the display area.

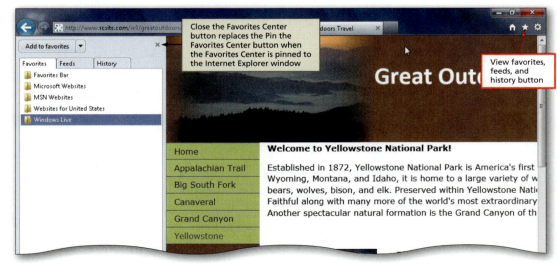

Figure 1–24

2

- Click the History tab to display the History list in the Favorites Center (Figure 1–25).

Q&A Why is the Favorites Center often hidden from the Internet Explorer window?

Internet Explorer reserves as much space as possible to display the Web pages in the display area. Continuously displaying the Favorites Center consumes space on the Web page, possibly resulting in the need to scroll the page horizontally to view all content.

Figure 1–25

3

- If necessary, click Today in the History list to display a list of Web sites that have been accessed today (Figure 1–26). Your History list might differ.

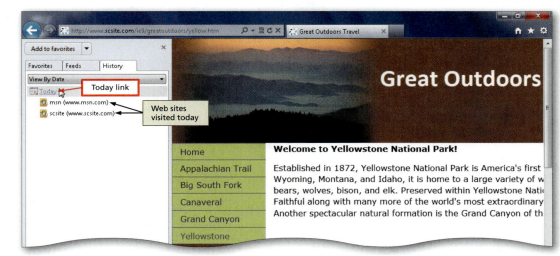

Figure 1–26

4

- Click scsite (www. scsite.com) to display the list of Web pages that were accessed from scsite.com.

- Click the third Great Outdoors Travel link to display the Great Outdoors Travel Web page (Figure 1–27).

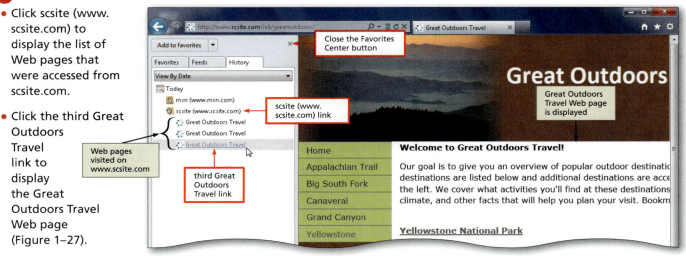

Figure 1–27

5

• Click the Close the Favorites Center button in the Favorites Center to close the Favorites Center (Figure 1–28).

Figure 1–28

Other Ways

1. Press ALT, click View, point to Explorer bars, click History
2. Press CTRL+SHIFT+H

Keeping Track of Favorite Web Pages

You can see from the previous figures that Web addresses can be long and cryptic. It is easy to make a mistake while entering complex Web addresses. Fortunately, Internet Explorer can keep track of favorite Web pages. You can store the Web addresses of favorite Web pages permanently in an area appropriately called the Favorites list.

A **favorite** consists of the title of the Web page and the Web address of that page. The title of the Web page is added to the Favorites Center. Your favorites appear in both the Favorites menu and the Favorites Center.

BTW

Suggested Sites

The Suggested Sites feature in Internet Explorer keeps a record of Web pages you frequently visit. It then uses this information to suggest other Web sites that might be of interest to you. To turn on Suggested Sites, click the 'View favorites, feeds, and history' button on the toolbar, and then click the Turn on Suggested Sites button.

To Add a Web Page to the Favorites Center

The following steps add a Web page to the Favorites Center, so that you easily can access the Web page in the future.

1
- Click the 'View favorites, feeds, and history' button on the toolbar to display the Favorites Center (Figure 1–29).

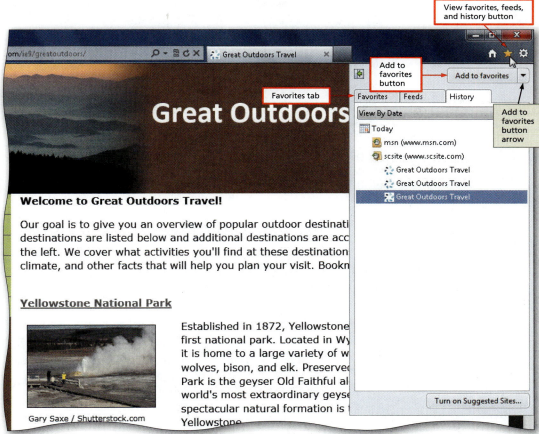

Figure 1–29

2
- Click the Favorites tab to display the list of Favorites.

- Click the 'Add to favorites' button in the Favorites Center to display the Add a Favorite dialog box (Figure 1–30).

Q&A How can I organize my favorites?

Clicking the 'Add to favorites' button arrow (shown in Figure 1–29) and then clicking the Organize favorites command displays the Organize Favorites dialog box, which allows you to move, rename, organize, and delete your favorites.

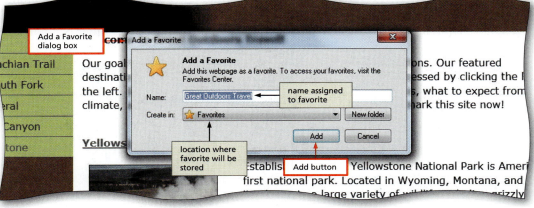

Figure 1–30

3

- Click the Add button (Add a Favorite dialog box) to add the Great Outdoors Travel Web page to the Favorites Center.

- Click the 'View favorites, feeds, and history' button on the toolbar, and then click the Favorites tab, if necessary, to display the Favorites Center and verify the new favorite is added (Figure 1–31).

- Close the Favorites Center.

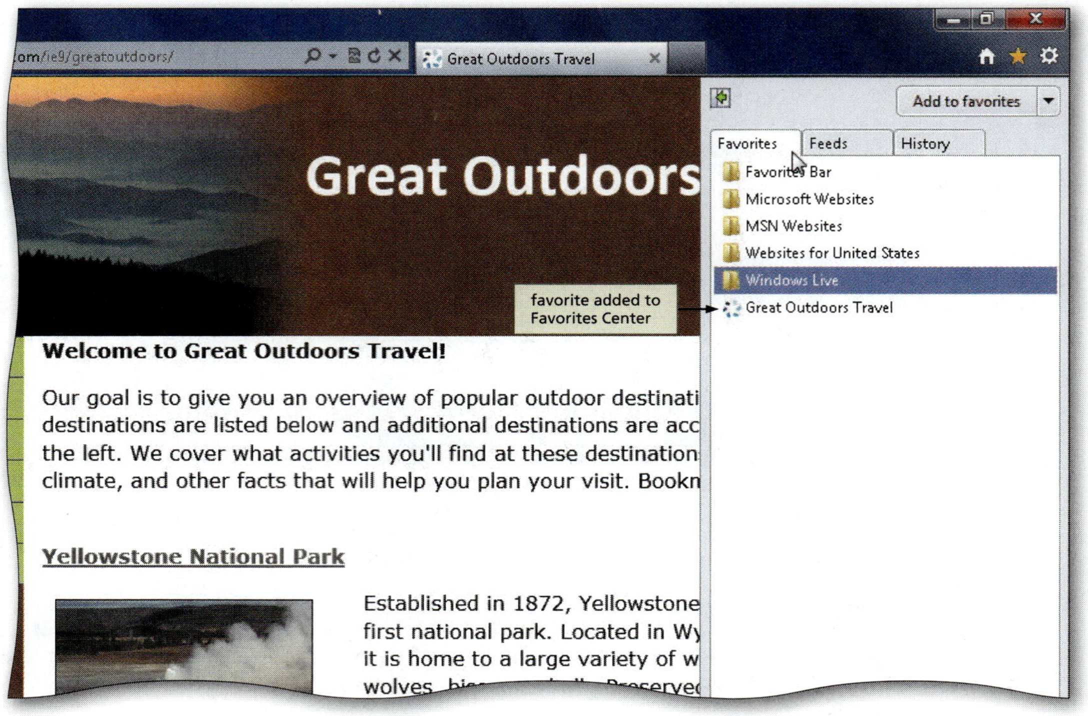

Figure 1–31

Experiment

- After you add the favorite, check the Favorites menu to verify that your new favorite appears in the list. Press the ALT key to display the menu bar, press A, verify that the favorite appears, and then press the ESC key twice to close the Favorites menu and hide the menu bar.

Other Ways

1. Press ALT, click Favorites on menu bar, and then click 'Add to favorites'
2. Press CTRL+D, press ENTER
3. Press ALT+A, press A, press ENTER

If you plan to store many favorites on your computer, you might choose to give your favorite Web sites meaningful names by renaming them and storing them in folders. In the Add a Favorite dialog box shown in Figure 1–30 on the previous page, clicking the New folder button displays the Create a Folder dialog box. Next, you can name the folder by typing an appropriate name in the Folder Name text box, and then clicking the Create button. After naming the folder, you can drag an existing favorite to the folder to store the favorite in that folder. You also can change the name of a folder or favorite in the Favorites Center by clicking a folder or favorite in the Organize Favorites dialog box, clicking Rename, typing the new name, and then pressing the ENTER key. For example, if you frequently visit many Web sites to read the news, you might choose to store the Web addresses of these sites as favorites in a News folder. If you are a student, for example, you might store school-related Web sites in an Academics folder.

BTW | **Importing and Exporting Favorites**
If you already have favorite Web sites set up on another computer or Web browser, or want to transfer your favorite Web sites to another computer, you can use Internet Explorer's Import/Export Wizard to preserve your favorites. Click the 'View favorites, feeds, and history' button on the toolbar, click the 'Add to favorites' list arrow in the Favorites Center, and then click 'Import and export' to start the Import/Export Wizard. Follow the steps in the wizard to import or export your favorites.

To Display the Home Page Using the Home Button

Many people designate the Web page they most frequently visit as their home page. The Home button on the toolbar provides a quick way to navigate to your home page. If you want to navigate back to your home page quickly and easily, perform the following step to display the home page in Internet Explorer's display area.

1

- Click the Home button on the toolbar to display the MSN. com home page in the Internet Explorer window (Figure 1–32). Your computer might display a different home page.

Q&A

Can I have more than one home page?

Yes. If you designate more than one Web page as your home page, Internet Explorer will open each home page in a separate tab when you start Internet Explorer or when you click the Home button on the toolbar. To create multiple home pages, click the Tools button on the toolbar, click the Internet options command, type the Web address for each Web page on its own line in the Home page text box, and then click the OK button. Alternatively, if you click the Use current button instead of typing the Web address, each tab you have open will be set as a home page.

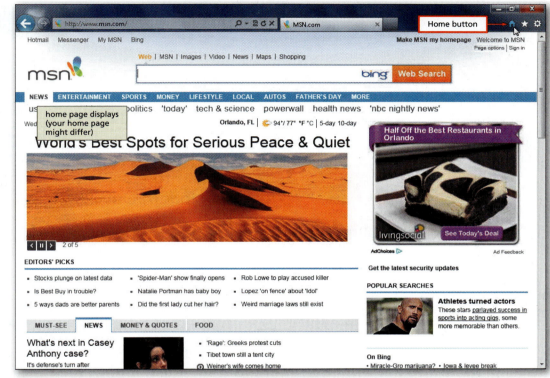

Figure 1–32

Other Ways

1. Press ALT, on View menu point to Go to, click Home Page on Go to submenu
2. Press ALT+V, press G, press H
3. Press ALT+HOME

To Display a Web Page Using the Favorites Center

The Favorites Center is used to display your list of favorite Web pages quickly, without having to type each Web address separately. Using a favorite to display a Web page is similar to using the History list to display a Web page. The following steps display the Great Outdoors Travel home page by using the Favorites Center.

1

- Click the 'View favorites, feeds, and history' button on the toolbar to display the Favorites Center.

- If necessary, click the Favorites tab in the Favorites Center to display the list of favorites (Figure 1–33).

Q&A What other favorites are displayed?

Additional favorites are displayed in the Favorites Center shown in Figure 1–33. Folders included in the Favorites list include the Favorites Bar folder, the Microsoft Websites folder, the MSN Websites folder, Websites for United States, and the Windows Live folder. Other folders and favorites might be displayed in the Favorites Center on your computer.

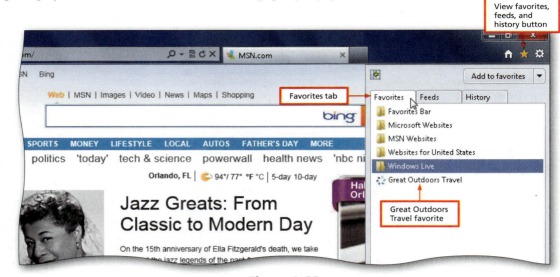

Figure 1–33

2

- Click Great Outdoors Travel in the Favorites Center to display the Great Outdoors Travel Web page in the display area (Figure 1–34).

Figure 1–34

Other Ways

1. Press ALT, on Favorites menu click favorite
2. Press ALT+A, click favorite
3. Press CTRL+I, click favorite

To Remove a Web Page from the Favorites Center

You could have a variety of reasons for wanting to remove a favorite from the Favorites Center. With the Web changing every day, the Web address that worked today might not work tomorrow, or perhaps the Web site is no longer of use to you, or your Favorites list is getting too big to be meaningful. Because not all operating systems are configured to handle deleted items in the same manner, you should not delete a favorite or a folder unless you are sure that you no longer want it. Once you decide that you no longer need a favorite, the following steps delete the favorite.

1

- Click the 'View favorites, feeds, and history' button on the toolbar to display a list of your favorites in the Favorites Center.

- Right-click the Great Outdoors Travel favorite in the Favorites Center to display a shortcut menu containing the Delete command (Figure 1–35).

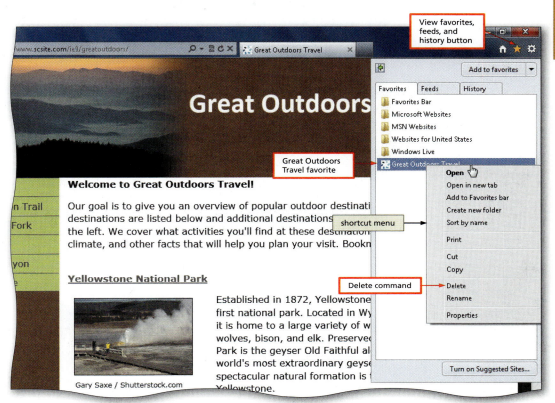

Figure 1–35

2

- Click Delete on the shortcut menu to move the Great Outdoors Travel Web Page favorite to the Recycle Bin (Figure 1–36).

Q&A

What happens when I delete a favorite?

Because favorites are stored as files on your computer, deleting a folder or favorite will move

Figure 1–36

it to the Recycle Bin. The Recycle Bin stores files marked for deletion before they are permanently deleted. While a file or folder is in the Recycle Bin, it can be restored by double-clicking the Recycle Bin icon on the desktop, clicking the item you want to restore, and then clicking the 'Restore this item' button.

3
- Click the 'View favorites, feeds, and history' button to close the Favorites Center (Figure 1–37).

Q&A
How can I delete a folder?

The steps required to delete a folder in the Favorites list are the same as those required to delete a favorite. If you delete a folder, however, Internet Explorer also will delete all favorites stored in that folder.

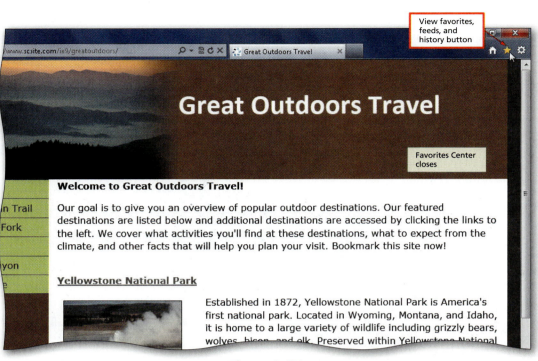

Figure 1–37

Other Ways
1. Press ALT, on Favorites menu click Organize Favorites, click favorite, click Delete button

Saving Information Obtained with Internet Explorer

BTW

Citing Web Pages
Whenever you use content from a Web site, you should cite the Web page as a source. Chapter 2 contains additional information about citing Internet sources.

The World Wide Web contains many different types of Web pages covering an infinite range of topics. Because these pages can help you gather information about areas of interest, there will be times when you will want to save the information you discover for future reference. The different types of Web pages and the various uses you have for the information require different methods of saving. Internet Explorer allows you to save an entire Web page, individual pictures, or selected pieces of text. Before saving a Web page or information from a Web page, you first should determine whether the information is available for you to use. If content on a Web page is protected by a copyright, or if the Web page displays a copyright symbol, you should contact the Web page author to obtain permission before copying or using the content. Copying an image that is protected by a copyright could carry legal consequences. If you are not sure whether content is protected by a copyright, you should seek permission before duplicating it. The following pages illustrate how to save an entire Web page, how to save a single picture, and how to save text.

To Save a Web Page

One method of saving information on a Web page is to save the entire page. The following steps save the Great Outdoors Travel home page on your computer so that you can access it even when you are not connected to the Internet.

1

- Click the Tools button on the toolbar to display the Tools menu.

- Point to File on the Tools menu to display the File submenu (Figure 1–38).

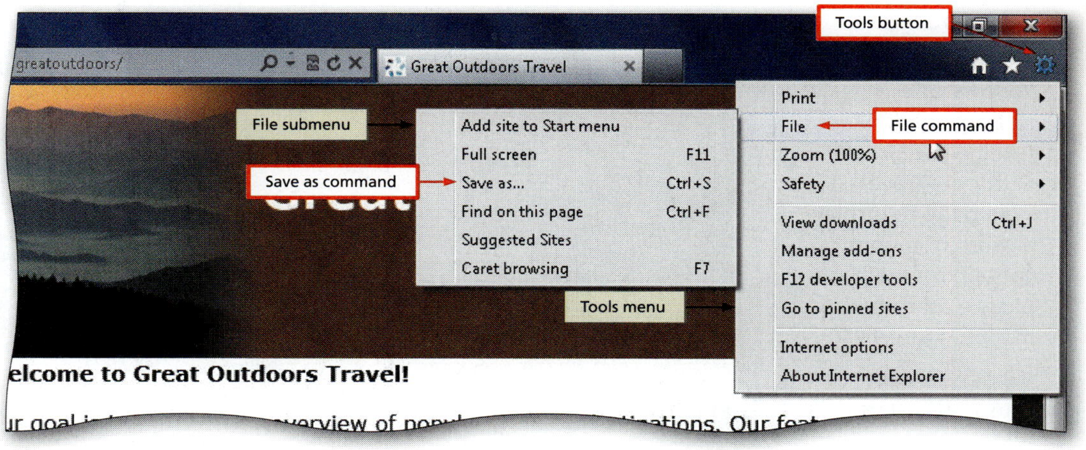

Figure 1–38

2

- Click Save as on the File submenu to display the Save Webpage dialog box. If the Save Webpage dialog box is not expanded, click the Browse Folders button to expand it.

- Click the Documents link below Libraries in the navigation pane to select the location for the saved Web page (Figure 1–39).

- Click the Save button (Save Webpage dialog box) to save the Web page to the Documents library on your computer.

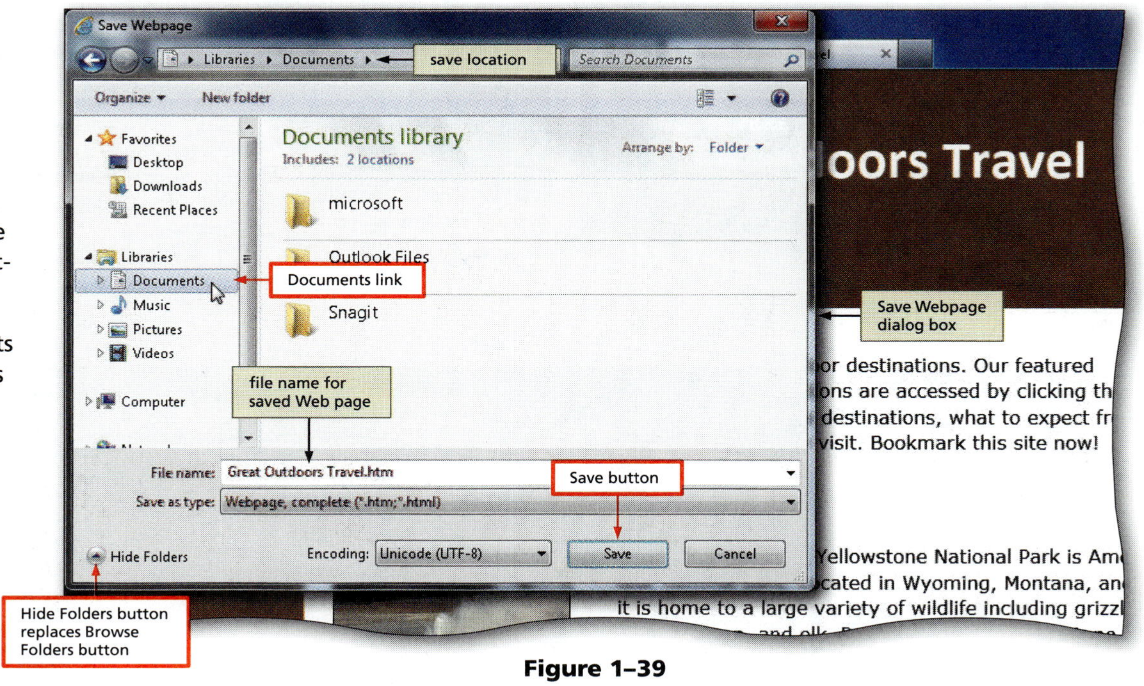

Figure 1–39

Q&A

How can I view the saved Web page?

Internet Explorer saves the instructions to display the saved Web page in the Great Outdoors Travel.htm file in the Documents library on your computer. You can view the saved Web page in the Internet Explorer window by double-clicking the Great Outdoors Travel.htm file in your Documents library. Internet Explorer also saves all files required for the Web page to display properly, such as images, in the Great Outdoors Travel_files folder in the Documents library.

Other Ways

1. Press CTRL+S

2. Press ALT+F, press A

To Save a Picture on a Web Page

In some cases, you might want to save just the image located on a Web page. The following steps save the Yellowstone National Park picture in the Pictures library on your computer in the Joint Photographic Experts Group (JPEG) file format using the file name Yellowstone.jpg. The JPEG file format is a method of encoding pictures that then can be displayed by a variety of programs. The following steps save a picture on a Web page.

1
- Right-click the Yellowstone National Park picture on the Great Outdoors Travel Web page to display a shortcut menu containing the 'Save picture as' command (Figure 1–40).

Q&A What else will Internet Explorer allow me to do with a picture?

From the shortcut menu, you can e-mail the picture, print the picture, navigate to your Pictures folder, or set the picture as your desktop background.

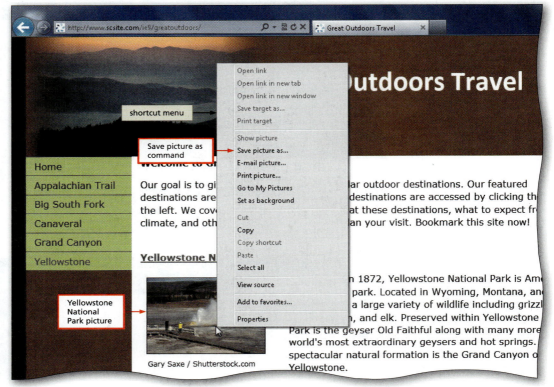

Figure 1–40

2
- Click 'Save picture as' on the shortcut menu to display the Save Picture dialog box (Figure 1–41).

Figure 1–41

3

- If necessary, click the Browse Folders button to expand the Save Picture dialog box.

- If necessary, click the Pictures link (Save Picture dialog box).

- Type **Yellowstone** in the File name text box to change the file name (Figure 1–42).

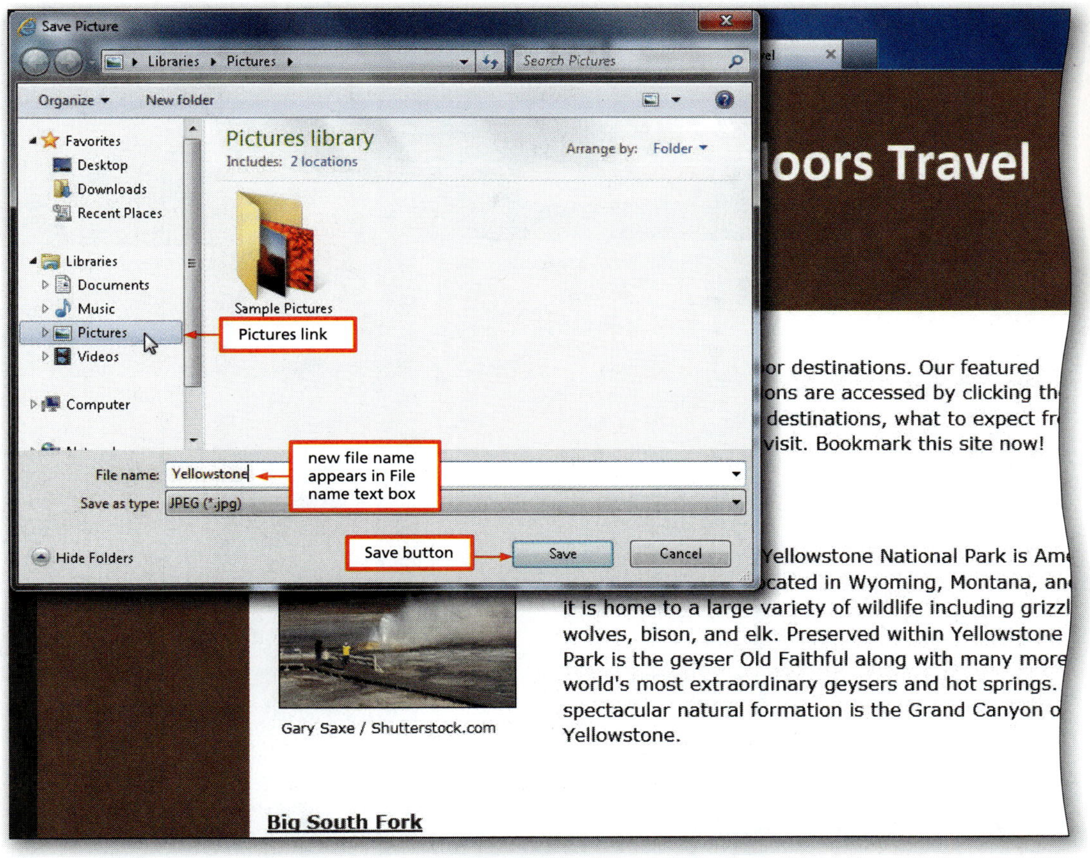

Q&A

Should I store all my pictures in the Pictures library?

Yes. Windows provides the Pictures library to help you organize your pictures and make backing up the pictures in the Pictures library to another storage device for safekeeping easy.

Three other libraries (Documents, Music, and Videos) are available to store document, music, and video files.

Figure 1–42

4

- Click the Save button (Save Picture dialog box) to save the picture in the Pictures library on your computer and to close the Save Picture dialog box.

Copying and Pasting Using the Clipboard

A third method of saving information, called the copy-and-paste method, allows you to copy an entire Web page, or portions of a page, and insert the information into any Windows document. The Clipboard is a storage area in main memory that temporarily holds the information being copied. The portion of the Web page you select is copied from the page to the Clipboard and then pasted from the Clipboard into the document. Information you copy to the Clipboard remains there until you add new information or clear it.

The following pages demonstrate how to copy text and pictures from the Yellowstone National Park Web page into a WordPad document using the Clipboard. WordPad is a word-processing program that is supplied with Microsoft Windows.

BTW

Copy and Paste Web Addresses
You can use the copy-and-paste operation to insert a Web address that appears in the Address bar into a document or e-mail message. You also can copy a Web address that appears in an e-mail message into the Address bar.

To Start WordPad

Before copying information from the Web page in Internet Explorer to the Clipboard, you first should start WordPad. The following steps start WordPad.

1

- Click the Start button on the Windows taskbar to display the Start menu.

- Click All Programs on the Start menu to display the All Programs list.

- Click Accessories on the All Programs list to display the Accessories list (Figure 1–43).

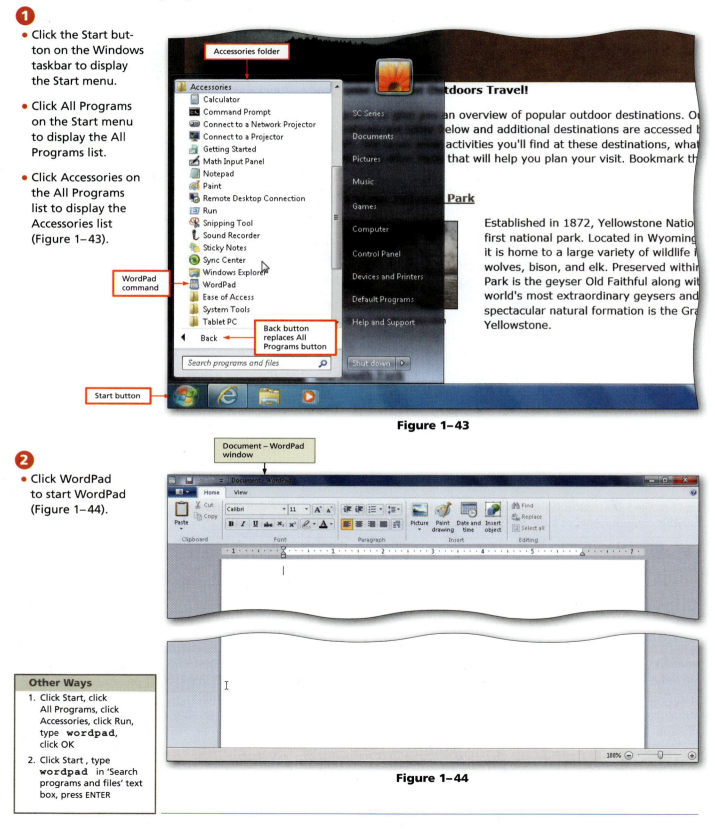

Figure 1–43

2

- Click WordPad to start WordPad (Figure 1–44).

Figure 1–44

Other Ways

1. Click Start, click All Programs, click Accessories, click Run, type **wordpad**, click OK

2. Click Start , type **wordpad** in 'Search programs and files' text box, press ENTER

To Display the Yellowstone National Park Web Page

Currently, the active Document – WordPad window is displayed on top of the inactive Great Outdoors Travel window. After starting WordPad and before copying text from a Web page to the Clipboard, make the Great Outdoors Travel window active and then display the Yellowstone National Park Web page. The following steps display the Yellowstone National Park Web page.

1

- Click the Internet Explorer button on the taskbar to make the Great Outdoors Travel window the active window (Figure 1–45).

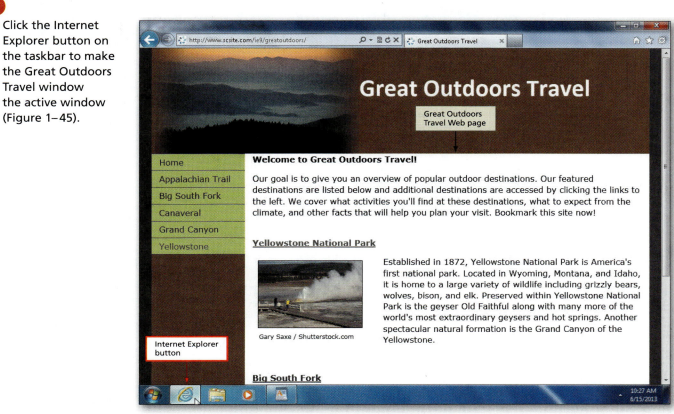

Figure 1–45

2

- Click the Yellowstone link on the Great Outdoors Travel Web page to display the Yellowstone National Park Web page (Figure 1–46).

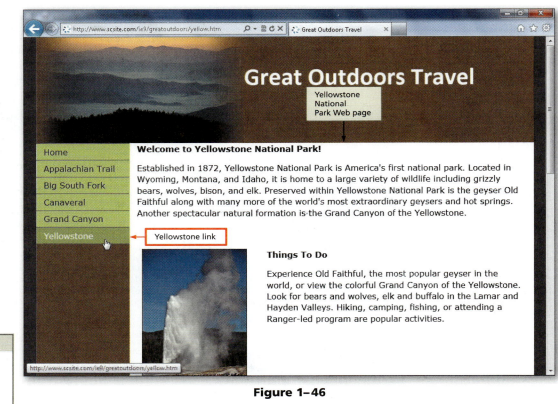

Figure 1–46

Other Ways

1. Press ALT+TAB, hold down ALT, press TAB to select
2. If visible, click window title bar

To Copy and Paste Text from a Web Page into a WordPad Document

With the Document – WordPad window open and the text you want to copy displayed on the Yellowstone National Park Web page, the next steps are to copy the text from the Yellowstone National Park Web page to the Clipboard, and then paste the text into the WordPad document. The following steps copy the text about Yellowstone National Park into the WordPad document.

1

- Position the mouse pointer (I-beam) to the left of the E in Established to prepare to select the text to be copied (Figure 1–47).

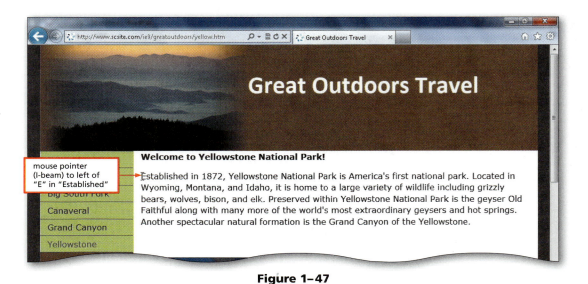

Figure 1–47

2

- Drag to select the text in the entire paragraph.

- Right-click the selected text to display a shortcut menu (Figure 1–48).

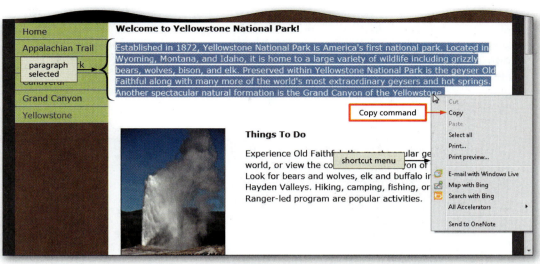

Figure 1–48

3

- Click Copy on the shortcut menu to copy the selected text to the Clipboard.

- Click the Document – WordPad button on the Windows taskbar to display the Document – WordPad window, and then right-click the empty text area in the Document – WordPad window to display a shortcut menu (Figure 1–49).

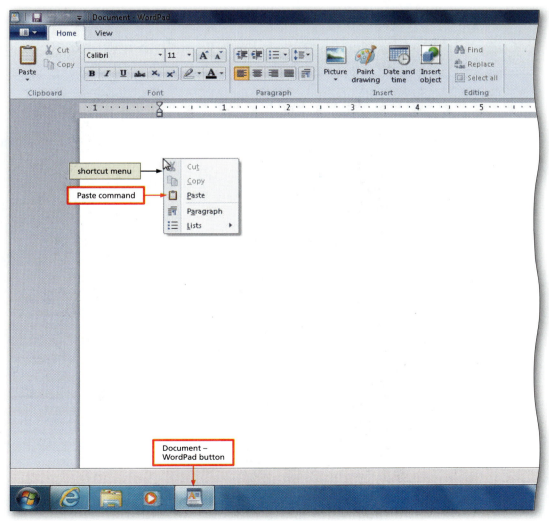

Figure 1–49

4

- Click Paste on the shortcut menu to paste the contents of the Clipboard in the Document – WordPad window (Figure 1–50).

text pasted into WordPad document →

Established in 1872, Yellowstone National Park is America's first national park. Located in Wyoming, Montana, and Idaho, it is home to a large variety of wildlife including grizzly bears, wolves, bison, and elk. Preserved within Yellowstone National Park is the geyser Old Faithful along with many more of the world's most extraordinary geysers and hot springs. Another spectacular natural formation is the Grand Canyon of the Yellowstone.

insertion point →

Figure 1–50

Other Ways

1. Select text, press CTRL+C, select paste area, press CTRL+V

To Copy and Paste a Picture from a Web Page into a WordPad Document

The steps to copy a picture from a Web page are similar to those used to copy and paste text. The following steps copy and then paste a picture from a Web page into a WordPad document.

1

- To activate the Yellowstone National Park Web page, click the Internet Explorer button on the Windows taskbar.

- Click outside the selected text to deselect the text.

- Right-click the picture to the left of the Things to Do area to display a shortcut menu (Figure 1–51).

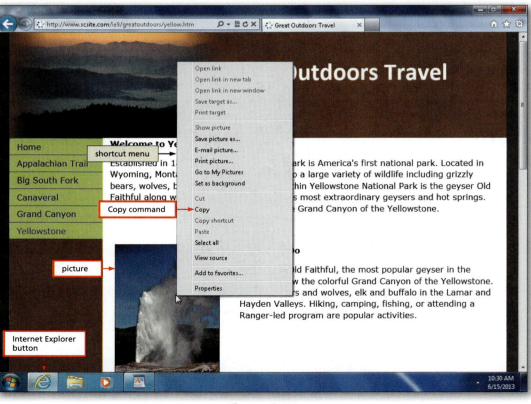

Figure 1–51

2

- Click Copy on the shortcut menu to copy the picture to the Clipboard.

- Activate the Document – WordPad window.

- Right-click an area below the insertion point in the Document – WordPad window to display a shortcut menu (Figure 1–52).

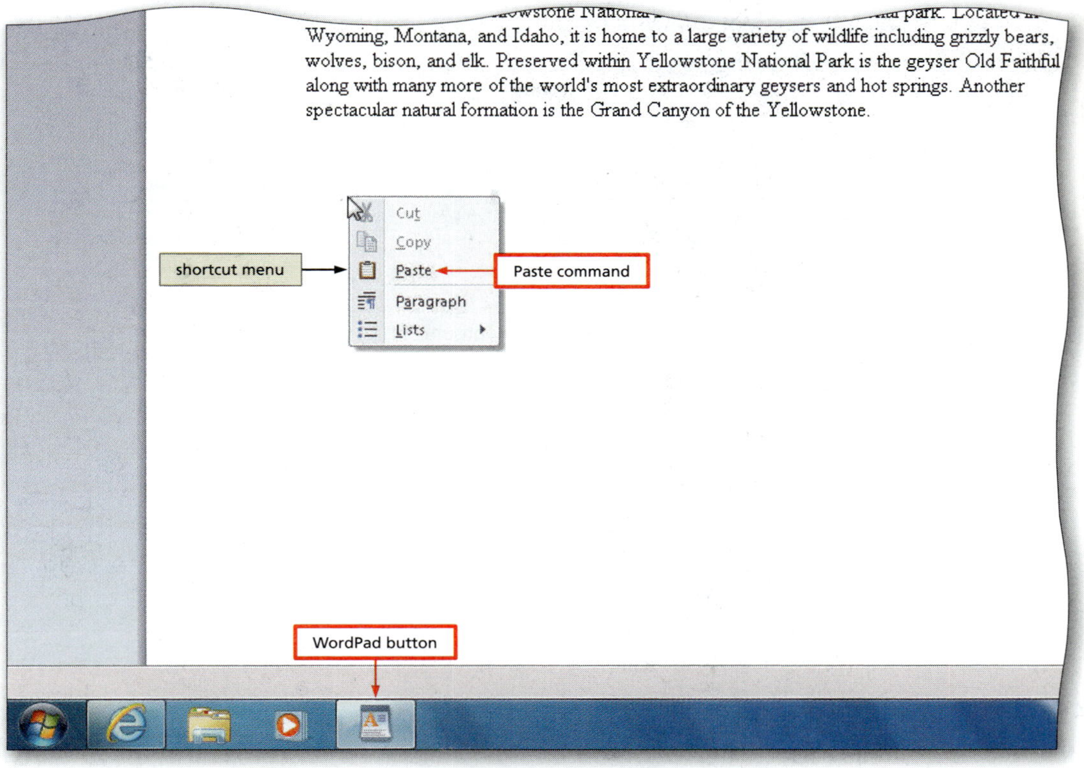

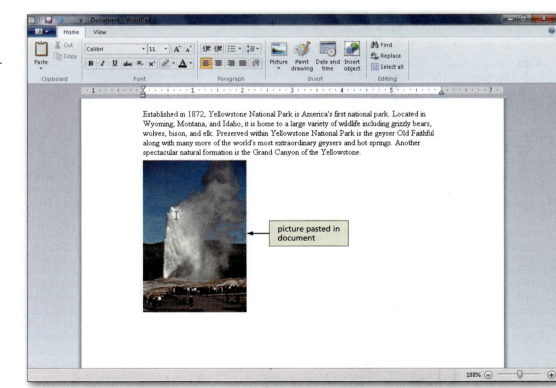

Figure 1–52

3

- Click Paste on the shortcut menu to paste the picture into the Document – WordPad window (Figure 1–53).

Figure 1–53

To Save the WordPad Document and Quit WordPad

When you are finished with the WordPad document, you can save it to your computer for later use and then quit WordPad. The following steps save the WordPad document using the Yellowstone National Park file name and then quit WordPad.

1

• Click the Save button on the Quick Access Toolbar in the Document – WordPad window to display the Save As dialog box (Figure 1–54).

Figure 1–54

2

• Type **Yellowstone National Park** in the File name text box (Figure 1–55).

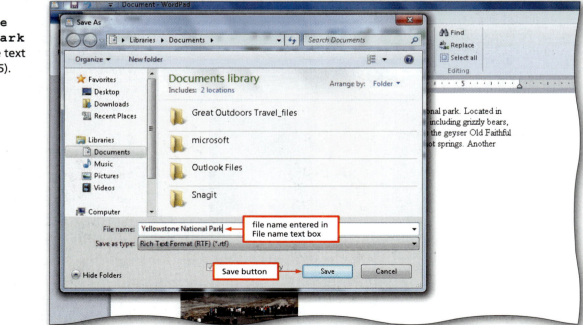

Figure 1–55

3
- Click the Save button (Save As dialog box) to save the WordPad document (Figure 1–56).

- Click the Close button on the Yellowstone National Park – WordPad title bar to quit WordPad.

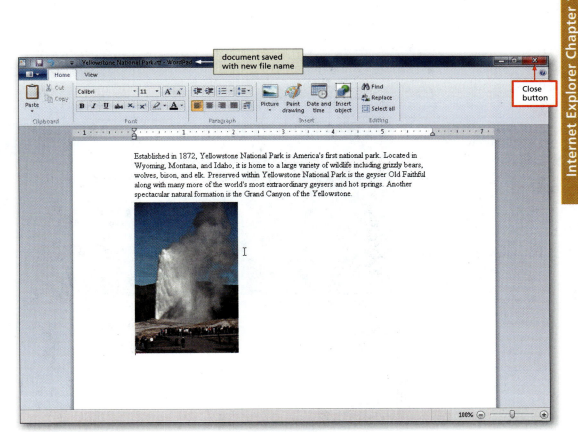

Figure 1–56

Other Ways

1. Press ALT+F, press A, type file name, press ENTER

2. Press CTRL+S, type file name, press ENTER

Printing a Web Page in Internet Explorer

As you browse the Web, you might want to print some of the Web pages you view. You might need to print driving directions, your airline ticket, or a record of your tax documents, if you submitted your taxes online. A printed version of a Web page is called a **hard copy** or printout.

You can suppress the title and Web address of a Web page from being displayed on a printout using the Page Setup dialog box. You can display the Page Setup dialog box by clicking the Tools button on the toolbar, pointing to Print, and then selecting the Page setup command. The Header and Footer buttons allow you to specify the information that is displayed in the header and footer areas of the printout.

BTW

Print Options
You can choose to print a table containing a list of all links on the Web page you are printing, or you can choose to print all documents with links on the Web page. Press CTRL+P, click the Options tab in the Print dialog box, and then click the 'Print all linked documents' check box or 'Print table of links' check box to print the documents or table.

To Print a Web Page

Internet Explorer allows you to print both the text and picture portions of a Web page. The following steps print the Yellowstone National Park Web page.

1

- Ready the printer according to the printer instructions.

- Click the Tools button on the toolbar to display the Tools menu.

- Point to Print on the Tools menu to display the Print submenu (Figure 1–57).

Q&A What other commands are available on the Print submenu?

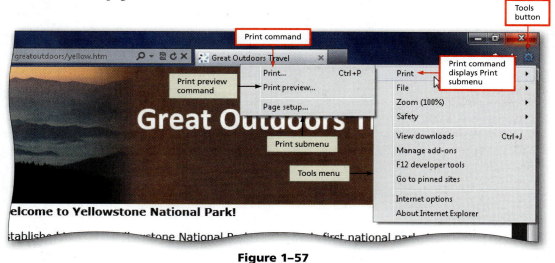

Figure 1–57

The Print submenu on the Tools menu also provides access to the Print preview and Page setup commands. The printing options available in the Print dialog box allow you to print the entire document, print selected pages of a document, print to a file, print multiple copies, change the printer properties, and cancel the print request.

2

- Click Print on the Print submenu to display the Print dialog box (Figure 1–58).

- Click the Print button (Print dialog box) to begin printing the document.

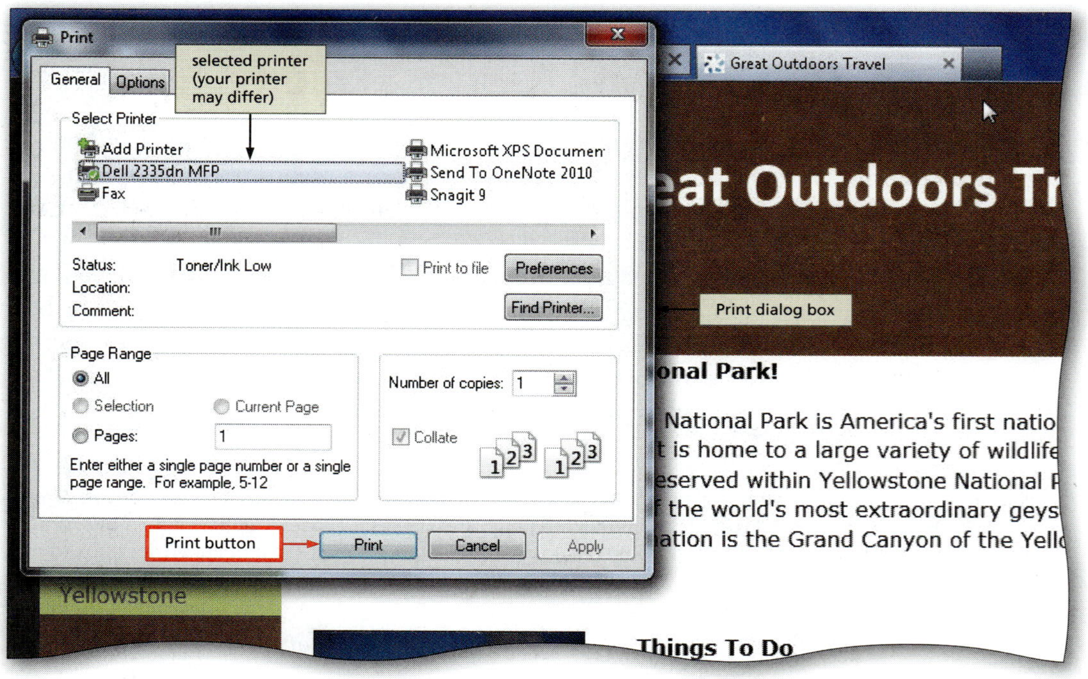

Figure 1–58

Other Ways

1. Press ALT, on File menu click Print, click Print button

2. Press CTRL+P, click Print button

Internet Explorer Help

Internet Explorer offers users many features and options. Although you will master some features and options quickly, it is not necessary for you to remember everything about all of them. Reference materials and other forms of assistance are available within Internet Explorer Help. Clicking the Help menu on the menu bar provides access to several additional commands related to Help, which are summarized in Table 1–3.

Table 1–3 Commands on the Help Menu	
Menu Command	**Function**
Internet Explorer Help	Displays the Windows Help and Support window
What's New in Internet Explorer 9	Displays a Web page highlighting new features in Internet Explorer 9
Online support	Displays Microsoft Support Web site
About Internet Explorer	Displays version, cipher strength, product ID, license information, and copyright information about Internet Explorer

To Access Internet Explorer Help

After opening the Windows Help and Support window, buttons on the Help toolbar allow you to perform activities such as going back to the most recent Help topic, going forward to a Help page you have visited prior to clicking the Back button, displaying the Windows Help and Support Center home page, printing the current page, browsing Help, requesting additional help, and accessing additional Help options. The following steps use Internet Explorer Help and the Windows Help and Support window to find more information about favorites.

1

- Press the ALT key to display the menu bar.

- Click Help on the menu bar to display the Help menu (Figure 1–59).

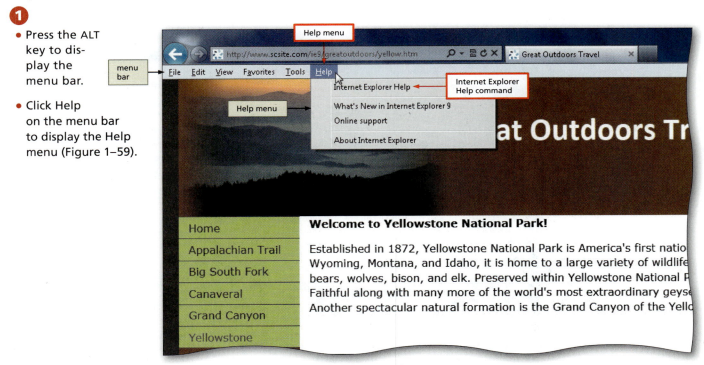

Figure 1–59

2

• Click Internet Explorer Help on the Help menu to open the Windows Help and Support window (Figure 1–60).

Q&A

What if the Windows Help and Support window is blank?

Click the button in the lower-right corner of the window and make sure Get offline Help is selected.

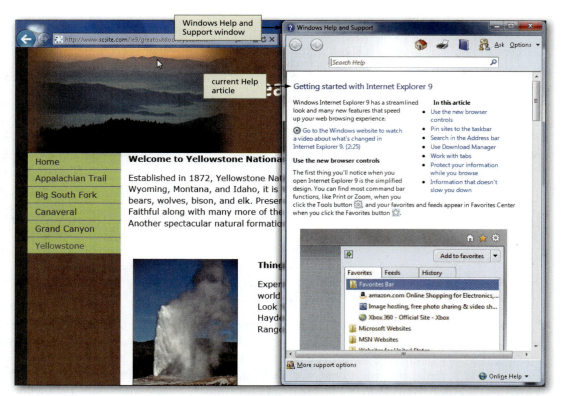

Figure 1–60

3

• Type **favorites** in the Search Help text box, and then press the ENTER key to display the search results matching your search text (Figure 1–61).

Q&A

Why do my search results differ?

When you search for help using Windows Help and Support, your search results also include online resources that match your search criteria. Microsoft regularly updates these online resources to provide you with an effective and up-to-date Help system.

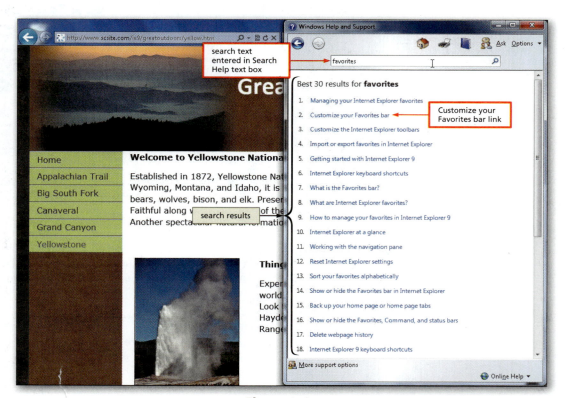

Figure 1–61

4

- Click the Customize your Favorites bar link in the list of Help topics to display information about favorites (Figure 1–62).

- When you are finished reading the information, click the Close button on the right side of the title bar to close the Windows Help and Support window.

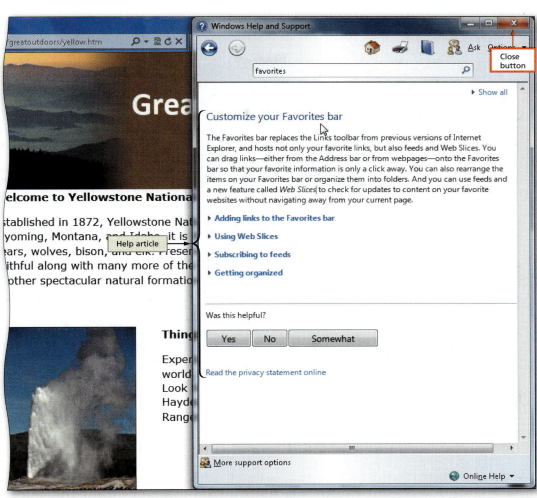

Figure 1–62

Other Ways

1. Press ALT+H, press I
2. Press F1

Quitting Internet Explorer

After browsing the Web and learning how to navigate Web sites, add favorites, copy and paste content, and print Web pages, you should quit Internet Explorer.

To Quit Internet Explorer

The following step quits Internet Explorer.

1

• Click the Close button in the upper-right corner of the Internet Explorer window to close the window (Figure 1–63).

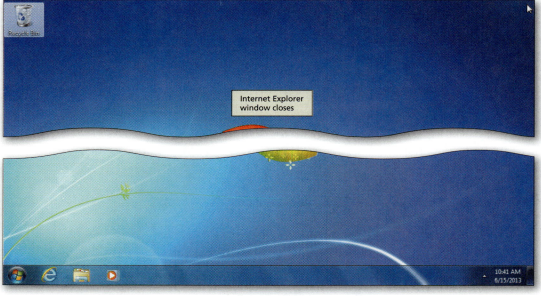

Internet Explorer window closes

Figure 1–63

Other Ways

1. Press ALT, click File menu, click Exit
2. Press ALT+F, press X

Chapter Summary

This chapter introduced you to the Internet and World Wide Web. You learned how to start Internet Explorer, use the commands on the toolbar, and enter a Web address to browse the Web. You learned how to add and remove favorites, save a picture and an entire Web page to the hard disk, copy and paste text from a Web page into a WordPad document, and print a Web page. In addition, you learned how to use Help to obtain help about Internet Explorer. The items listed below include all the new Internet Explorer skills you have learned in this chapter.

1. Start Internet Explorer (IE 11)
2. Browse the Web by Entering a Web Address (IE 15)
3. Refresh a Web Page (IE 20)
4. Use the Navigation Buttons to Find Recently Displayed Web Pages (IE 21)
5. Display a Web Page Using the Address Bar Autocomplete List (IE 22)
6. Display a Web Page Using the History List (IE 24)
7. Add a Web Page to the Favorites Center (IE 27)
8. Display the Home Page Using the Home Button (IE 29)
9. Display a Web Page Using the Favorites Center (IE 30)
10. Remove a Web Page from the Favorites Center (IE 31)
11. Save a Web Page (IE 33)
12. Save a Picture on a Web Page (IE 34)
13. Start WordPad (IE 36)
14. Display the Yellowstone National Park Web Page (IE 37)
15. Copy and Paste Text from a Web Page into a WordPad Document (IE 38)
16. Copy and Paste a Picture from a Web Page into a WordPad Document (IE 40)
17. Save the WordPad Document and Quit WordPad (IE 42)
18. Print a Web Page (IE 44)
19. Access Internet Explorer Help (IE 45)
20. Quit Internet Explorer (IE 48)

Learn It Online

Test your knowledge of chapter content and key terms.

Instructions: To complete the following exercises, please visit `cengagebrain.com`. On the CengageBrain.com home page, enter the book title `Windows Internet Explorer 9 Introductory` or the ISBN `0-538-48239-7` and then click the Find button. On the product page for this book, click the Access Now button below the Study Tools heading. On the Book Companion Site Web page, click the drop-down menu, select Chapter 1, and then click the link for the desired exercise.

Chapter Reinforcement TF, MC, and SA

A series of true/false, multiple-choice, and short-answer questions that test your knowledge of the chapter content.

Flash Cards

An interactive learning environment where you identify key terms from the chapter associated with displayed definitions.

Practice Test

A series of multiple-choice questions that test your knowledge of chapter content and key terms.

Who Wants To Be a Computer Genius?

An interactive game that challenges your knowledge of chapter content in the style of the television quiz show.

Wheel of Terms

An interactive game that challenges your knowledge of key terms from the chapter in the style of the television show *Wheel of Fortune*.

Crossword Puzzle Challenge

A crossword puzzle that challenges your knowledge of key terms presented in the chapter.

Apply Your Knowledge

Reinforce the skills and apply the concepts you learned in this chapter.

Browsing the World Wide Web Using Web Addresses and Links

Instructions: You work part-time for *USA Today*, one of the nation's leading sources of news. Your editor has asked you to search for information on several informational Web sites and print pages from each Web site.

Perform the following tasks:
Part 1: Use the Address Bar to Find Web Pages
1. If necessary, connect to the Internet and start Internet Explorer.
2. Click the Address bar, type `www.fbi.gov` to enter the Web address, and then press the ENTER key to display the Federal Bureau of Investigation's home page (Figure 1–64 on the next page).

Continued >

Apply Your Knowledge *continued*

Federal Bureau
of Investigation
home page

ABOUT US link

Figure 1–64

3. Point to the ABOUT US link and then click the Quick Facts link to display the Web page that contains facts about the FBI.

4. Click the Tools button, point to Print, click Print on the submenu, and then click the Print button to print the Web page.

5. Use the Back button on the toolbar to display the FBI home page.

6. Click the Tools button, point to Print, click Print on the submenu, and then click the Print button to print the Web page.

7. Click the Address bar, type **www.nbc.com** to enter the Web address, and then press the ENTER key to display the NBC home page (Figure 1–65).

NBC home page

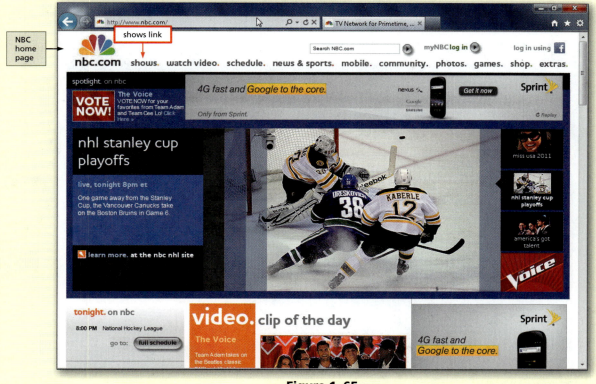

Figure 1–65

8. Click the shows link, and then click the Dateline link in the NBC Web site to display the Web page about the television show, *Dateline*.

9. Click the Tools button, point to Print, click Print on the submenu, and then click the Print button to print the Web page.

10. Click the Address bar, type `www.weather.com` in the box, and then press the ENTER key to display the weather.com home page (Figure 1–66 on the next page).

Continued >

STUDENT ASSIGNMENTS

Apply Your Knowledge *continued*

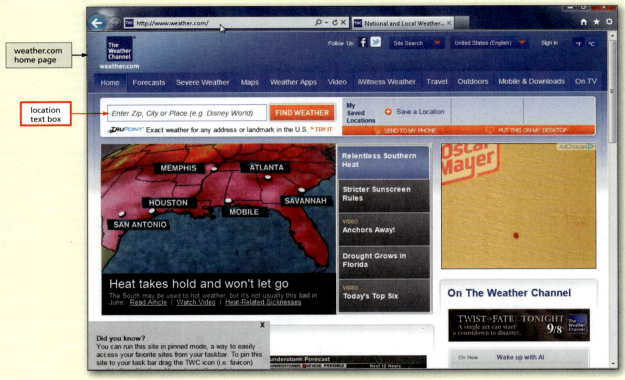

weather.com home page

location text box

Figure 1–66

11. Type your ZIP code in the location text box, and then click the FIND WEATHER button to display the Web page containing the weather report for your area.

12. Record information about the weather forecast for your area.

13. Click the Address bar, type `www.abc.com` to enter the Web address, and then press the ENTER key to display the ABC home page (Figure 1–67).

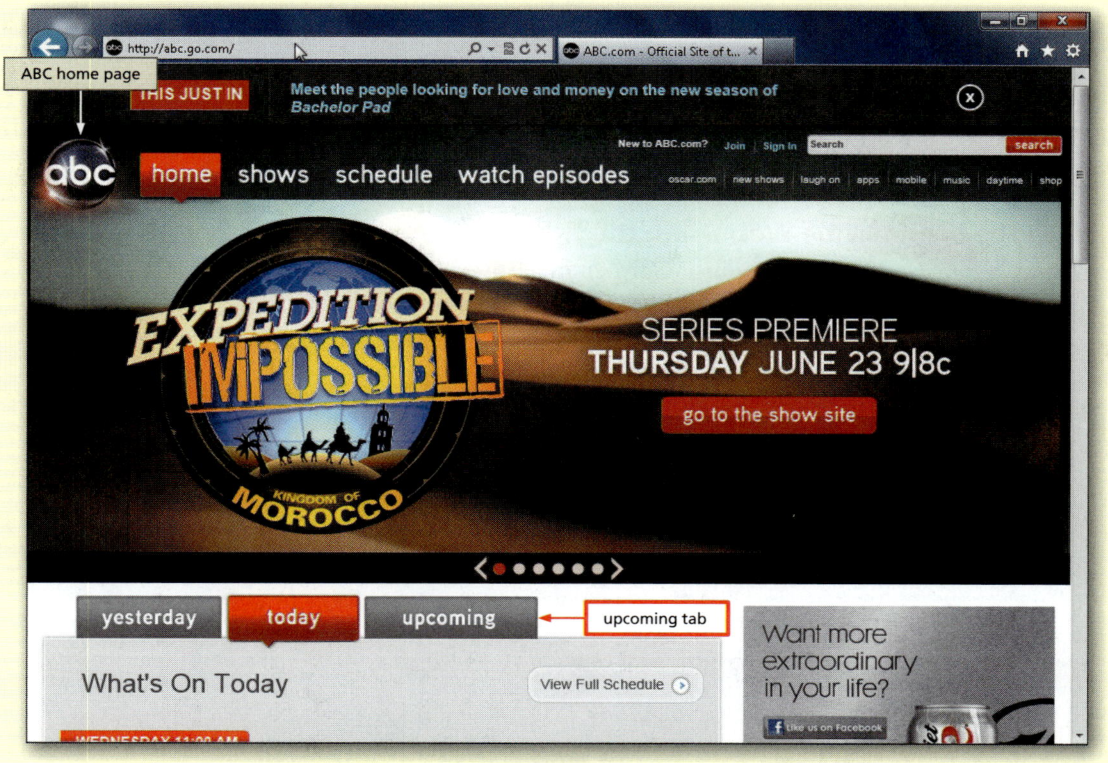

Figure 1–67

14. Click the upcoming tab to display the Web page containing information about upcoming shows.

15. Write down a list of upcoming shows on ABC.

Part 2: Use the History List to Find a Web Page

1. Click the Home button on the toolbar to display your default home page.

2. Click the 'View favorites, feeds, and history' button on the toolbar, click the History tab to display the History list, click Today, click the nbc (www.nbc.com) folder name in the History list, and then click the TV Network for Primetime, Daytime and Late Night Television Shows – NBC Official Site link to display the NBC home page.

3. Print the first page of this Web page.

4. If necessary, click the Close button in the Favorites Center.

Part 3: Use the Back Button to Find a Web Page

1. Click and hold the Back button, and then click the ABC.com – Official Site of the ABC Network entry on the menu to display the ABC home page.

Part 4: Use the Show Address Bar Autocomplete Button to Find a Web Page

1. Click the Show Address bar Autocomplete button and then click http://www.weather.com in the list of Web addresses to display the weather.com home page.

2. Print only the second page of this Web page.

3. Click the Close button in the Internet Explorer window.

4. Submit the printed pages to your instructor.

STUDENT ASSIGNMENTS

Extend Your Knowledge

Extend the skills you learned in this chapter and experiment with new skills. You might need to use Help to complete the assignment.

Browsing the World Wide Web Using the Address Bar

Instructions: Concerned about keeping your personal information and your computer safe when you access the Internet, you decide to visit the Web site of a leading computer security company.

Perform the following tasks:

1. Use the Address bar to locate the official McAfee Web site. What keywords did you type to locate this page?

2. Navigate to the McAfee home page (Figure 1–68).

McAfee home page →

Figure 1–68

3. View the Web page in Print Preview. What buttons appear at the top of the Print Preview window? How many pages will it take to print this Web page?

4. Print the McAfee home page from the Print Preview window, and then close the Print Preview window.

5. Use the links on the McAfee home page to answer the following questions for home users:

   a. What are the five most recent threats?

   b. On what date was the latest virus discovered?

   c. How does McAfee measure the severity of threats?

   d. What must you do to protect your computer from viruses? What programs does McAfee offer to help you protect your computer?

   e. What is the current Threat Meter level?

   f. If your computer already has been infected by a threat, such as a virus or spyware, what should you do?

6. Use the History list to navigate back to the McAfee home page.

7. Browse McAfee's Web site for a page that discusses an example of current malware. Print the Web page.

8. Navigate back to the McAfee home page, and add the Web page to your Favorites Center.

9. Remove the Web page from your Favorites Center.

10. Organize your printed Web pages and submit them, along with the answers to the questions in this exercise, to your instructor.

In the Lab

Use Internet Explorer to navigate the World Wide Web by using the guidelines, concepts, and skills presented in this chapter. Labs are listed in order of increasing difficulty.

Lab 1: Using the History List to Locate Previously Viewed Web Pages

Instructions: Your instructor would like you to practice browsing the Internet and using the History list. As proof of completing this assignment, you should print the first page of each Web site you visit.

Perform the following tasks:
Part 1: Clear the History List
1. Click the Tools button on the toolbar and then click Internet options to display the Internet Options dialog box (Figure 1–69).

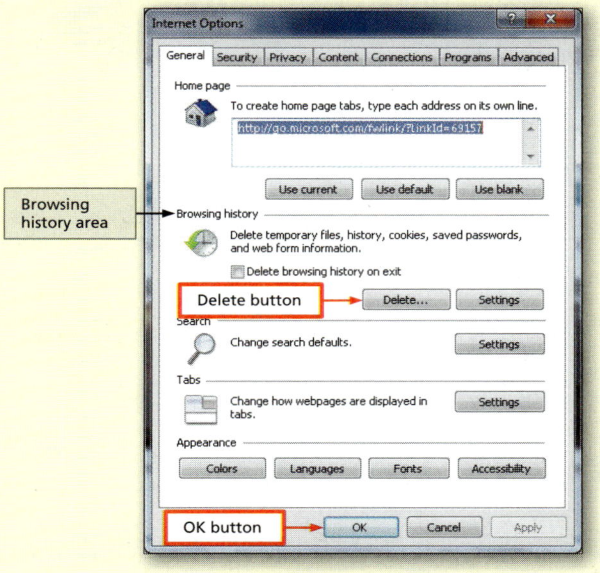

Figure 1–69

Continued >

In the Lab *continued*

2. Click the Delete button in the Browsing history area and then click the Delete button in the Delete Browsing History dialog box. (*Hint:* If a notification bar appears at the bottom of the display area indicating that Internet Explorer has finished deleting the selected browsing history, click the Close button on the Notification bar to close the bar.)

3. Click the OK button to close the Internet Options dialog box.

Part 2: Browse the World Wide Web

1. Click the Address bar, type **www.youtube.com** to enter the Web address, and then press the ENTER key to display the YouTube home page.

2. Click the Address bar, type **www.ku.edu** to enter the Web address, and then press the ENTER key to display the The University of Kansas home page.

3. Click the Address bar, type **www.geocaching.com** to enter the Web address, and then press the ENTER key to display the Geocaching home page.

4. Click the Address bar, type **www.foxsports.com** to enter the Web address, and then press the ENTER key to display the FOX Sports home page.

Part 3: Use the History List to Print a Web Page

1. Click the 'View favorites, feeds, and history' button on the toolbar, click the History tab, and then click Today to display the current History list. Click the Pin the Favorites Center button to pin the Favorites Center (Figure 1–70).

History list displays in Favorites Center

Figure 1–70

2. Click the ku (www.ku.edu) folder in the History list and then click the www.ku.edu link. Print the first page of the Web page.

3. Click the youtube (www.youtube.com) folder in the History list and then click the YouTube – Broadcast Yourself link. Print the first page of the Web page.

4. Click the msn.foxsports (msn.foxsports.com) folder in the History list and then click the FOX Sports on MSN link. Print the first page of the Web page.

5. Delete the geocaching (www.geocaching.com) folder. (*Hint:* Right-click the folder, click Delete, and then click the Yes button in the WARNING dialog box.)

6. Click the Close the Favorites Center button.

Part 4: Clear the History List

1. Click the Tools button on the toolbar, point to Safety, and then click 'Delete browsing history' to display the Delete Browsing History dialog box.

2. If necessary, click the History check box so that it contains a check mark, and then click the Delete button.

3. Submit the printed Web pages to your instructor.

In the Lab

Lab 2: Adding, Viewing, Printing, and Removing Your Favorites

Instructions: Your instructor would like you to practice browsing the Internet and adding Web sites to the Favorites Center. As proof of completing this assignment, print out the first page of each Web site you visit.

Perform the following tasks:
Part 1: Create a Folder in the Favorites Center
1. Click the 'View favorites, feeds, and history' button on the toolbar, click the 'Add to favorites' list arrow, and then click Organize favorites to display the Organize Favorites dialog box (Figure 1–71).

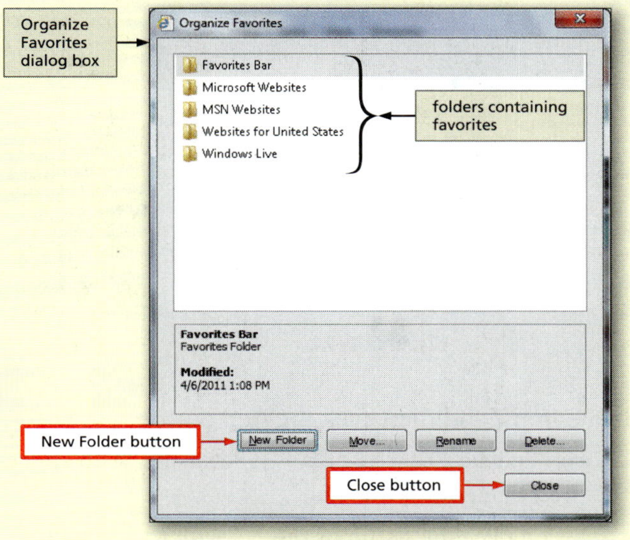

Figure 1–71

2. Click the New Folder button in the Organize Favorites dialog box to create a folder titled New folder, type your first and last name as the folder name, and then press the ENTER key.
3. Click the Close button to close the Organize Favorites dialog box.

Part 2: Add Favorites to Your Folder
1. Click the Address bar, type **www.defense.gov** to enter the Web address, and then press the ENTER key to display the U.S. Department of Defense home page.
2. Add a U.S. Department of Defense favorite to the folder identified by your name by clicking the 'View favorites, feeds, and history' button on the toolbar, and then clicking the 'Add to favorites' button (Figure 1–72). Click the Create in drop-down list button to display the Create in list.

Continued >

In the Lab continued

Figure 1–72

3. Click your folder in the Create in list and then click the Add button.

4. Click the Address bar, type `www.priceline.com` to enter the Web address, and then press the ENTER key to display the priceline.com home page.

5. Add this Web page as a favorite, change the name of the favorite to Priceline, and then create the favorite in your folder.

6. Click the Home button on the toolbar to display your default home page.

Part 3: Display and Print a Favorite from Your Folder

1. Click the 'View favorites, feeds, and history' button on the toolbar to display the Favorites Center. If necessary, click the Favorites tab.

2. Click your folder in the Favorites Center and then click The Official Home of the Department of Defense.

3. Print the first page of the Web page.

4. If necessary, click the 'View favorites, feeds, and history' button on the toolbar to display the Favorites Center.

5. Click Priceline in the Favorites Center.

6. Print the first page of the Web page.

Part 4: Delete a Folder in the Favorites Center

1. If necessary, display the Favorites Center.

2. Right-click your folder name, click Delete on the shortcut menu, and then click the Yes button in the Delete Folder dialog box.

3. If necessary, close the Favorites Center.

4. Verify that you have deleted your folder.

5. Submit the printed pages to your instructor.

In the Lab

Lab 3: Printing and Saving the Current U.S. Weather Map

Instructions: You are interested in finding a current United States weather map to use on a road trip starting in Leavenworth, Kansas, and ending in Orlando, Florida. You want to print the map and save it on your hard disk.

Perform the following tasks:

1. Type **www.weather.com** in the Address bar and then press the ENTER key to display the weather.com home page.

2. Point to Maps and then click the US Current Temperatures link to display an enlarged weather map for the United States. If necessary, scroll down to view the weather map (Figure 1–73). The map that is displayed on your computer might differ from Figure 1–73.

Figure 1–73

3. Right-click the weather map, click Print picture on the shortcut menu, and then click the Print button in the Print dialog box to print the weather map.

4. Right-click the weather map and click 'Save picture as' on the shortcut menu to display the Save Picture dialog box. Click the Pictures library in the left pane of the Save Picture dialog box, type **U.S. Weather map** as the file name, and then click the Save button (Save Picture dialog box) to save the picture on your hard disk.

5. Submit the printed weather map to your instructor.

STUDENT ASSIGNMENTS

In the Lab

Lab 4: Collecting Biographical Information

Instructions: To complete an assignment in history class, you must locate the Biography.com Web site and select a person whose biography is on the Web site. When you find the biography of your chosen person, copy his or her picture and the text of the biography into WordPad, and then print the WordPad document.

Perform the following tasks:

Part 1: Retrieve a Web Page

1. Type **www.bio.com** in the Address bar and then press the ENTER key to display the bio.com home page (Figure 1–74).

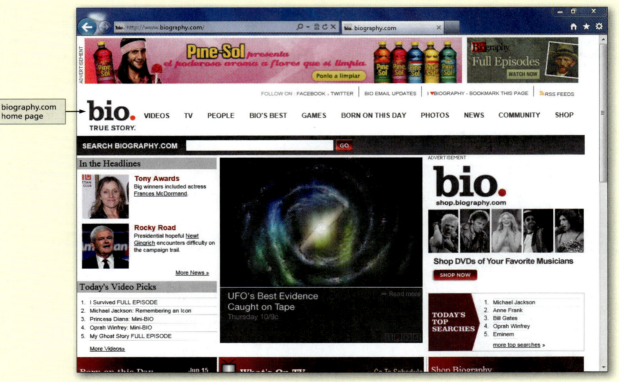

biography.com home page

Figure 1–74

2. Using the links on the Web site, search for the biography of a person in whom you are interested. (Suggestions: Maya Angelou, Amelia Earhart, Thomas Edison, Albert Einstein, Frida Kahlo, Elvis Presley, Jackie Robinson, Eleanor Roosevelt, George Washington)

Part 2: Copy a Picture and Text to Microsoft WordPad

1. If a picture of the person is available, copy the picture to the Clipboard.

2. Start Microsoft WordPad.

3. Paste the picture from the Clipboard into the WordPad document, click anywhere off the picture, and then press the ENTER key.

4. Switch back to the Internet Explorer window.

5. Copy the biography text to the Clipboard.

6. Switch to the WordPad window.

7. Paste the text on the Clipboard into the WordPad document.

8. Save the WordPad document on your hard disk using the file name, `Biography Assignment`.

9. Print the WordPad document.

10. Quit WordPad.

11. Submit the WordPad document to your instructor.

In the Lab

Lab 5: Searching the Web for a Job in Database Administration

Instructions: You are job-hunting for a position that uses your expertise in database administration. Instead of using the newspaper to find a job, you decide to search for jobs on the Internet. You decide to visit three Web sites in hopes of finding the perfect job.

Perform the following tasks:

1. Click the Address bar, type `www.computerjobs.com` to enter the Web address, and then press the ENTER key to display the computerjobs.com home page (Figure 1–75).

Figure 1–75

2. Type `database administrator` in the Keywords text box and then press the ENTER key. Print the first page of the database administrator listings.

3. Type `www.monster.com` in the Address bar and then press the ENTER key.

Continued >

STUDENT ASSIGNMENTS

In the Lab *continued*

4. Type **database administrator** in the Any Skills/Keywords text box and then click the SEARCH button. Print the first page of the database administrator listings.

5. Type **www.careerbuilder.com** in the Address bar and then press the ENTER key.

6. When the careerbuilder.com page displays, type **database administrator** in the Keywords text box, and then click the Find Jobs button. Print the first page of the database administrator listings.

7. Submit the printouts to your instructor.

In the Lab

Lab 6: Using Windows Help and Support to Find Information about Internet Explorer

Instructions: Because you do not know much about Internet Explorer, you decide to learn more by using Windows Help and Support to search for the following topics: InPrivate Browsing, SmartScreen Filter, Tracking Protection, Download Manager, and keyboard shortcuts.

Perform the following tasks:

1. Press the F1 key to display the Windows Help and Support window, which contains general information about Internet Explorer (Figure 1–76).

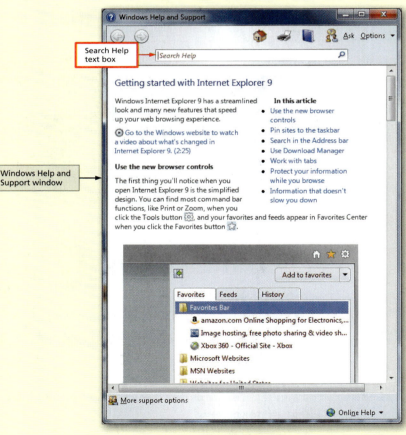

Figure 1–76

2. Type `InPrivate Browsing` in the Search Help text box, press the ENTER key, and browse the topics necessary to answer the following questions.

   a. What is InPrivate Browsing?

   b. What is InPrivate Filtering?

3. Select the text in the Search box, type `SmartScreen Filter`, press the ENTER key, and browse the search results to answer the following questions.

   a. What is the SmartScreen Filter?

   b. How do you report a phishing Web site?

4. Select the text in the Search box, type `Tracking Protection`, press the ENTER key, and browse the search results to answer the following questions.

   a. What is tracking protection?

   b. How do you turn on tracking protection?

5. Select the text in the Search box, type `Download Manager`, press the ENTER key, and browse the search results to answer the following questions.

   a. What is the Download Manager?

   b. How can you choose where downloads are stored?

6. Select the text in the Search box, type `keyboard shortcuts`, press the ENTER key, and browse the search results to answer the following questions.

   a. What is the keyboard shortcut to select the text in the Address bar?

   b. What is the keyboard shortcut to open an InPrivate Browsing window?

   c. What is the keyboard shortcut to delete the browsing history?

7. Close the Windows Help and Support window.

8. Close the Internet Explorer window.

9. Submit the answers to the questions to your instructor.

Cases and Places

Apply your creative thinking and problem-solving skills to browse for information.

1: Browsing the Web for Stock Information

Academic

Your assignment in your finance class is to find fundamental stock information about three companies of your choice—for example, Microsoft Corporation (MSFT), Google Inc. (GOOG), or Apple Inc. (AAPL). Use the Yahoo! Finance Web site (finance.yahoo.com) to obtain today's stock price, dividend rate (look for Div value), daily volume, 52-week range, and the P/E (price earnings ratio). To display this information, enter the stock symbol and then click the GET QUOTES button to display the information. Print the detailed results for each stock. In addition, click the first article under the Headlines heading for the stock of your choice and then print the page.

Continued >

Cases and Places *continued*

2: Browsing the Web for a New Car

Personal

Your old car broke down and you are in the market for a new one. Navigate to **www.autotrader.com** to display the AutoTrader home page. Select your favorite make, type your ZIP code, and then click the Next button. On the following Web page, use the form fields to search for a new car. Select two competitors of the car you chose. Print the information on your favorite car and its two competitors.

3: Browsing the Web for Travel Specials

Professional

You are planning a business trip to Belize. You want to leave exactly one month from today and plan to stay seven days, including the travel days. Check with at least two different travel Web sites such as Orbitz (www.orbitz.com) and Expedia (www.expedia.com) for travel specials to Belize. Print any Web pages containing flight information and then summarize the information you find in a brief report.

2 | Internet Research

Objectives

You will have mastered the material in this chapter when you can:

- Describe the 13 general categories of Web sites

- Evaluate a Web resource

- Describe the three basic types of search tools

- Search the Web using both a directory and keywords

- Use tabbed browsing features

- Use the Address bar to search for a Web page

- Refine a search

- Describe the techniques used for successful keyword searches

- Describe how to create a working bibliography

- Compile a list of works cited for Web resources

- Search the Web for specific information

- Add, use, and remove an Accelerator

2 | Internet Research

Introduction

Research is an important tool for success in academics, or in any career. Writing papers, preparing speeches, and doing homework assignments all are activities that rely heavily on research. When researching, you are seeking information to support an idea or position, to prove a point, or to learn about a topic or concept. Traditionally, research was accomplished using books, newspapers, periodicals, and other materials found in libraries. The World Wide Web provides a new and useful resource for supplementing those traditional print materials.

Although the Web is a valuable resource with billions of Web pages covering every conceivable topic, you should not rely solely on the Web for your research. The information found on Web pages is not always up to date, accurate, or verifiable. In addition, Web sites change quite frequently, which means Web pages might become unavailable.

This chapter demonstrates successful techniques for locating information on the Web about space exploration and then evaluating the Web page for its usefulness as a source.

Overview

As you read this chapter, you will learn how to search the Web and use Windows Internet Explorer by performing these general tasks:

- Search the Web, using Web search tools
- Use tabbed browsing
- Refine a Web search, using advanced search techniques
- Evaluate a Web resource
- Create a working bibliography

Plan Ahead

> **Internet Research Guidelines**
> Internet research involves searching for Web sites using appropriate search engines and specific search criteria, as well as evaluating your search results for timeliness and accuracy. Understanding search techniques will help you find relevant search results. Before starting your research, you should consider these general guidelines:
>
> 1. **Determine the information you need.** Before you can effectively search the Internet for information and locate relevant Web sites, you must determine what information you will need. You also should consider whether you are looking for factual information or an opinion. If you are seeking factual information, be sure to identify credible Web sites.
>
> 2. **Decide upon an appropriate search method.** The Internet offers many different types of resources to use when beginning your research. Before deciding on a site or sites to perform your search, you should learn about the types of searches that each search engine offers. You also can search the Internet from your Web browser, without navigating first to a search engine Web site.
>
> *(continued)*

(continued)

3. **Identify search engines that are best suited for delivering the results you want.** The Internet contains Web sites that allow you to search for information, pictures, video, addresses, and maps. Some Web sites are better for performing certain types of searches than others. For example, some users prefer to find the definition of a word using the Dictionary.com Web site. If you have never searched the Internet, consider experimenting with various search engines to identify the ones you prefer.

4. **Determine whether the information you find is accurate, up to date, and valid.** Anyone can post information on the Internet, so it is important that you evaluate the accuracy of any information you plan to use from an Internet source. In addition, because some Web pages on the Internet can date back many years, you also should evaluate the information for currency. The Web can be a valuable resource for information, but you must know where to look.

5. **Determine how you will need to cite your work.** If you are performing research on the Internet to write a paper for a class or to submit a report to your boss, you should plan to cite the sources you utilize. When you submit a report with information from various outside sources, you typically will need to follow a standard documentation style such as **Modern Language Association** (**MLA**) or **American Psychological Association** (**APA**). It can be helpful to first obtain information on the style that you are required to use before beginning your Internet research.

Plan Ahead

Understanding Web Resources

In general, Web sites can be loosely categorized into 13 categories, based upon their content and purpose: portal, news, informational, business/marketing, educational, entertainment, advocacy, blog, wiki, online social network, content aggregator, personal, and Web applications (Figure 2–1). In addition, the Web provides other resources through which you can access useful information when doing research. The following sections describe each category of Web site in greater detail.

Portals   A **portal** is a Web site that offers a variety of Internet services from a single, convenient location (Figure 2–1a). Most portals offer the following free services: search engine and/or directory; news and sports headlines; weather; Web publishing; reference tools such as yellow pages, stock quotes, and maps; shopping; and e-mail and other forms of online communications. Popular portals include iGoogle, My Yahoo!, and MSN.com.

Many portals have online communities. An **online community** is a Web site that allows a group of people with similar interests or relationships to communicate with each other. These communities may offer online photo albums, chat rooms, and other services to facilitate communications among members. A wireless portal is a portal designed for Internet-enabled mobile devices.

Figure 2–1 (a) portal

**Figure 2–1 (b)
news**

**Figure 2–1 (c)
informational**

**Figure 2–1 (d)
business/
marketing**

**Figure 2–1 (e)
blog**

Figure 2–1 (f) wiki

News Web Sites   A news Web site contains topical material such as articles, pictures, and video that relates to current events, life, money, sports, and the weather (Figure 2–1b). Many magazines and newspapers provide Web sites that offer summaries of articles that appeared in the print edition, as well as articles that are online only. Newspapers, television news programs, and radio stations are some of the media that maintain news Web sites.

Informational Web Sites   An informational Web site contains factual information (Figure 2–1c). Many United States government agencies have informational Web sites providing factual information such as census data, tax codes, and the congressional budget. Other examples of factual information you can find online include public transportation schedules and published research findings.

Business/Marketing Web Sites   A business/marketing Web site contains content that promotes or sells products or services (Figure 2–1d). Nearly every business has a business/marketing Web site. Allstate Insurance Company, Dell Inc., General Motors Corporation, Kraft Foods Inc., and Walt Disney Company all have business/marketing Web sites. Many of these companies use their Web sites to sell products or services online.

Blogs   A **blog**, short for Web log, is an informal Web site consisting of time-stamped articles, or posts, in a diary or journal format, usually listed in reverse chronological order (Figure 2–1e). A blog that contains video is called a **video blog**, or vlog. The term **blogosphere** refers to the worldwide collection of blogs.

Blogs reflect the interests, opinions, and personality of their authors, called **bloggers**, who post observations, essays, images, and links for their online audiences, which can number in the hundreds of thousands for the most popular bloggers. Blogs have become an important means of worldwide communication. Businesses create blogs to communicate with employees, customers, and vendors. Teachers create blogs to collaborate with other teachers and students. Home users create blogs to share aspects of their personal life with family, friends, and others.

Wikis   A **wiki** is a collaborative Web site that allows users to create, add to, modify, or delete the Web site content via their Web browser. One popular wiki is Wikipedia, a free Web encyclopedia (Figure 2–1f). Although many wikis are open to modification by the general public, nonpublic wikis are used by project teams to communicate on large, complex projects. Wikis usually collect recent edits on a Web page so a moderator can review them for accuracy. The difference between a wiki and a blog is that readers of blogs cannot modify original posts made by the blogger.

Online Social Networks   An **online social network**, also called a **social networking Web site**, is a Web site that encourages members in its online community to share their interests, ideas, stories, photos, music, and videos with other registered users (Figure 2–1g). Most online social networks include chat rooms, newsgroups, and other communications services. Facebook is a popular social networking Web site, which has more than 500 million active users. In some social networking Web sites, such as Second Life, users assume an imaginary identity and interact with other users in a role-playing environment. A **media-sharing Web site** is a specific type of online social network that enables members to share media such as photos, music, videos, and even bookmarks. Flickr, Fotki, and Webshots are popular photo-sharing communities; Google Video and YouTube are popular video-sharing communities; and Delicious is a social networking Web site for sharing bookmarks.

Educational Web Sites   An educational Web site offers exciting, challenging avenues for formal and informal teaching and learning (Figure 2–1h). On the Web, you can learn how rockets travel into space or how to cook a meal. For more structured learning experiences, many colleges offer online classes and degrees, whereas in class, instructors often use the Web to enhance classroom teaching by publishing course materials, grades, and other pertinent class information. Similarly, some companies provide specialized online training programs for employees.

Entertainment Web Sites   An entertainment Web site offers an interactive and engaging environment (Figure 2–1i). Popular entertainment Web sites offer music, videos, sports, online games, ongoing story lines (known as Web episodes or Webisodes), sweepstakes, chats, and more. Sophisticated entertainment Web sites often partner with other technologies. For example, you can cast your vote online for a contestant you watched on a television show.

Advocacy Web Sites   An advocacy Web site contains content that describes a cause, opinion, or idea (Figure 2–1j). These Web sites usually present views of a particular group or association. Sponsors of advocacy Web sites include the Democratic National Committee, the Republican National Committee, the American Society for the Prevention of Cruelty to Animals, and the Human Rights Watch.

Figure 2–1 (g) online social network

Figure 2–1 (h) educational

Figure 2–1 (i) entertainment

Figure 2–1 (j) advocacy

**Figure 2–1 (k)
Web
application**

**Figure 2–1 (l)
content
aggregator**

Figure 2–1 (m) personal

Figure 2–1   Types of Web sites (continued)

Web Applications   A **Web application**, or **Web app**, is a Web site that allows users to access and interact with fully functional software through a Web browser on any computer or device connected to the Internet, unlike typical software that must be installed on your computer before it can be used. Some Web applications are free, whereas others offer part of their software free and charge for access to more comprehensive features or when a particular action is requested (Figure 2-1k). For example, TurboTax Online might let you prepare your taxes on its Web site for free, but then charge you to file them electronically. In addition to TurboTax Online, other examples of Web applications include Google Docs (word processing, spreadsheets, presentations) and Windows Live Hotmail (e-mail).

Content Aggregators   A **content aggregator** is a business that gathers and organizes Web content. Some content aggregators also then distribute, or feed, the content to subscribers for free or for a fee. Examples of distributed content include news, music, video, and images (Figure 2–1l). Subscribers select content in which they are interested. Whenever this content changes, it is downloaded automatically (pushed) to the subscriber's computer or mobile device.

Personal Web Sites   An individual or family might maintain personal Web sites (Figure 2–1m), or single Web pages, for a variety of reasons. Some people are job hunting, whereas others simply want to share life experiences with their friends, extended family, or the world. Some authors of personal Web sites add updates to their Web pages in a blog-type format. It can be rewarding to start a personal Web page to keep family and friends updated about your activities. In addition, people seeking jobs might choose to post an online résumé for potential employers to review. Because the Web is accessible to everyone, be cautious about posting too much personal information on any Web site.

Other Web Resources

A number of other resources are available on the Internet. File Transfer Protocol (FTP) sites, newsgroups, and for-profit database services all contain information and files that you can use for research purposes.

Papers, documents, manuals, and complete ready-to-execute programs are available using File Transfer Protocol. **File Transfer Protocol** (**FTP**) is an Internet standard that permits file uploading and downloading (transferring) with other computers on the Internet. **Downloading** is the process of transferring documents, graphics, and other objects from a computer on the Internet to your computer. Uploading is the opposite of downloading; that is, **uploading** is the process of transferring documents, graphics, and other objects from your computer to another computer on the Internet.

A **newsgroup** is an online forum where users are engaged in written discussions about a particular subject. Many experts and professionals read the threads in newsgroups pertaining to their areas of expertise and are willing to answer questions and supply information. To participate in a discussion, or **thread**, a user sends a message to the newsgroup, and other users in the newsgroup read and reply to the message. Although some newsgroups might require that you access them through a special program, other newsgroups are available simply by visiting a Web site. For example, Yahoo! Groups and Google Groups provide easy access to discussions about almost any topic. Some major topic areas include news, recreation, society, business, science, and computers.

A number of **database services**, such as Dow Jones and LexisNexis (Figure 2–2), are available on the Web. Before these services were available on the Web, users needed specialized software to access these databases. For a fee, these database services allow you to search a wide variety of sources, including publications and journals, financial and public records, and legal documents. Colleges and universities often subscribe to database services and make the search services available to faculty, staff, and students. Ask a librarian how to access these database services.

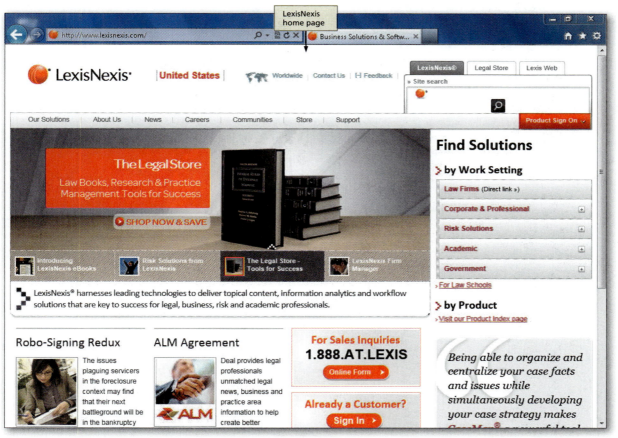

Figure 2–2

Most Web sites have multiple objectives. News Web sites include advertising. Personal Web pages might advocate a cause or opinion. A business/marketing Web site might contain factual information that is verifiable from other sources. However, identifying the general category in which the Web page falls can help you evaluate the usefulness of the Web page as a source of information for a research paper.

Evaluating a Web Resource

Once a promising Web page is found, you should evaluate it for its reliability, validity, and content. Remember, anyone can put a page on the Web, and Web pages do not have to be reviewed for accuracy or verified by editors. You have an obligation to ensure that the information and other materials you use are accurate, attributable, and verifiable.

Just as criteria exist for evaluating printed materials, criteria also exist for evaluating Web pages. These criteria include authorship, accuracy of information, currency of information, and topic and scope of coverage. Table 2–1 shows the information you should look for when evaluating Web resources.

Table 2–1 Criteria for Evaluating Web Pages	
Criterion	**Information to Evaluate**
Authorship	• Is the name of the person or organization publishing the page legitimate? • Does a link exist to a page that describes the goals of the organization? • Does the page include a statement of official approval from the parent organization? • Is there a copyright notice? • What are the author's qualifications? • Are any opinions and biases clearly stated? • Does the page contain advertising? If so, is it differentiated from content? • Is the information provided as a public service?
Accuracy of information	• Are any sources used and are they listed on the page? • Does the page contain links to other Web sites that verify the information on the page? • Are data and statistics clearly displayed and easy to read? • Is the page grammatically correct?
Currency of information	• When was the page written? • When was the page placed on the Web? • When was the page last updated? • Does the page include dates associated with the information on the Web page?
Topic and scope of coverage	• What is the purpose of the Web page? • Does the page declare a topic? • Does the page succeed in describing or discussing the declared topic? • Are points clear, well stated, and supported? • Does the page contain links to related resources? • Is the page under construction?

You can use an evaluation worksheet to aid in assessing the Web pages you find as potential resources. Figure 2–3 shows a sample evaluation worksheet template created from the criteria listed in Table 2–1. You can make copies of this worksheet, or create a new worksheet to use each time you find a possible research source.

Web Resource Evaluation Worksheet

Web Page Title:

Web Page URL:

Type of Web Resource

      Advocacy   Blog   Business/Marketing   Content Aggregator   Educational

      Entertainment   Informational   News   Personal   Portal   Social Network

      Web Application   Wiki

      Reasons:

Authorship

      What are the author's qualifications?

      Is there a sponsoring organization? Does the page link to the organization?

      Are any opinions and biases clearly stated?

      Does the page contain a copyright notice?

Accuracy of Information

      What sources verify the information on the Web page? Does the page link to those
      sources?

      Is the page grammatically correct?

Currency of Information

      What date was the page placed on the Web?

      What date was the page last updated?

      What date did you visit the page?

Topic and Scope

      What is the purpose of the page?

      Does the page succeed in describing and discussing the topic?

      Are points clear, well stated, and supported?

      Does the page include links to other related pages?

Figure 2–3

Using Web Search Tools

Finding a valuable resource among the many Web pages available on the World Wide
Web can be quite a challenge. One of the best ways to find a relevant resource from
among all those pages is to use one of the many Web search tools to guide you to the
information you are seeking.

    As stated previously, the Web contains billions of Web pages. To find information
for a term paper, learn more about a topic of interest, or locate the Web site of a

governmental agency, you must know either the Web address, or Uniform Resource Locator (URL), of the Web page with the information you are seeking or you must use a search tool. A **search tool** is a specialized Web site that helps you find Web pages relevant to your research. Search tools fall into two general categories:

- Directory
- Search engine

The first type of search tool, called a **directory**, uses an alphabetical index to organize related Web resources. Figure 2–4 shows a directory (Yahoo! Directory) that is organized into broad categories. When using a directory, you must decide which category would include your search topic and then click the corresponding link. When you click the link, another page of links is displayed that contains more specific categories from which to choose. You continue drilling down into your chosen topic until you find the information you want.

Figure 2–4

Web Search Engines
Fierce competition exists among search engines. Each search engine claims to have the largest index of Web resources. This competition ensures that there are large, up-to-date indexes of Web resources.

One of the benefits of using a directory is that because you select topics from a list of categories, you do not have to determine which terms to use to find the most relevant Web sites. On the other hand, it's possible that you might navigate through several levels of categories only to discover that the directory does not contain links to any Web sites relevant to your topic.

A second type of search tool, called a **search engine**, retrieves and displays a list of links to Web pages based on a query. A **query** is a word, set of words, or phrase, also known as **keywords**, that describes your chosen topic. When you enter your query in a search engine, the search engine then uses the query to search an index of Web resources in its database for best-matching Web pages. Some of the more popular search engines include Google, Yahoo!, Bing, Ask.com, AltaVista, and Wolfram|Alpha.

When you use a search engine that performs searches based on queries, instead of a directory, you can explore the Web and display links to Web pages without having to maneuver through any intermediate pages. You provide one or more relevant words, or keywords, about your chosen topic, and the search engine returns links that point directly to pages containing those keywords. Figure 2–5 shows a **keyword search form** (Google Advanced Search) used to enter keywords to search the Web.

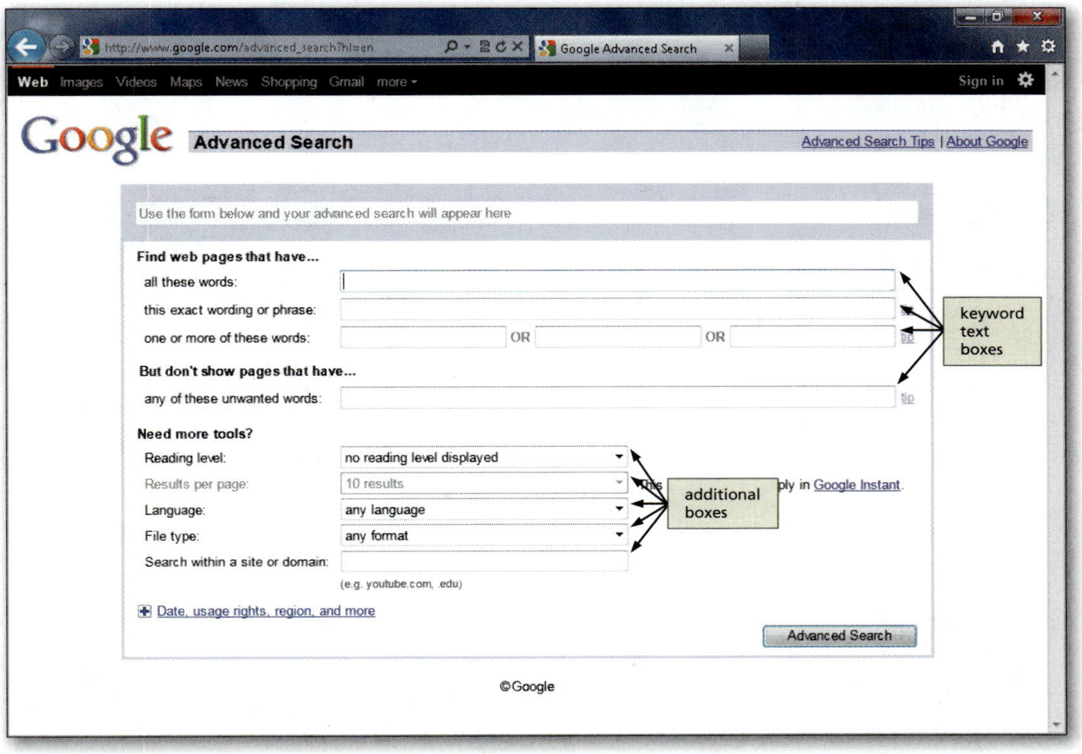

Figure 2–5

The index used by a search engine is created using several techniques. An automated program, called a **robot** or **spider**, travels around the Web, automatically following links and adding entries to the index. Individuals also can request that their Web pages be added to a directory or index, usually for a fee. Many businesses pay a fee to advertise on search engines. For example, if you perform a search on Google using the keyword, cruises, you might notice that a link to priceline.com, a popular travel Web site, displays in the Ads column on the right side of the page, indicating that the company pays a fee for a link to its Web site to display in that area when specific keywords are entered.

Most of the popular portal Web sites have both a search engine and a directory. Most portals also include specialized search tools that display maps and directions (MapQuest), provide information about businesses (Yellow Pages), and help find people (People Finder).

Internet Explorer's Address bar also can be used as a search tool. If you type a keyword into the Address bar, Internet Explorer uses Bing (or the search engine you have designated as your default search provider) to search for your keyword and then displays a Web page containing a list of search results. Most people find it efficient to search directly from the Address bar, rather than first navigating to a search engine.

BTW

Google Products
In addition to providing search capabilities for various resources, Google also offers productivity tools such as an e-mail service, a calendar, and programs that create documents, presentations, and spreadsheets. To view a list of Google products, navigate to the Google Web page, click the more link, and then click the even more link.

To Start Internet Explorer

The following step starts Internet Explorer using the method described at the beginning of Chapter 1.

1

- To start Internet Explorer, click the Internet Explorer button on the Windows taskbar (Figure 2–6).

- If the Internet Explorer window is not maximized, click the Maximize button to maximize it.

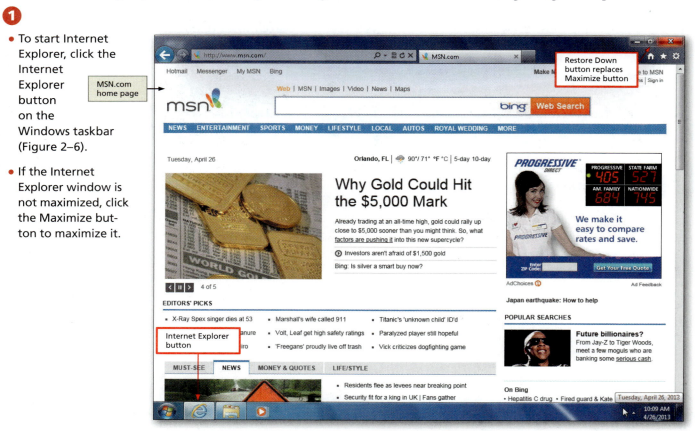

Figure 2–6

Searching the Web Using a Directory

BTW

Search Engines
Today, most search engines offer both a directory and the capability of performing keyword searches.

Yahoo! is respected for its directory because it is created and maintained by real people, rather than by using an automated system. Starting with general categories and becoming increasingly more specific as links are selected, the Yahoo! Directory offers a drill-down approach to searching the Web. Because the Yahoo! Directory uses a series of menus to organize links to Web pages, you can find information without entering keywords.

To Display the Yahoo! Directory Home Page

The following step displays the Yahoo! Directory home page.

1

- Click the Address bar, type **dir.yahoo.com** as the Web address, and then press the ENTER key to display the Yahoo! Directory Web page (Figure 2–7).

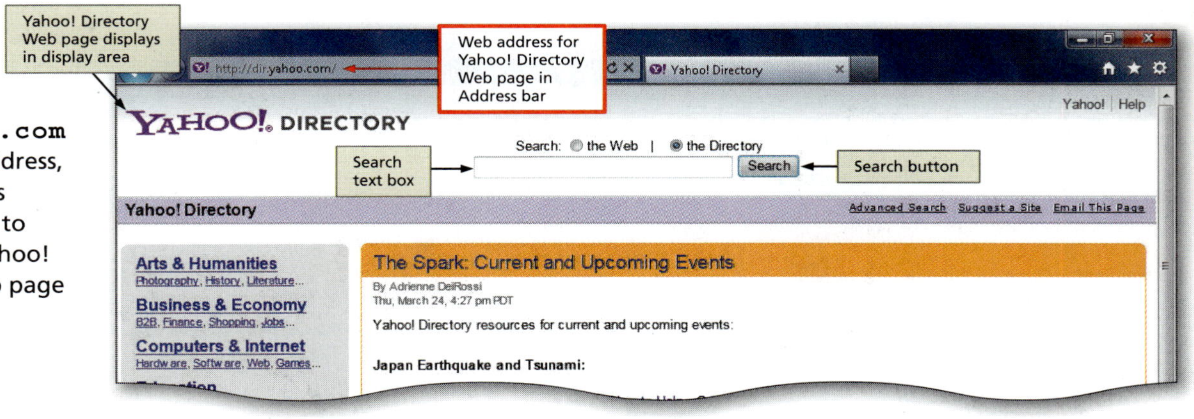

Yahoo! Directory Web page displays in display area

Web address for Yahoo! Directory Web page in Address bar

http://dir.yahoo.com/

YAHOO!® DIRECTORY

Yahoo! | Help

Search: ○ the Web | ● the Directory

Search text box

Search button

Yahoo! Directory

Advanced Search   Suggest a Site   Email This Page

Arts & Humanities
Photography, History, Literature...

Business & Economy
B2B, Finance, Shopping, Jobs...

Computers & Internet
Hardware, Software, Web, Games...

The Spark: Current and Upcoming Events

By Adrienne DelRossi
Thu, March 24, 4:27 pm PDT

Yahoo Directory resources for current and upcoming events:

Japan Earthquake and Tsunami:

Figure 2–7

When you type a Web address in the Address bar and then press the ENTER key, **AutoComplete** remembers the Web address you typed. As a result, when you type the Web address for the Yahoo! Directory home page in the Address bar in Figure 2–7, AutoComplete might display a list of previously entered Web addresses in a box below the Address bar. If this happens, you can select a Web address from the list in the Address bar by clicking the Web address, or you can continue to type the Web address using the keyboard.

The Search text box and Search button next to the Yahoo! Directory title allow you to perform a keyword search. Several links appear along the left side of the Web page. Scrolling the Web page displays the remainder of the Yahoo! Directory (Figure 2–8 on the next page). The Yahoo! Directory is organized into broad categories, such as Art & Humanities, Business & Economy, Computers & Internet, and Education.

BTW

Yahoo!
In 1994, two graduate students at Stanford University organized lists of their favorite Web sites into a hierarchy and started Yahoo!. Their endeavor became a corporation in 1996, and Yahoo! is now a household name among Web users.

To Search Using the Yahoo! Directory

You decide to start your search on space exploration with the major category Science. The following steps navigate through the Yahoo! Directory to retrieve information about space experiments.

1

• If necessary, scroll the Web page to display the Science link (Figure 2–8).

Figure 2–8

2

• Click the Science link to view the links in the Science category (Figure 2–9).

Q&A What are the numbers that appear in parentheses?

The numbers in parentheses represent the number of search results found in that category.

Figure 2–9

3

- If necessary, scroll to display the Space link.

- Click Space to view the links in the Space subcategory (Figure 2–10).

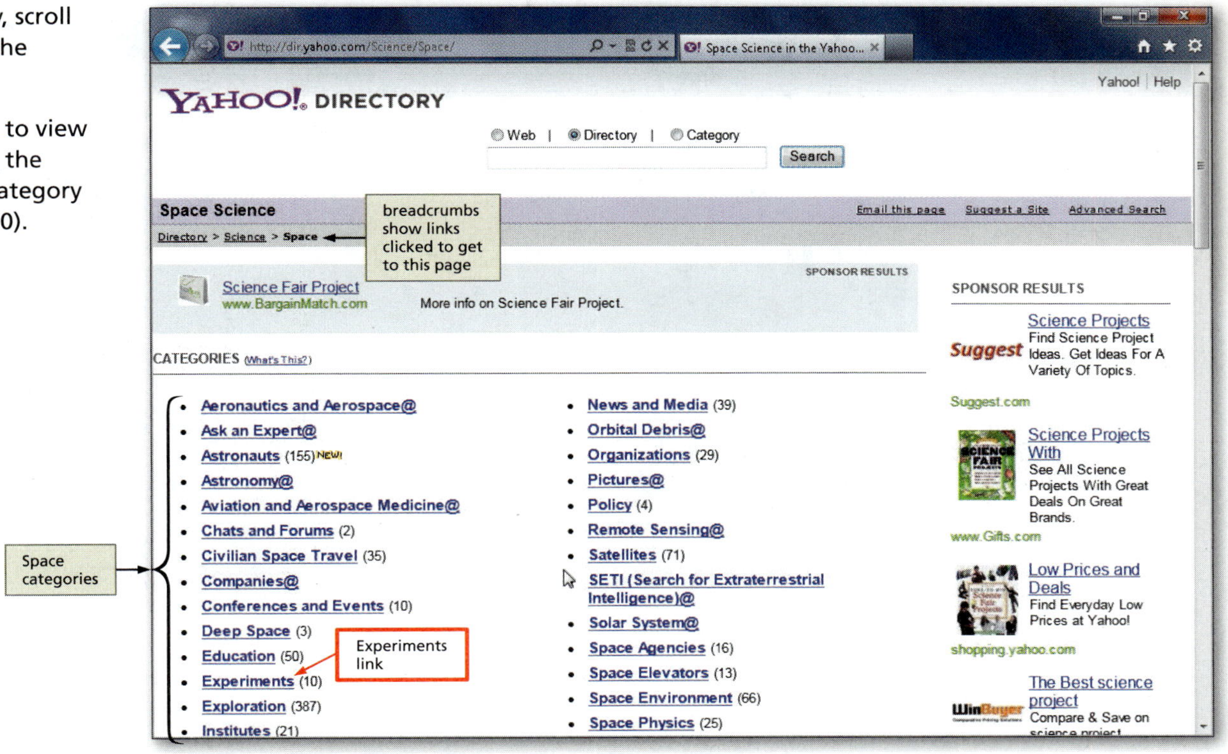

Space categories

Experiments link

breadcrumbs show links clicked to get to this page

Figure 2–10

4

- Click Experiments to view the links in the Experiments subcategory (Figure 2–11).

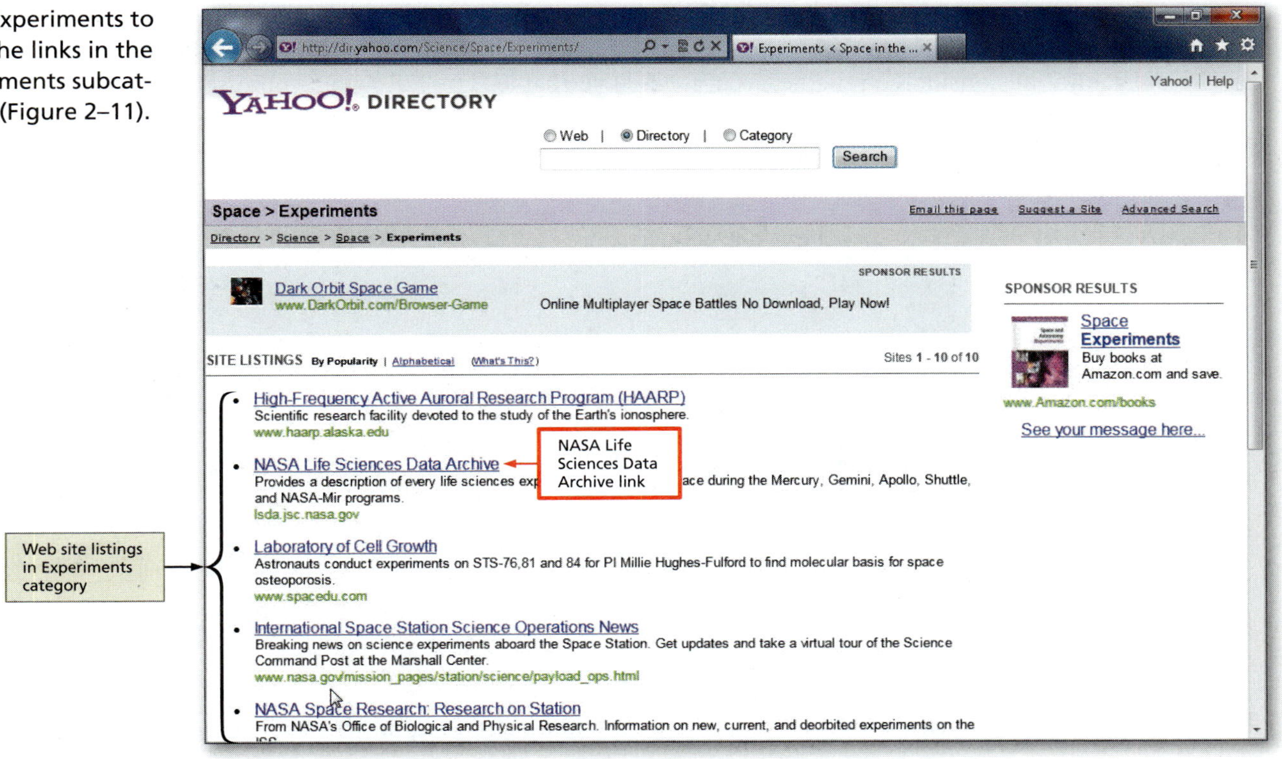

Web site listings in Experiments category

NASA Life Sciences Data Archive link

Figure 2–11

5

• Click the NASA Life Sciences Data Archive link to display the Life Sciences Data Repositories Web page (Figure 2–12).

Experiment

• Click the Back button and visit the various Web sites listed in the Space > Experiments sub-category. Once you have finished exploring these Web sites, return to the Life Sciences Data Repositories Web page.

Figure 2–12

To Evaluate a Web Resource

Now that you have located a potentially informative Web site, you need to evaluate the Web page to see if it can be used as a source. Many Web pages do not meet the necessary criteria to be a source for a research paper. You will discard many promising Web pages because after evaluating the site, you will discover that the information on the site cannot be considered reliable, accurate, and verifiable. The following steps use the sample evaluation worksheet (Figure 2–3 on page IE 73) to evaluate the Life Sciences Data Repository page for accuracy, validity, and reliability.

1

• If necessary, scroll the Web page to display the bottom of the Life Sciences Data Repositories Web page (Figure 2–13).

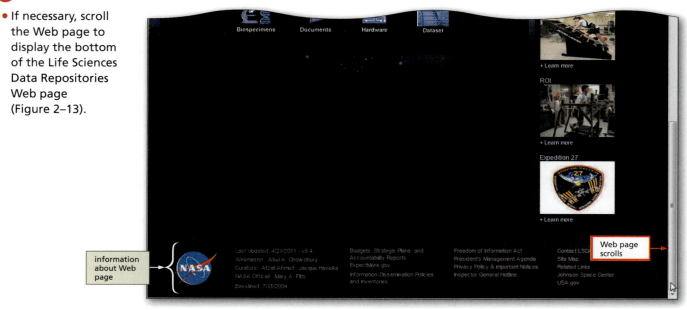

Figure 2–13

2

• Use this information on the Life Sciences Data Repositories Web site to complete the evaluation worksheet (Figure 2–14).

Web Resource Evaluation Worksheet

Web Page Title: NASA Life Sciences Data Archive

Web Page URL: http://lsda.jsc.nasa.gov

Type of Web Resource

Advocacy   Blog   Business/Marketing   Content Aggregator   Educational

Entertainment ⟨ Informational ⟩ News   Personal   Portal   Social Network

Web Application   Wiki

Reasons: Contains information about life sciences experiments

Authorship

What are the author's qualifications? NASA officials

Is there a sponsoring organization? Does the page link to the organization? Yes – NASA; Yes

Are any opinions and biases clearly stated? Yes

Does the page contain a copyright notice? No

Accuracy of Information

What sources verify the information on the Web page? Does the page link to those sources?

Is the page grammatically correct? Yes

Currency of Information

What date was the page placed on the Web?

What date was the page last updated?

What date did you visit the page? April 26, 2013

Topic and Scope

What is the purpose of the page? NASA Human Research Program

Does the page succeed in describing and discussing the topic? Yes

Are points clear, well stated, and supported? Yes

Does the page include links to other related pages? Yes

Figure 2–14

The information gathered so far is summarized on the worksheet illustrated in Figure 2–14. Based on the current worksheet criteria, the Life Sciences Data Repositories Web page is an exceptionally strong resource.

If you are doing a large amount of Web research, consider creating an electronic version of the worksheet. Then you can record the evaluation details for each Web resource you use and save the document using a file name that identifies the Web site.

Searching the Web

In addition to performing an Internet search using a directory, you also can search the Internet using one or more keywords. A search engine uses keywords to find relevant Web pages. The following section discusses how to search the Web using keywords and how to use the tabs feature in Internet Explorer while doing so.

Google is one of the more widely used search engines. It has an index of billions of Web pages. Each day, its robots visit millions of sites, capturing Web addresses and corresponding text to update its index. Robot programs also check for Web addresses that no longer work, known as **dead links** or **broken links**. Google is not only capable of locating Web sites containing textual information that matches your search criteria, but it also can return results for various other resources such as images, videos, maps, books, items for sale, and patents.

To Search Using the Google Simple Search Form

As with most search engines, Google has both a simple search form and an Advanced Search form. The simple search form is displayed on its home page and consists of a text box, the Google Search button, and the I'm Feeling Lucky button. When you type a keyword in the text box and click the Google Search button, Google will search for the keyword and display a list of links to Web pages that contain the keyword.

By default, Google Instant search enhancement is enabled. This search enhancement allows Google to display results as you enter your search keywords. In addition, Google will help provide suggestions to narrow your search and reduce the number of search results. The following steps use Google to search for Web pages that contain the keywords, nasa space exploration.

1

- Click the Address bar, type **google.com**, and then press the ENTER key to display the Google Web page (Figure 2–15).

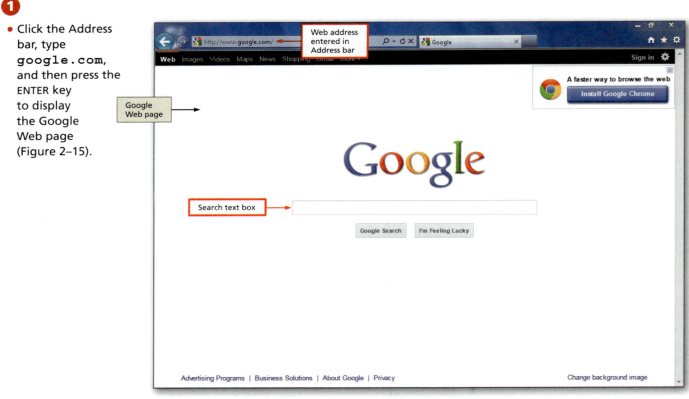

Figure 2–15

2

• Type **nasa space exploration** in the Search text box (Figure 2–16).

Q&A

What will happen if I click the I'm Feeling Lucky button?

If Google Instant search is turned off and you click the I'm Feeling Lucky button instead of the Google Search button after entering your search text, Google will display the Web page for the first search result it locates.

Figure 2–16

3

• Press the ENTER key to initiate Google's search and to display a Web page containing the search results (Figure 2–17). Your search results might differ.

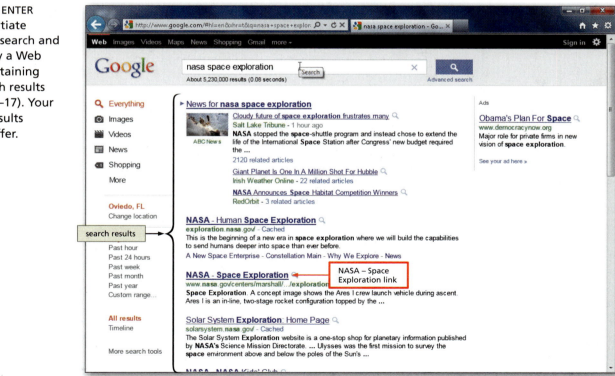

Figure 2–17

Using Tabbed Browsing to Help Search the Web

Searching the Web for an exact topic is not always easy when search engines return numerous hits. A **hit** is the term used when a search engine returns a Web page that matches the search criteria. The **tabbed browsing** feature provides a way to navigate between the search results and associated Web page(s) within a single browser window. When a Web page opens in a new tab, the tab is added in the tab row, which appears to the right of the Address bar.

Internet Explorer makes it easy to manage tabs by using tab groups. **Tab groups** are two or more tabs that are related to each other. For example, if you right-click a link on a Web site and open the link in a new tab, the two tabs would be part of a tab group, identified by a unique color.

To Open a Link in a New Tab and Create a Tab Group

Because the first Web page you view might not contain the information you are looking for, it might be necessary to return to the Google search results page to continue evaluating additional Web pages. Internet Explorer's tabbed browsing feature allows you to open multiple Web pages within the same browser window, instead of opening a new browser window for each page. The following steps open a link in a new tab and create a new tab group.

- Right-click the NASA – Space Exploration link to display a shortcut menu (Figure 2–18).

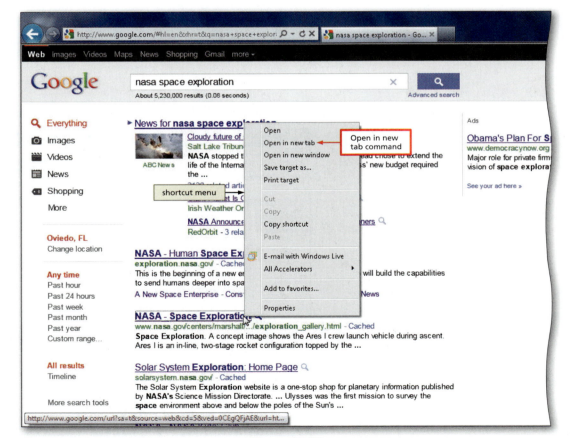

Figure 2–18

2

- Click the 'Open in new tab' command to open the NASA – Space Exploration Web page in a new tab.

- If necessary, click the NASA – Space Exploration tab to make it the active tab (Figure 2–19).

Q&A

How can I open a new tab before navigating to a Web page of my choice?

Clicking the New Tab button on the tab row, or pressing CTRL+T, will open a new tab. Once the new tab opens, you can type the Web address of the Web page you want to visit in the Address bar, and then press the ENTER key to display the Web page.

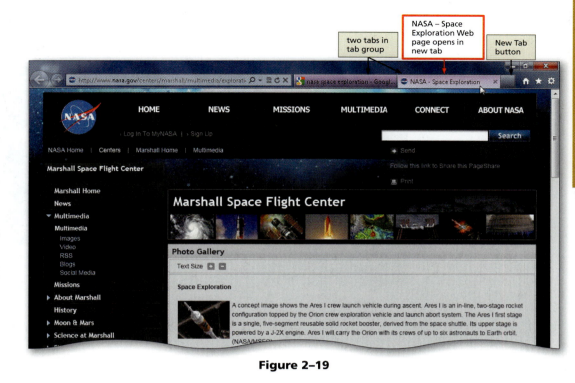

Figure 2–19

Other Ways
1. While holding down CTRL key, click NASA – Space Exploration link

To Switch Between Tabs

Currently, the nasa space exploration – Google Search tab is inactive and the NASA – Space Exploration tab is active. A tab is considered active when the contents of the tab are displayed in the browser window and the tab is in the foreground of the tab row. When you want to switch to another tab, click the tab. The clicked tab becomes the active tab and the contents of the tab are displayed in the browser window. The following steps switch between the two open tabs.

1

- Click the nasa space exploration – Google Search tab to display the Web page containing the Google search results (Figure 2–20).

Figure 2–20

2

- Click the NASA – Space Exploration tab to return to the NASA – Space Exploration Web page (Figure 2–21).

Figure 2–21

Other Ways

1. Press CTRL+TAB, press CTRL+TAB

2. Press CTRL+1, press CTRL+2

To Show Tabs on a Separate Row

As you add additional tabs to the tab row in Internet Explorer, the size of the tabs decreases, and you might not be able to read all of the text displayed on each tab — making it difficult to identify which Web page corresponds to which tab. Internet Explorer provides an option to show the tabs on a separate row, below the Address bar, to allow more space to view the text that displays on each tab. The following steps show tabs on a separate row.

1

- Right-click the tab row to display a shortcut menu (Figure 2–22).

Figure 2–22

2

● Click 'Show tabs on a separate row' to move the tab row below the Address bar (Figure 2–23).

Figure 2–23

To Show Tabs Next to the Address Bar

If you no longer have many tabs open and want to maximize the browser's display area, you can move the tab row so that it appears next to the Address bar. The following steps move the tab row back to its original location.

1 Right-click the tab row to display a shortcut menu.

2 Click 'Show tabs on a separate row' to remove the check mark and move the tab row back to its original location.

To Tear Off a Tab

If you have multiple tabs open in one window, one way to reduce the clutter on the tab row is to display a tab in a new Internet Explorer window by tearing off a tab. The following steps tear off a tab.

1

● Drag the NASA – Space Exploration tab downward and off of the tab row until the tab and its contents appear separated from the Internet Explorer window (Figure 2–24).

Figure 2–24

- Release the mouse
button to tear
off the tab
(Figure 2–25).

Figure 2–25

To Switch Between Web Pages Using the Windows Taskbar

If you have multiple tabs open in two or more browser windows, you might forget which browser window contains the tab you want to display. If the Windows 7 Aero interface is supported on your computer, you can view thumbnails of each open tab using the Windows taskbar. If the Aero interface is not supported or displayed, the Windows taskbar can display the title of each tab open in Internet Explorer. The following steps switch between tabs using the Windows taskbar.

- Point to the
Internet Explorer
button on the
Windows taskbar to
display a thumbnail
for each open Web
page (Figure 2–26).

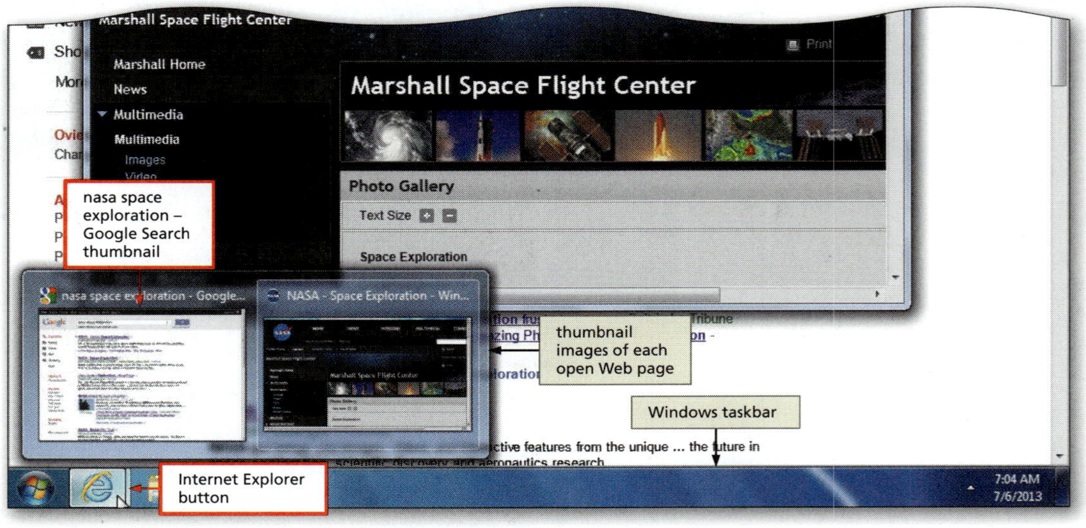

Figure 2–26

2

- Click the nasa space exploration – Google Search thumbnail to display the Google search results (Figure 2–27).

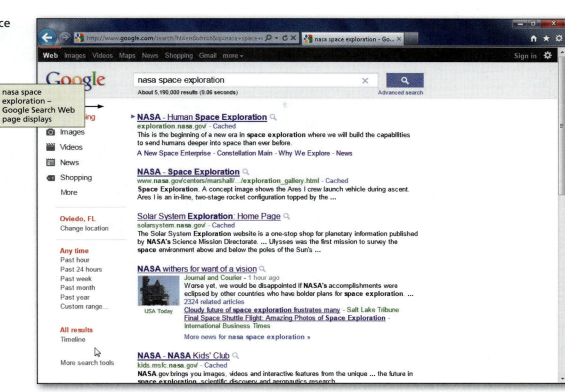

nasa space exploration – Google Search Web page displays

Figure 2–27

3

- Point to the Internet Explorer button on the Windows taskbar to display a thumbnail for each open Web page (Figure 2–28).

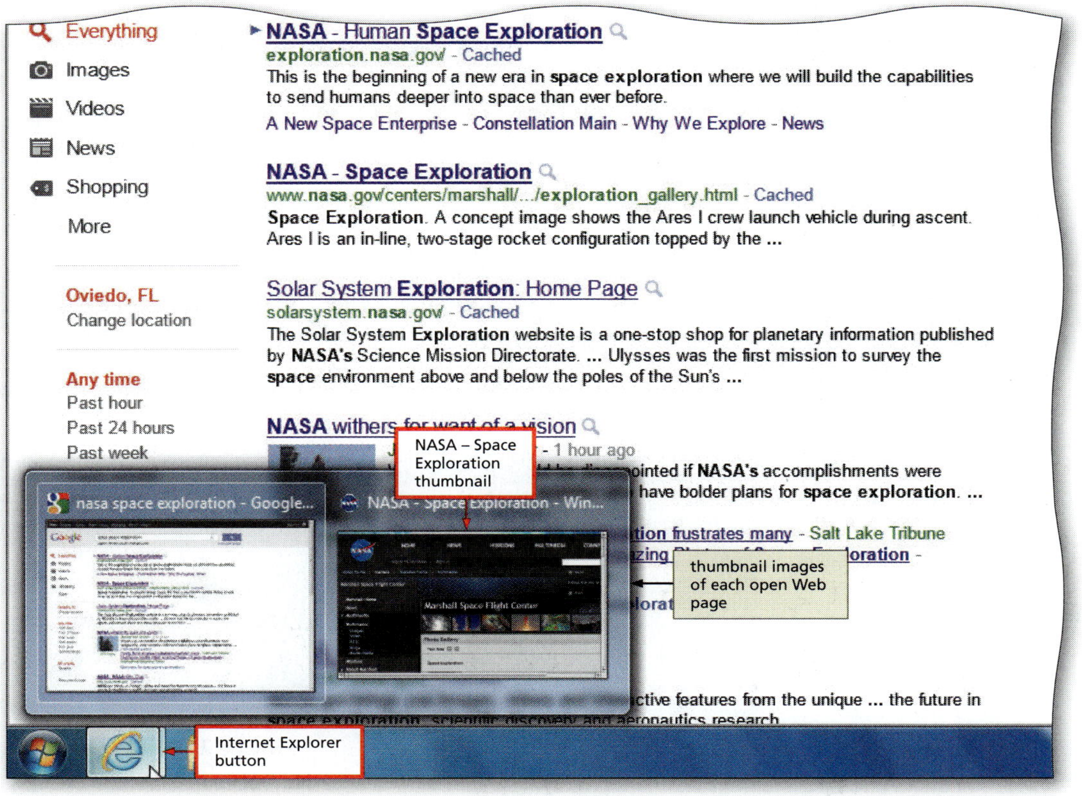

NASA - Human **Space Exploration**
exploration.nasa.gov/ - Cached
This is the beginning of a new era in **space exploration** where we will build the capabilities to send humans deeper into space than ever before.
A New Space Enterprise - Constellation Main - Why We Explore - News

Everything
Images
Videos
News
Shopping
More

NASA - **Space Exploration**
www.**nasa**.gov/centers/marshall/.../**exploration**_gallery.html - Cached
Space Exploration. A concept image shows the Ares I crew launch vehicle during ascent. Ares I is an in-line, two-stage rocket configuration topped by the ...

Oviedo, FL
Change location

Solar System **Exploration**: Home Page
solarsystem.**nasa**.gov/ - Cached
The Solar System **Exploration** website is a one-stop shop for planetary information published by **NASA's** Science Mission Directorate. ... Ulysses was the first mission to survey the **space** environment above and below the poles of the Sun's ...

Any time
Past hour
Past 24 hours
Past week

NASA withers for want of a vision
- 1 hour ago
...pointed if **NASA's** accomplishments were ...have bolder plans for **space exploration**. ...

NASA – Space Exploration thumbnail

nasa space exploration - Google...   NASA - Space Exploration - Win...

tion frustrates many - Salt Lake Tribune
zing ... **lorat**ion -

thumbnail images of each open Web page

Internet Explorer button

Figure 2–28

4

- Click the NASA – Space Exploration thumbnail to display the NASA – Space Exploration Web page (Figure 2–29).

Figure 2–29

To Drag a Tab from One Window to Another Window

If you have multiple Internet Explorer windows open, and want to consolidate your open tabs into one window, you can drag tabs between windows. The following step consolidates the windows by dragging a tab from one open window into the other open window.

1

- If necessary, arrange the windows on the screen so that the nasa space exploration – Google Search window is maximized in the background, and the NASA – Space Exploration Web page is in the foreground, but not maximized, as shown in Figure 2–29.

- Drag the NASA – Space Exploration tab to the right of the nasa space exploration – Google Search tab in the background window.

- Release the mouse button to move the NASA – Space Exploration tab from its own window to the tab row in the existing window (Figure 2–30).

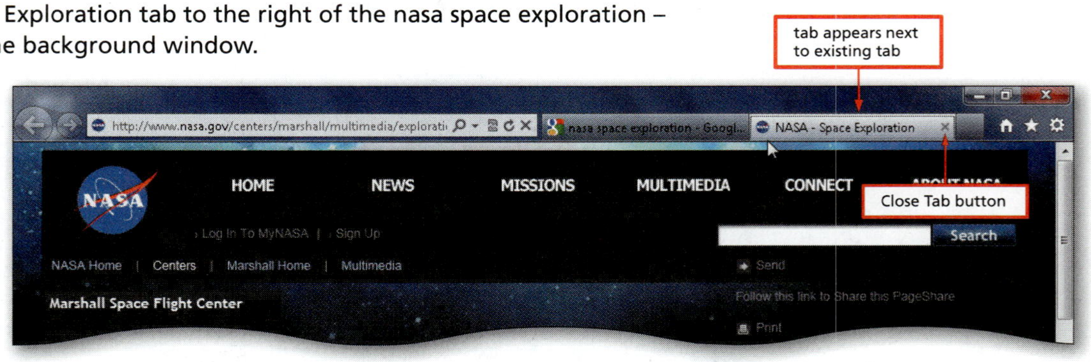

tab appears next to existing tab

Close Tab button

Figure 2–30

To Close a Tab

When you are finished viewing the contents of a Web page in a tab, you should close the tab to keep the tab row free from clutter. Having too many tabs open at one time makes it difficult to locate a particular tab. The following step closes an open tab.

1

• Click the Close Tab button on the NASA – Space Exploration tab to close the tab (Figure 2–31).

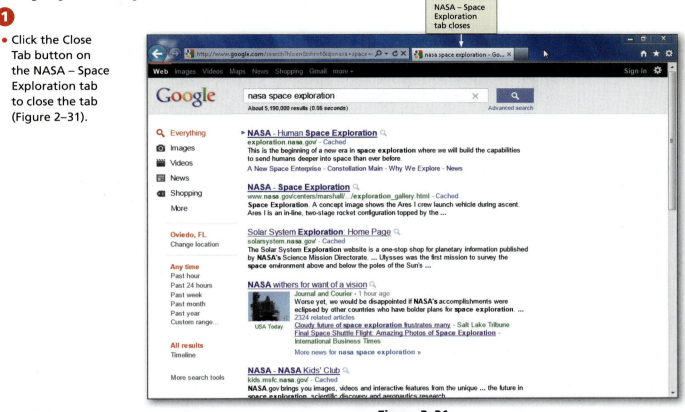

NASA – Space Exploration tab closes

Figure 2–31

Other Ways
1. Right-click tab to close, click Close tab
2. Select tab to close, press CTRL+W

Using the Address Bar to Search the Web

The Address bar also allows you to search for information on the Web. You have entered Web addresses in the Address bar and displayed the associated Web page. Now you will enter keywords or phrases into the Address bar to gain access to Bing, or another search engine, to perform a search relating to the keyword or phrase. The Address bar allows you to search for Web pages directly from the browser interface without first navigating to a search engine's Web page. In addition, Internet Explorer allows you to customize the Address bar by adding other search engines. The Address bar can perform searches on Web sites such as Bing, Wikipedia, eBay, Yahoo!, Facebook, and Google. By default, Bing is the default search provider when you search for keywords using the Address bar. Table 2–2 on the next page lists some of the additional search engines that you can add to the Address bar.

Table 2–2 Additional Search Engines Available for the Address Bar	
Topic Search	**Description**
About.com	Search consumer advice and information
Amazon	Search Amazon's online stores
CareerJunction	Search jobs online
CNET	Search tech news, reviews, and downloads
eBay	Search online auctions
ESPN	Search sports online
Expedia	Search your favorite travel destinations
Facebook	Search Facebook
Getty Images	Search images online
Microsoft	Search Microsoft
MTV	Search music, videos, and TV shows
Myspace	Search for friends, bands, video, and more
The New York Times	Search news online
Target	Search and shop Target.com
USA Today	Search news online
Wal-Mart	Search Walmart.com
Weather.com	Search local weather, forecasts, news, and video
Wikipedia	Search the free encyclopedia

To Customize the Address Bar by Adding a Search Engine

The following steps add the Ask.com search engine to the Address bar.

1

• Click the Show
Address bar
Autocomplete
button on the
Address bar to dis-
play the Address
bar Autocomplete
feature and a
list of installed
search providers
(Figure 2–32).

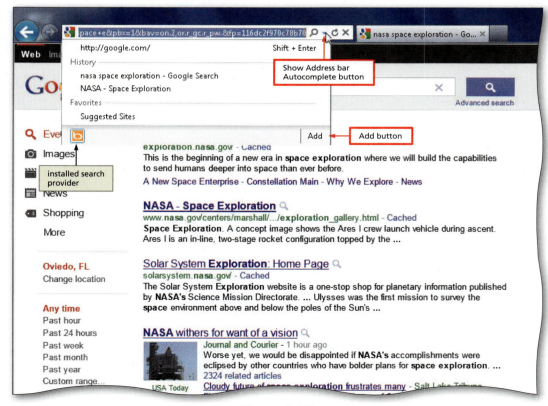

Figure 2–32

2

- Click the Add button to display the Internet Explorer Gallery Add-ons Web page in a new tab (Figure 2–33).

Figure 2–33

3

- Click the search link to display a list of search providers (Figure 2–34).

Figure 2–34

4

- If necessary, scroll to the right until the Ask.com search provider is displayed (Figure 2–35).

Figure 2–35

5

- Click the Ask.com button in the Internet Explorer Gallery Add-ons window to display information about the add-on (Figure 2–36).

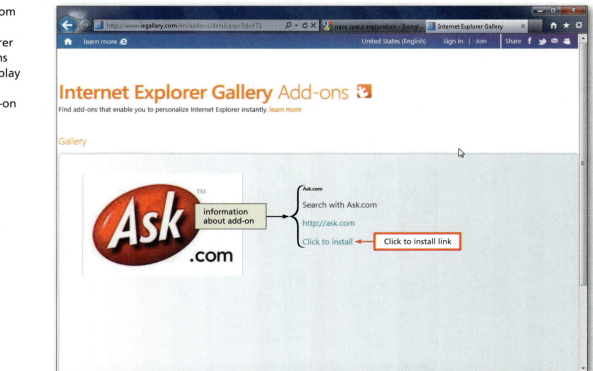

Figure 2–36

6

- Click the 'Click to install' link to display the Add Search Provider dialog box (Figure 2–37).

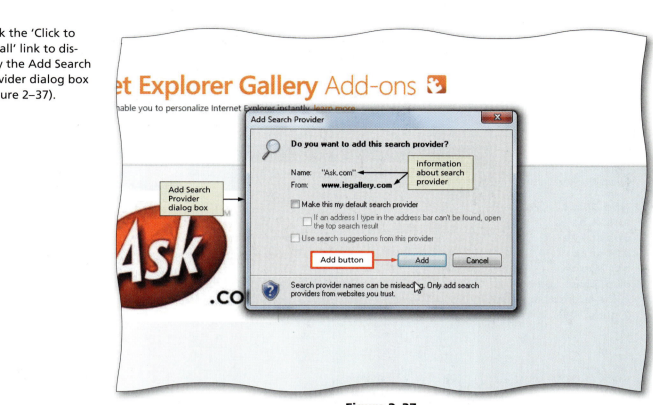

Figure 2–37

7

- Click the Add button to add the search provider to the Address bar (Figure 2–38).

Figure 2–38

To Search for Web Pages Using the Ask.com Search Engine

The Ask.com search engine allows you to perform a search by using natural language as your search criteria, whereas other search engines expect you to enter keywords. For instance, you can enter a statement (Give me information about space exploration.) or a question (When did space exploration begin?). The search engine searches for and displays a list of links to Web pages that pertain to the words, phrase, statement, or question. The following steps use the Address bar to search Ask.com for Web pages about the positive effects of space exploration.

 1

- Click the text in the Address bar to select the text.

- Type **What are the positive effects of space exploration?** in the Address bar (Figure 2–39).

Figure 2–39

2

- Click the Ask.com button on the Address bar list to change the active search provider in the Address bar (Figure 2–40).

Figure 2–40

❸

- Press the ENTER key to display the Ask. com Web page containing the search results (Figure 2–41).

🔍 **Experiment**

- Hold the CTRL key and click a search result to open a new tab containing a Web page that discusses the positive effects of space exploration. After you view the Web page, close the tab and return to the search results.

Q&A   How can I open the page containing my search results in a new tab?

After you enter your search text, hold down the ALT key while pressing the ENTER key to display your search results in a new tab.

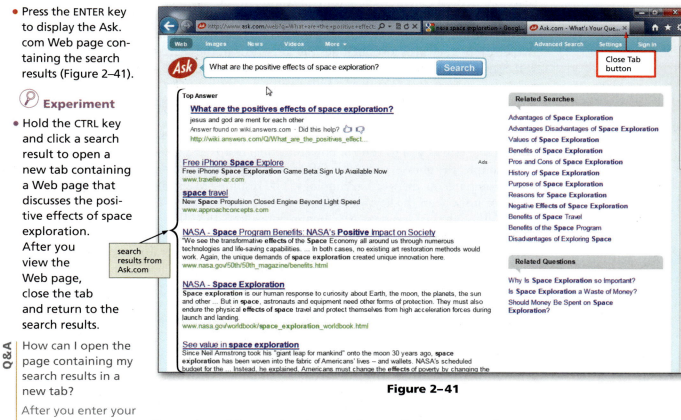

Figure 2–41

❹

- Close the tab containing the search results.

Refining a Web Search

You **refine** a search by providing more information for the search engine to use to return a narrower, more focused set of results. Most search engines, when performing a search using multiple keywords, will give each word the same weight, or level of importance. When each keyword contains the same weight, Web pages containing any one of the keywords or any combination of the keywords will satisfy the search engine and be returned as a successful match. Any Web page that contains the word, exploration, for example, will be included in the hundreds of thousands of links returned by the search, even though some of those pages will have nothing to do with space exploration. To eliminate these Web pages, the keywords you use to search need to be more specific and better organized.

In addition to entering keywords, Google, along with many other search engines, allows the use of operators, advanced operators, and some compound search criteria to refine a search.

Operators increase the accuracy of a search by fine-tuning the keywords in the search. Operators include the + (plus), – (minus), and ~ (tilde) symbols and the OR logical operator. Typing the **+ (plus) symbol** before a keyword guarantees the keyword will be included in the search results. Alternatively, placing quotation marks around two or more keywords also includes the keywords in the search, but the search engine will search for those keywords in that same order. Placing the **– (minus) symbol** before a keyword guarantees that the keyword will be excluded from the search. Placing the **~ (tilde) symbol** immediately preceding a keyword causes a search for the keyword and any synonyms.

The **OR operator**, one example of a **Boolean operator**, is a compound search criteria that allows you to control how individual words in a keyword phrase are used. For example, the phrase, computer OR technology, finds Web pages containing either the word, computer, or the word, technology. The resulting Web pages can contain both keywords or just one of the keywords.

Although the Google search engine only allows the OR operator, other search engines allow the use of additional Boolean operators. These logical operators include AND, NOT, and NEAR. The **AND operator**, like the OR operator, allows you to create keyword searches containing compound conditions. Whereas the OR operator expands your search and increases the number of results, the AND operator narrows your search and reduces the number of results. The **NOT operator** is used to exclude keywords from the resulting Web pages. The **NEAR operator** is used to find pages in which two keywords appear within close proximity of each other. Table 2–3 describes the Boolean operators and gives an example of each one.

Table 2–3 Boolean Operators and Examples	
Boolean Operator	**Example**
AND	Finds only those Web pages that contain all of the specified words or phrases. Peanut AND butter finds Web pages where both the word, peanut, and the word, butter, appear.
OR	Finds Web pages containing at least one of the specified words or phrases. Peanut OR butter finds Web pages containing either peanut or butter. The resulting Web pages can contain both words, but only have to contain one of the words.
NOT	Excludes Web pages containing the specified word or phrase. Peanut AND NOT butter finds Web pages where the word, peanut, appears but the word, butter, does not. With some search engines, NOT cannot be used alone. It must be used in conjunction with another operator, such as AND.
NEAR	Finds Web pages containing both specified words or phrases within 10 words of each other. Peanut NEAR butter would find Web pages on peanut butter, but probably not any other kind of butter such as apple butter.
( )	Use parentheses to group complex Boolean phrases. For example, (peanut AND butter) AND (jelly OR jam) finds Web pages with the words, "peanut butter and jelly," or, "peanut butter and jam," or both.

Another useful feature is the **wildcard character**. Several search engines allow you to use the asterisk (*) to replace one or more characters in a word. For example, searching for immun* will return hits for immune, immunize, immunization, immunology, immunologist, and any other word beginning with the letters, i-m-m-u-n. Many people use wildcards if the entire spelling of a keyword is unknown. Table 2–4 offers useful search tips.

Table 2–4 Successful Search Techniques	
Tip or Wildcard	**Example**
Use wildcard characters	Use an asterisk (*) to broaden a search. To find any words that start with gold, use gold* to find matches for gold, goldfinch, goldfinger, golden, and so on. Use this character if the word you are searching for could have different endings (for example, do not search for dog, search for dog* to include the plural).
Use quotation marks to surround a phrase	If you know a certain phrase will appear on the page you are looking for, put the phrase in quotation marks (for example, try entering song lyrics such as "you ain't nothin' but a hound dog").
Use either specific or general keywords	Conduct searches using specific keywords to obtain fewer, more precise links, or general keywords to obtain numerous, less precise links. For example, if you are searching for a Web page about mushrooms, a generic keyword might be "mushroom," whereas a specific keyword might be "portobello."

Advanced operators are query words that have special meaning in search engines. The advanced operators modify a search or perform a different type of search. Google's advanced operators include cache, link, related, info, define, stocks, site, allintitle, intitle, allinurl, and inurl. For example, entering the phrase, link:www.google.com, in the Google Search text box finds Web pages that have links to Google's home page.

Most search engines have a link on their search pages to access advanced search options. Clicking the Advanced Search Tips link on the Google Advanced Search page (Figure 2–42) displays information about advanced searching.

To Display the Google Advanced Search Form

The following step displays the Google Advanced Search form.

1

- Click the Advanced search link, located below the Search button on the Google search results Web page, to display the Advanced Search form (Figure 2–42).

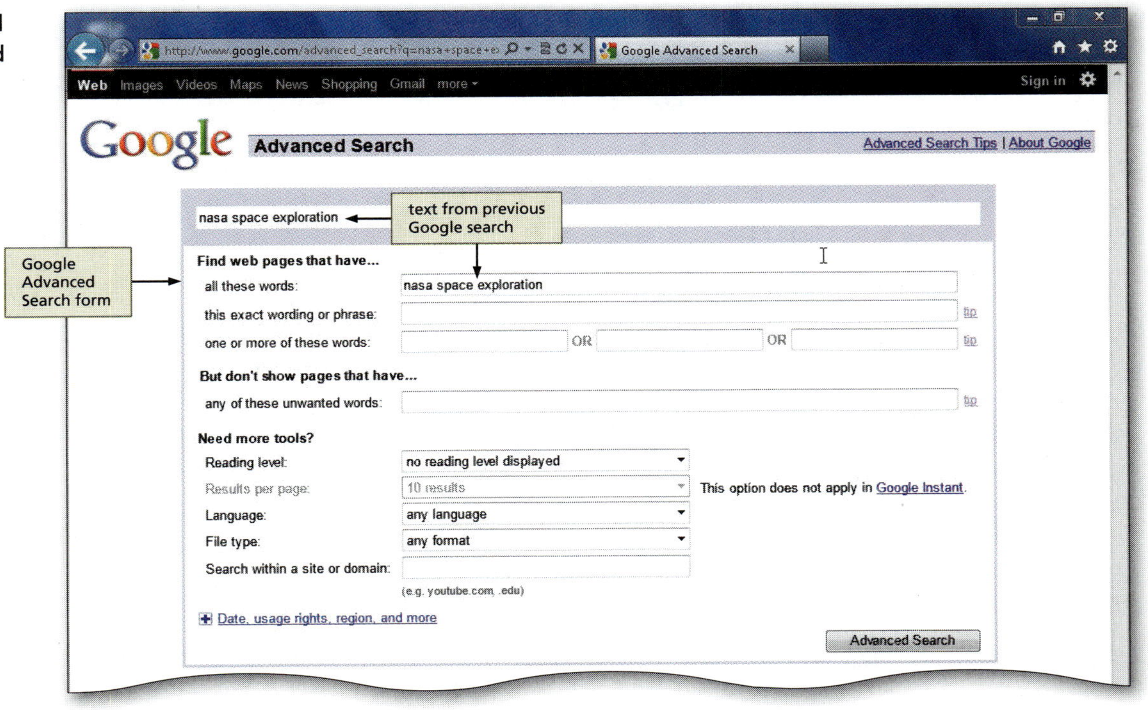

Figure 2–42

The Google Advanced Search page contains multiple text boxes. As you enter your search criteria, Google displays the keywords and operators used to perform the search in a text box at the top of the Google Advanced Search Web page. Table 2–5 describes the text box descriptions and gives an example of each search rule.

Table 2–5 Google Advanced Search Form Text Boxes	
Text Box Description	**Search Rules**
all these words	Web pages must contain all the words you typed in the text box.
this exact wording or phrase	Web pages must contain the exact words in the order they were typed in the text box.
one or more of these words	Web pages must contain at least one of the words in the text box.
any of these unwanted words	Web pages must not contain the word or words in the text box.

To Search Using the Google Advanced Search Form

The following steps use the Google Advanced Search form to refine the search and find information about Neil Armstrong, a famous figure in the history of space exploration.

1

- Select the existing text in the 'all these words' text box.

- Type **Neil Armstrong** in the 'all these words' text box.

- Click the 'this exact wording or phrase' text box.

- Type **space exploration** in the text box (Figure 2–43).

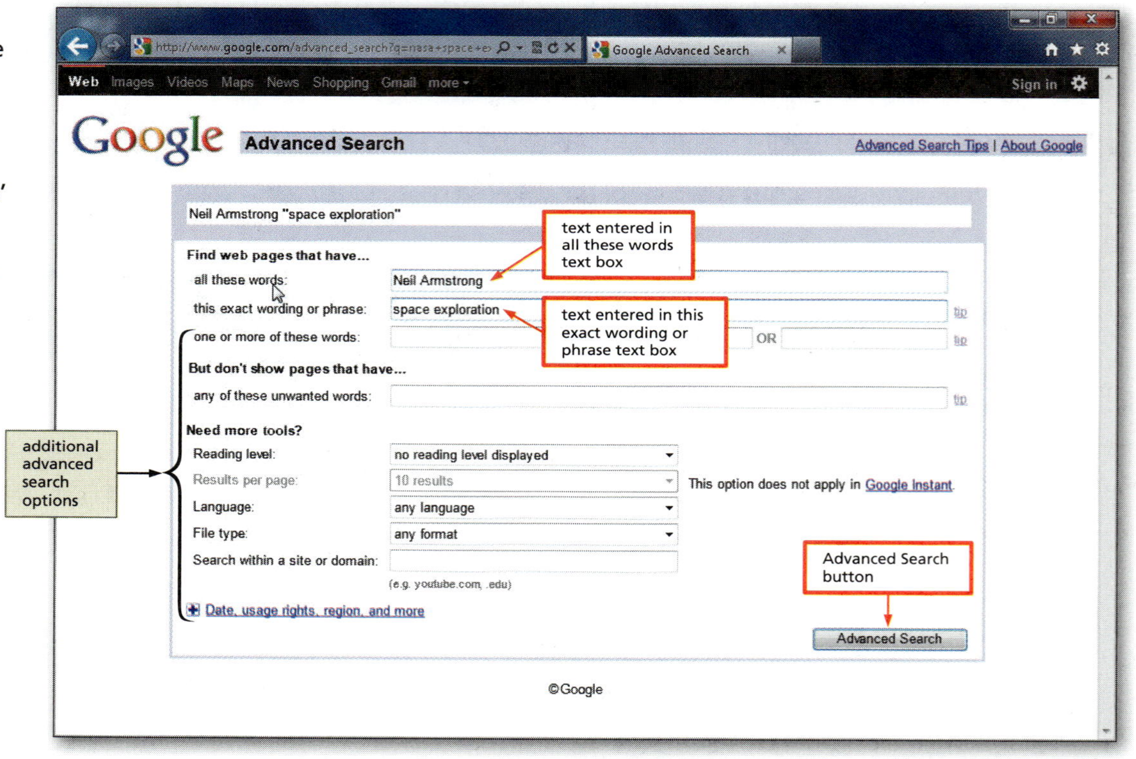

Figure 2–43

2

- Click the Advanced Search button to display the search results.

- Click the NASA – NASA Honors Neil Armstrong With Exploration Award link (Figure 2–44).

Figure 2–44

Focusing Your Search Results

Searching using the names, Neil Armstrong, in the 'all these words' text box results in a search for both names and displays Web pages that contain both names. The phrase, space exploration, in the 'this exact wording or phrase' text box results in a list of Web pages that contain the exact phrase.

Recall that the initial search for space exploration using the Google simple search form returned millions of links. The second attempt using the Google Advanced Search form returned far fewer links, and the pages were more useful because they met more specific search criteria, illustrating how important it is to *be as specific as possible with keywords*. Put some thought into what small group of words most represents the topic or is used frequently with it. Choose the best words from this group to use with the search engine.

If you receive only a couple or no useful links, make the keywords slightly more general and try again. For example, if you wanted to find information about tax-exempt municipal bonds, a general-to-specific list of keywords might include investments, bonds, tax-free investments, municipal bonds, or tax-exempt bonds.

Creating a Working Bibliography

Once you find a good Web source, you should record it. A **bibliography** is a list of sources referred to in the creation of a paper. As you do research online, creating a working bibliography will help you organize and compile the resources you find. For Web resources, you should note the author or authors, title of the page, Web address, date of publication, date of the last revision, date you accessed the resource, heading of any part or section where the relevant information is located, navigation instructions necessary to find the resource, and other pertinent information.

Often, when you are compiling the information, you will need to locate the name of the person who authored the material on the Web page. If the author's information is not readily available, you might have to write to the person responsible for the Web site, or **webmaster**, and ask for the author's name. First, display the home page of the Web site to see if a directory or contact section is listed. If you do not find a directory or contact section, display the bottom of the Web page or other pages in the Web site. Many Web pages include the e-mail address of the webmaster at the bottom of the page.

In the past, index cards were used to record relevant information about a work, and you still can use index cards to record Web research. There are a variety of ways you can keep track of the Web sites you use and the information you gather:

- You can send the information that you need in an e-mail message to yourself and store the messages in separate folders. Use one folder for each point or category you are researching.
- You can store the information in separate document files using copy-and-paste techniques. Use a separate file for each point or category you research.
- You can create a folder in the Favorites Center and then place related favorites you find on the Web in that folder.
- You can print the Web page and file the hard copy.

To Record Relevant Information in WordPad about a Web Research Source

To demonstrate how to record relevant information about a Web resource, the following steps copy information from the NASA – NASA Honors Neil Armstrong With Exploration Award Web page and paste it into a WordPad document.

1

- Open WordPad by clicking the Start button on the Windows taskbar, clicking All Programs on the Start menu to display the All Programs list, clicking Accessories on the All Programs list to display the Accessories list, and then clicking WordPad on the Accessories list.

- If necessary, maximize the WordPad window (Figure 2–45).

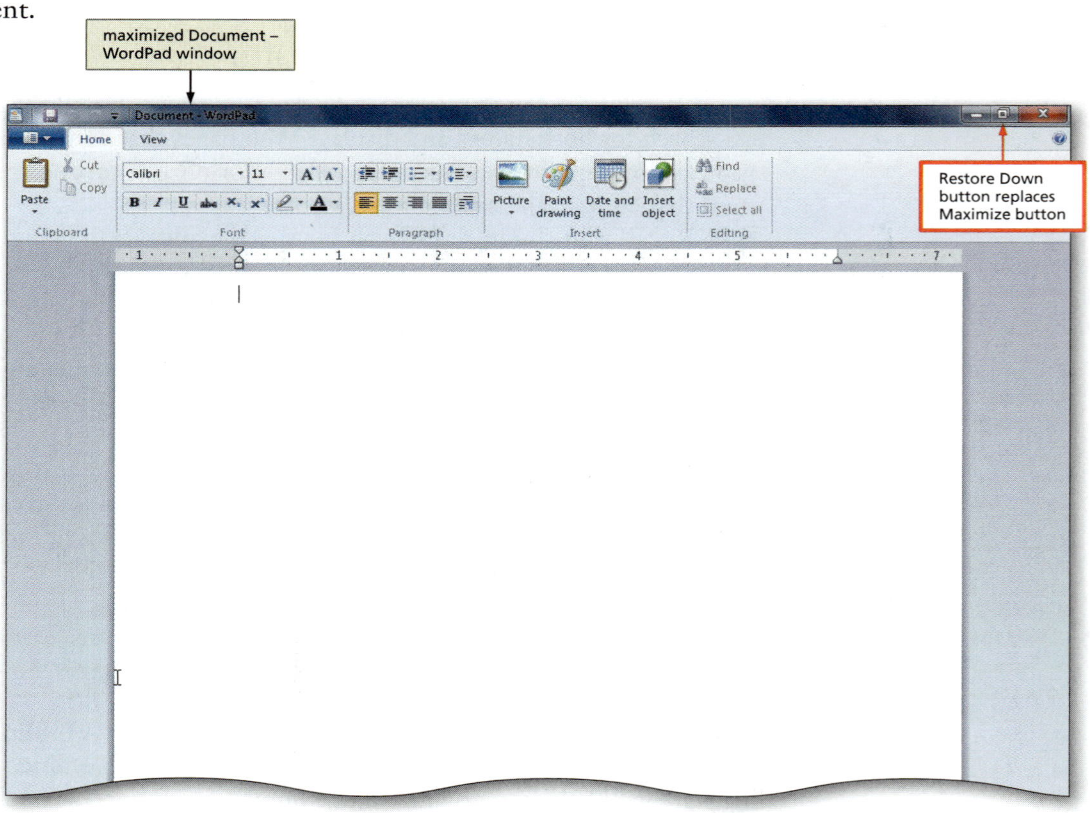

maximized Document – WordPad window

Restore Down button replaces Maximize button

Figure 2–45

2

- Click the Internet Explorer button on the taskbar to move the Document – WordPad window to the background and display the Internet Explorer window in the foreground.

- If necessary, scroll to display the beginning of the article (Figure 2–46).

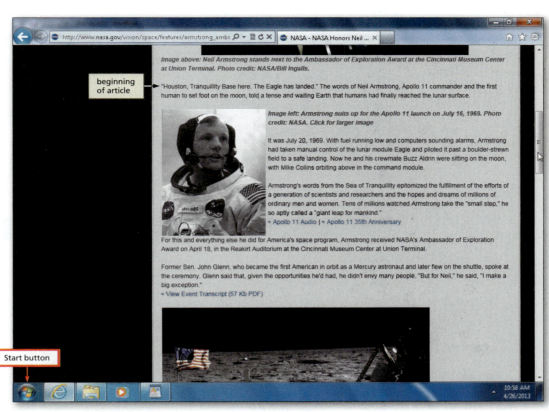

Figure 2–46

3

- Select the entire first paragraph.

- Right-click the selected text to display a shortcut menu (Figure 2–47).

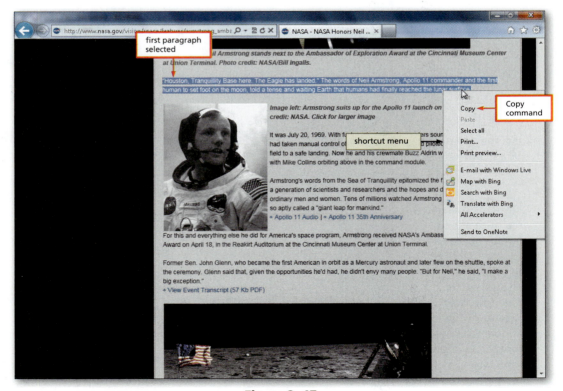

Figure 2–47

4

- Click Copy on the shortcut menu to copy the selected text to the Clipboard.

- Click the Document – WordPad button on the taskbar to display the Document – WordPad window (Figure 2–48).

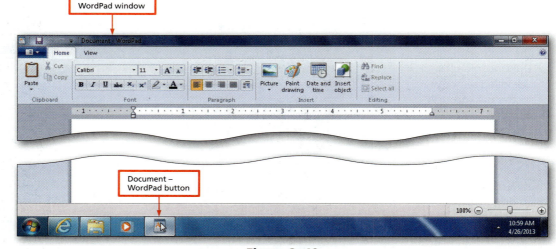

Figure 2–48

5

- Type `http://www.nasa.gov/vision/space/features/armstrong_ambassador_of_exploration.html` in the WordPad document.

- Press the ENTER key and then type **NASA Honors Neil Armstrong With Exploration Award** in the WordPad document.

- Press the ENTER key and then type today's date in the WordPad document.

- Press the ENTER key twice (Figure 2–49).

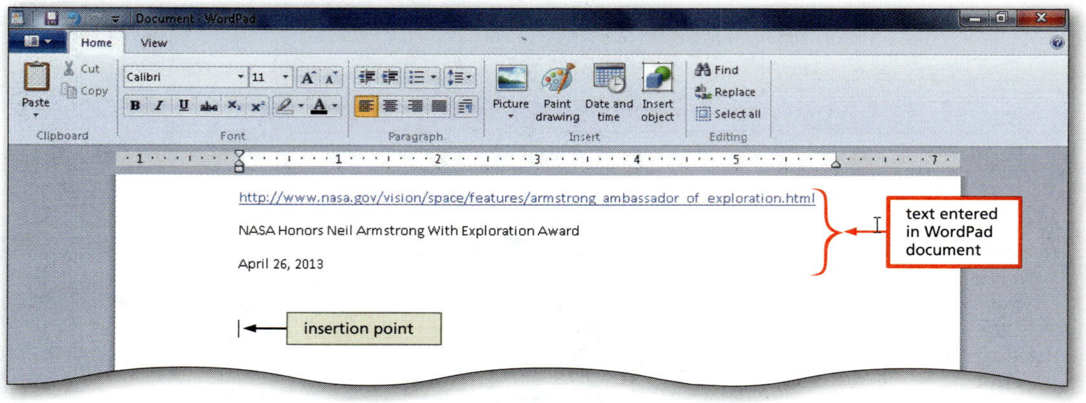

Figure 2–49

6

- Right-click a blank area of the document to display a shortcut menu, and then click Paste on the shortcut menu to paste the contents of the Clipboard in the WordPad window at the location of the insertion point (Figure 2–50).

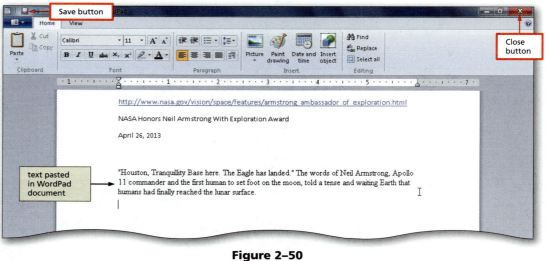

Figure 2–50

To Save a WordPad Document

The following steps save the WordPad document in the Documents library on your computer using the file name, Neil Armstrong – Exploration Award. If you have a lot of research to do, consider saving both the evaluation criteria and the research information for a particular Web site in the same document.

1 Click the Save button on the Quick Access Toolbar.

2 If necessary, select the Documents Library.

3 Type `Neil Armstrong – Exploration Award` in the File name box.

4 Click the Save button in the Save As dialog box to save the new file to the Documents Library on your computer.

5 Click the Close button on the WordPad title bar to quit WordPad.

Citing Web Sources

Standards for citing Web resources have been developed and published by most of the documentation style authorities, like the Modern Language Association (MLA) and the American Psychological Association (APA). You can find these guides to documentation style at a library or on the Web at mla.org and apa.org, respectively.

An example of citing a Web resource using the MLA documentation style appears in Figure 2–51. The example documents the source of the criteria for Neil Armstrong's exploration award.

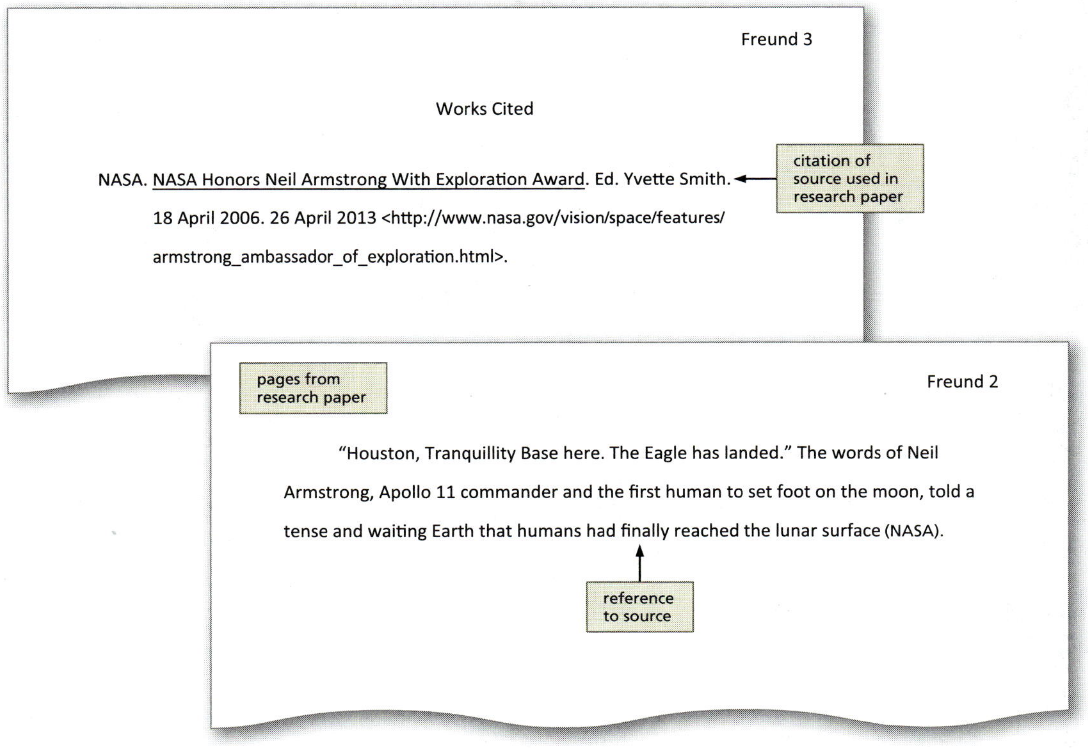

Freund 3

Works Cited

NASA. NASA Honors Neil Armstrong With Exploration Award. Ed. Yvette Smith.

18 April 2006. 26 April 2013 <http://www.nasa.gov/vision/space/features/

armstrong_ambassador_of_exploration.html>.

[citation of source used in research paper]

Freund 2

[pages from research paper]

"Houston, Tranquillity Base here. The Eagle has landed." The words of Neil

Armstrong, Apollo 11 commander and the first human to set foot on the moon, told a

tense and waiting Earth that humans had finally reached the lunar surface (NASA).

[reference to source]

Figure 2–51

BTW

Citing Web Sources
Both of the style guides mentioned in the text differ slightly from one another on the format of the citation of a Web source. Check with your instructor for his or her preferred format.

Searching the Web for Specific Information

You also can search the Web for Web sites published during a particular time period, mailing addresses, maps, words, and images. Using a specialized Web site for this purpose can produce more targeted and relevant results over generic search engines such as Yahoo! or Google.

To Locate Events Using Google Timeline

Once you perform a Google search, you might want to locate information relating to your search topic during a specific time period. **Google Timeline** applies a filter to display the search results in chronological order. The following steps use Google Timeline to locate news about Neil Armstrong during a specific time period.

1

- Type **google. com** in the Address bar and then press the ENTER key to display the Google Web page.

- Type **Neil Armstrong** and then press the ENTER key to display the search results.

- If necessary, scroll to display the Timeline link.

- Click the Timeline link to display a timeline of search results relating to Neil Armstrong (Figure 2–52).

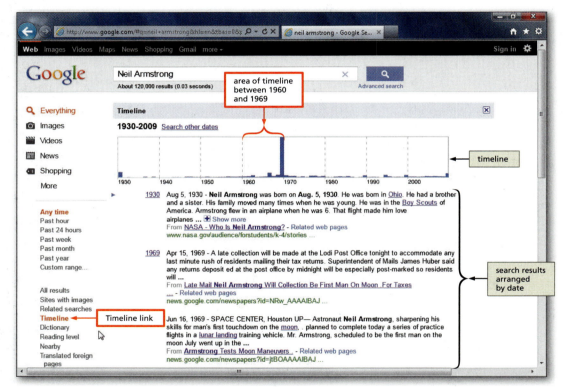

Figure 2–52

2

- Click the area on the timeline between 1960 and 1969 to display search results that date from those years (Figure 2–53).

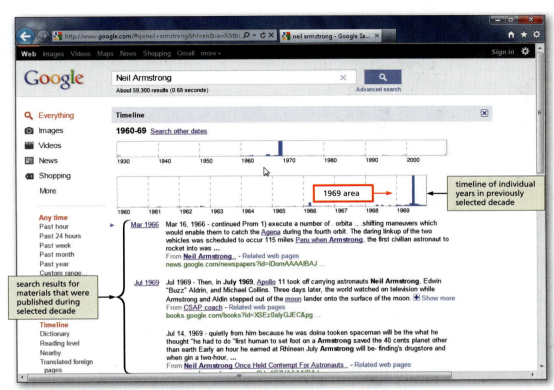

Figure 2–53

3

- Click the 1969 area on the timeline to display search results dated from 1969 (Figure 2–54).

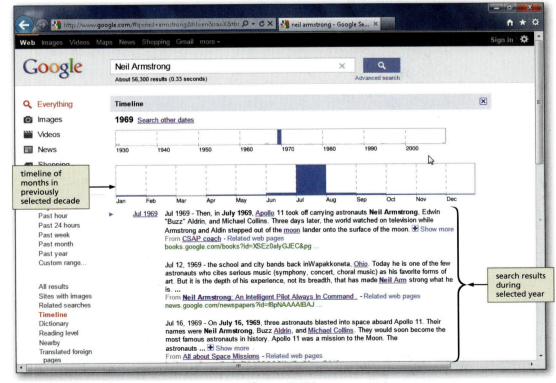

Figure 2–54

4

● Click the Jul area on the timeline to display search results dating from July of 1969 (Figure 2–55).

Q&A

How are the dates associated with the search results determined?

The timeline displays dates when the information was published. Recent events will have more search results than older events because there is less information available online for events that occurred before the emergence of the Internet as a news repository.

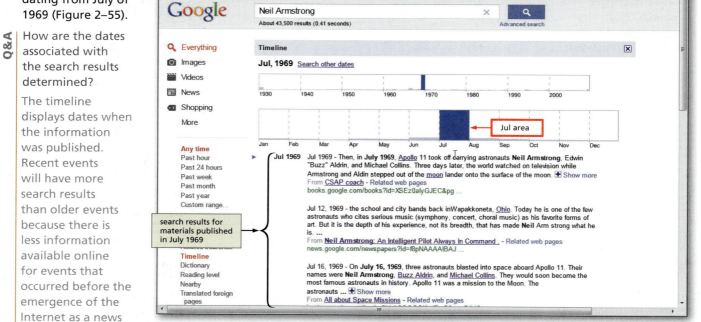

Figure 2–55

To Search the Web for an Address

You can use Web sites such as Superpages and WhitePages to find locations of businesses or people. The following steps use Superpages to search for the location of the Kennedy Space Center.

1

- Type **superpages. com** in the Address bar and then press the ENTER key to display the Superpages Web page (Figure 2–56).

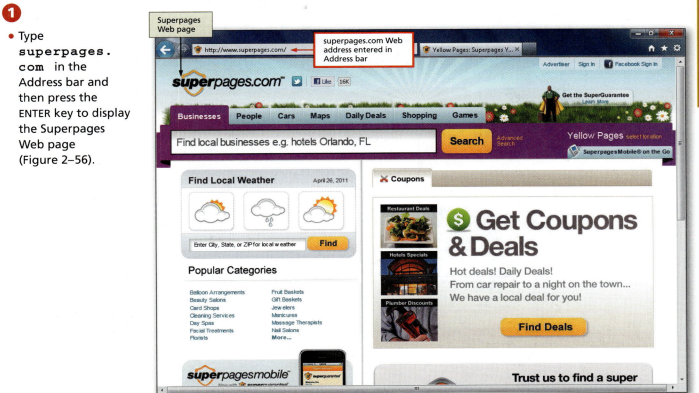

Figure 2–56

2

- Click the Search text box and then type **Kennedy Space Center** (Figure 2–57).

Figure 2–57

3

- Click the Search button.

- If necessary, scroll the Web page to display the search results (Figure 2–58).

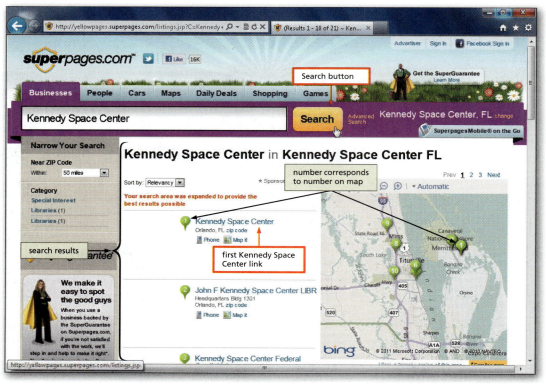

Figure 2–58

4

- Click the first Kennedy Space Center link to display the location information about the Kennedy Space Center (Figure 2–59).

Figure 2–59

To Search the Web for a Map of a Place or Landmark

When you plan to visit a landmark in a new city or state, you can use the Internet to provide a map of the area you plan to visit. Many people use Google Maps or MapQuest for finding maps. The following steps use Google Maps to search for a map of the Kennedy Space Center Visitor Complex in Titusville, Florida.

1

- Type **maps. google.com** in the Address bar and then press the ENTER key to display the Google Maps Web page (Figure 2–60).

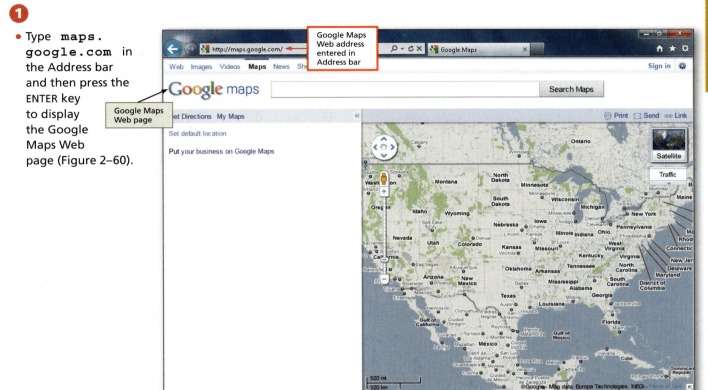

Figure 2–60

2

- Type **Kennedy Space Center Visitor Complex** in the Search box (Figure 2–61).

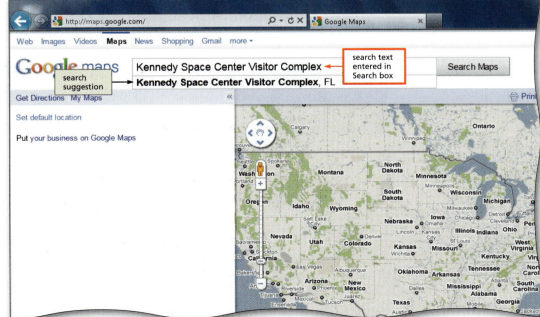

Figure 2–61

3

- Click the Search Maps button to search the Google Maps database and display the search results (Figure 2–62).

Experiment

- In the Internet Explorer window, click the Zoom In and Zoom Out buttons multiple times to zoom the map in and out.

Experiment

- Click the Satellite button to view satellite imagery of the area surrounding the Kennedy Space Center Visitor Complex.

Figure 2–62

To Search the Web for a Definition of a Word

Online dictionaries, like Dictionary.com and Merriam-Webster Online, allow you to search for definitions, encyclopedia articles, or synonyms and antonyms. The following steps use Dictionary.com to find the definition of the word, rocket.

1

- Type **dictionary. com** in the Address bar and then press the ENTER key to display the Dictionary.com Web page (Figure 2–63).

Figure 2–63

2

- Type `rocket` in the text box at the top of the Dictionary.com Web page (Figure 2–64).

Figure 2–64

3

- Click the Search button to search for the word, rocket.

- If necessary, scroll down to display the first definition (Figure 2–65).

Experiment

- Scroll down the Web page and click the first Cite This Source link, which appears below the definition for Richard. The citation for the definition is displayed in multiple styles, including APA and MLA.

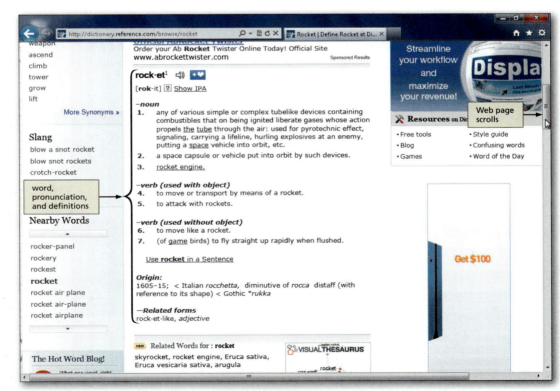

Figure 2–65

To Search the Web for an Image

When you want to search for an image, many search engines are able to include images as search results. The following steps use Bing to search for images related to space exploration.

1

- Type **bing.com** in the Address bar and then press the ENTER key to display the Bing Web page (Figure 2–66).

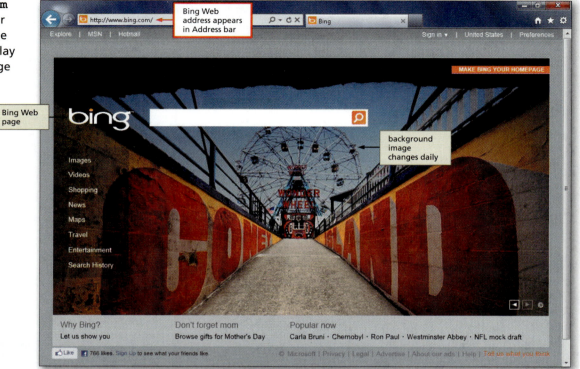

Figure 2–66

2

- Click the Images link to limit the search results to images (Figure 2–67).

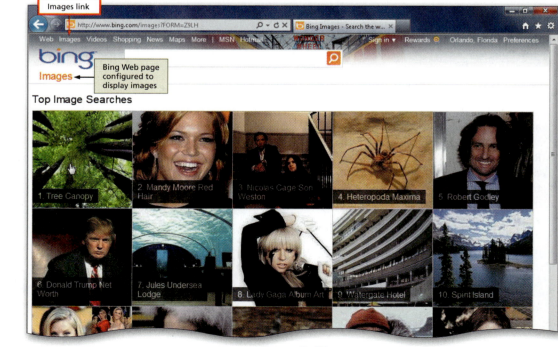

Figure 2–67

3

• Type **space exploration** in the Search text box (Figure 2–68).

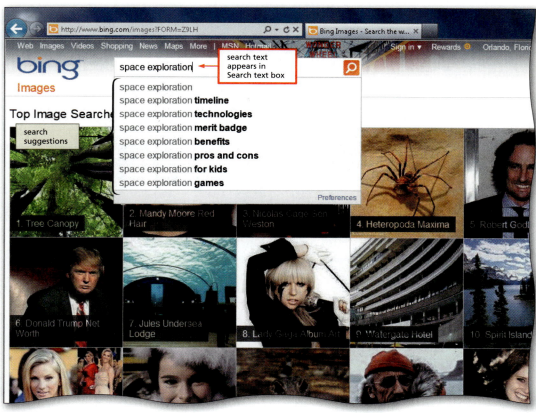

Figure 2–68

4

• Click the Search button to initiate the Bing image search and display the search results (Figure 2–69).

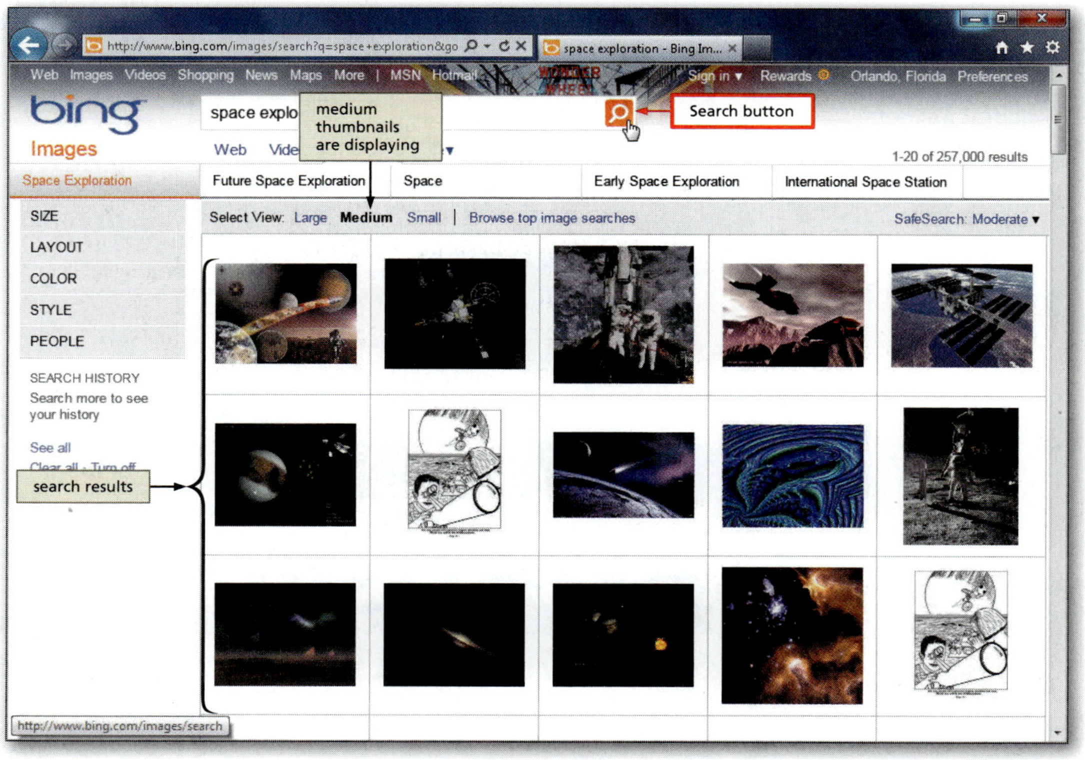

Figure 2–69

5

- Point to one of the images to display a larger thumbnail of that image, along with the image title, size, and link (Figure 2–70).

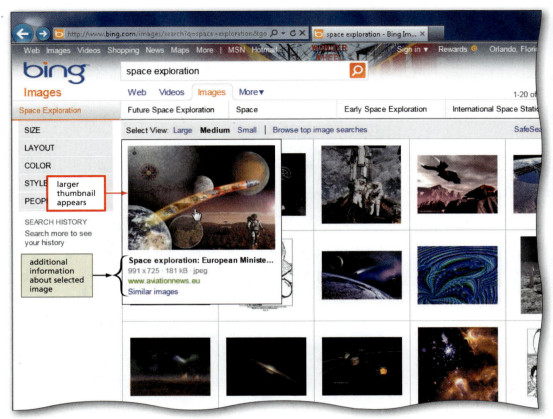

Figure 2–70

6

- Click the image to see a larger version of the image and additional details (Figure 2–71).

Figure 2–71

7

- Click the 'See full size image' link to view the image in a new tab (Figure 2–72).

- Click the Close Tab button to close the tab displaying the full-size image.

Q&A

Can I use the images that a search engine returns for personal or business-related use?

You always should obtain permission from the person or company hosting the Web site containing the image before using it for your own purposes. Many images on the Internet are protected by copyright regulations and are unavailable for use without permission.

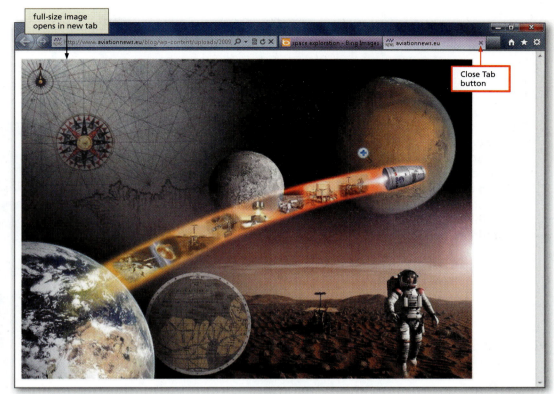

full-size image opens in new tab

Close Tab button

Figure 2–72

Accelerators

The **Accelerator** feature in Internet Explorer 9 allows you to perform a Web search using text shown on a Web page by first selecting the text on the page and then choosing an Accelerator to search for the selected text. Web sites such as eBay, Facebook, Bing, and more create Accelerators. For example, if you are visiting the Armstrong Air and Space Museum's Web site and want to display a map with its location, you can do so by selecting the address, clicking the Accelerator icon, and then selecting the Map with Bing command. In addition to performing searches on the Web, Accelerators also enable you to send content from a Web page to another program, translate text, or create a blog entry about a particular topic.

To Search the Web Using an Accelerator

Using an Accelerator to search the Web can decrease the amount of time it takes you to find your search results. For example, to display search results for a keyword, you previously navigated to a search engine, typed search text into a text box, and then clicked the Search button. Using an Accelerator, you can search right from the Web page containing the term. The following steps use an Accelerator to search for a keyword.

1

- Type **exploration. nasa.gov** in the Address bar and then press the ENTER key to display the NASA - Exploration Web page (Figure 2–73).

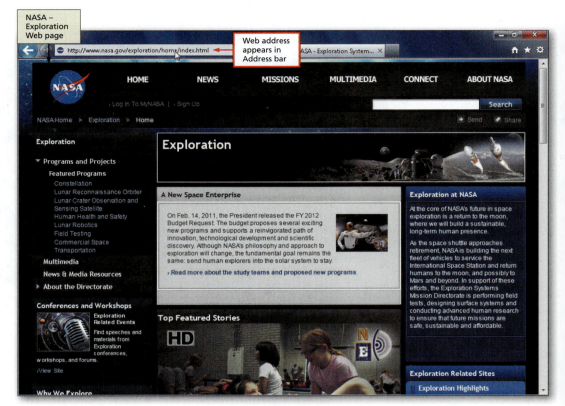

Figure 2–73

2

- Select the word, exploration, on the Web page to search the Web using that word as a keyword. After you select the text, the blue Accelerator icon will appear (Figure 2–74).

Figure 2–74

3

- Click the Accelerator icon to display the Accelerator menu (Figure 2–75).

Q&A

What should I do if the Accelerator icon does not appear?

If you move your mouse too quickly, or the Accelerator icon does not appear for some other reason, you still can access the Accelerators installed on your computer by right-clicking the selected text, and then selecting your chosen Accelerator from the shortcut menu.

Figure 2–75

4

- Click the Search with Bing command to display the Bing Web page containing the search results for the selected keyword (Figure 2–76).

- When you are done viewing the search results, click the Close Tab button on the tab containing the search results.

Q&A

Why do some Accelerators display results while the mouse pointer is hovering over the command in the shortcut menu?

Some Accelerator providers allow you to preview the information you are seeking by hovering over the command on the menu. However, other Accelerators require that you open a new tab or browser window to display the information.

Figure 2–76

To Add a New Accelerator

In addition to the Accelerators that are installed with Internet Explorer 9, you can download and install Accelerators that are developed by third parties such as eBay, Facebook, and Yahoo!. The following steps add the Bing Translator Accelerator to Internet Explorer.

1

- Click the Tools button to display the Tools menu (Figure 2–77).

Figure 2–77

2

- Click the Manage add-ons command to display the Manage Add-ons dialog box (Figure 2–78).

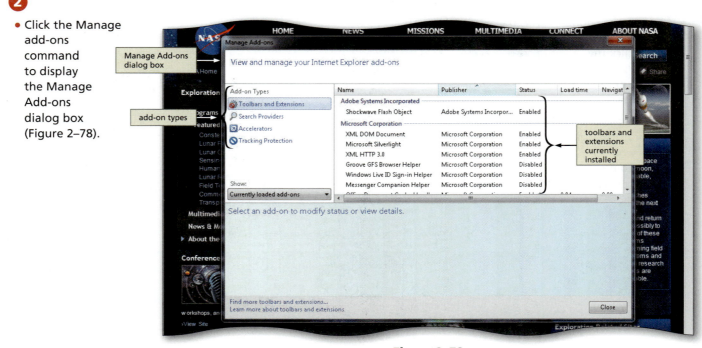

Figure 2–78

3

- Click the Accelerators add-on type to display a list of Accelerators that can be managed (Figure 2–79).

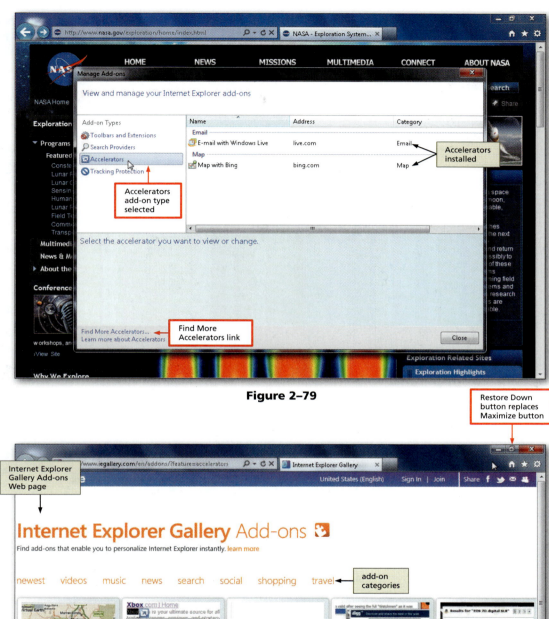

Figure 2–79

4

- Click the Find More Accelerators link to display the Internet Explorer Gallery Add-ons Web page in a new browser window.

- If necessary, maximize the browser window (Figure 2–80).

Figure 2–80

5

- If necessary, scroll to display the Bing Translator Accelerator.

- Click the Bing Translator thumbnail to display more information about the selected Accelerator (Figure 2–81).

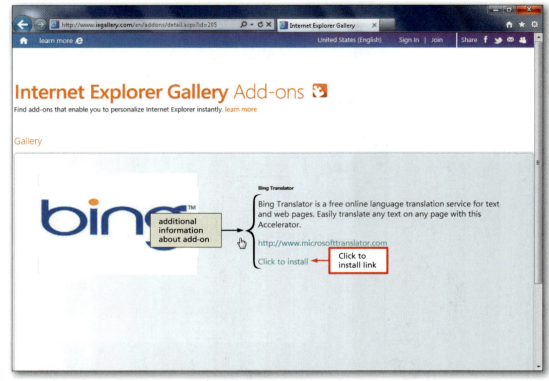

Figure 2–81

6

- Click the 'Click to install' link to display the Add Accelerator dialog box (Figure 2–82).

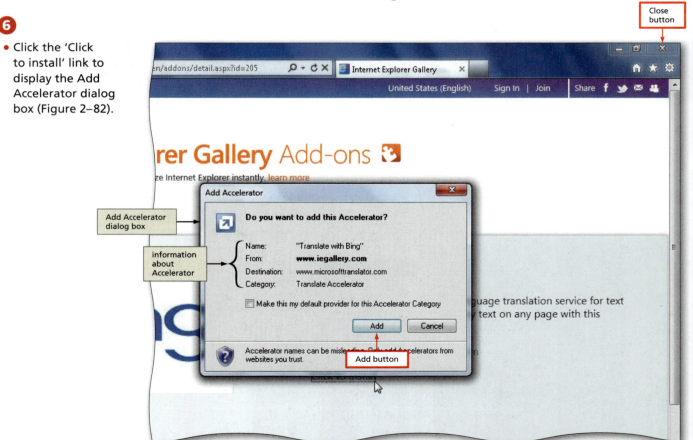

Figure 2–82

7
- Click the Add button to install the Accelerator.
- Click the Close button to close the Internet Explorer Gallery – Add-ons window (Figure 2–83).
- Click the Close button to close the Manage Add-ons dialog box.

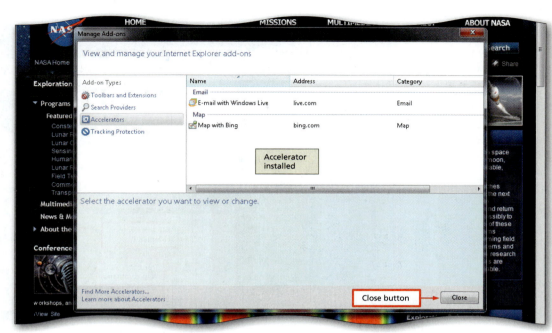

Figure 2–83

Other Ways
1. Select text on Web page, click Accelerator icon, point to All Accelerators, click Find more Accelerators, click Accelerator to add

To View the Accelerators Installed on Your Computer

When you click the Accelerator icon after selecting one or more words on a Web page, an abbreviated list of the Accelerators installed on your computer is displayed. The following steps display all Accelerators currently installed on your computer.

1
- If necessary, select a word on the displayed Web page to display the Accelerator icon (Figure 2–84).

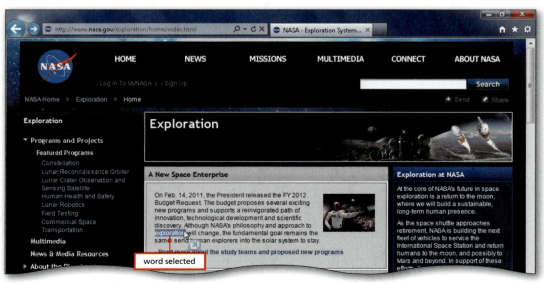

Figure 2–84

2

- Click the Accelerator icon to display the Accelerator menu.

- Point to the All Accelerators command to display the All Accelerators submenu (Figure 2–85).

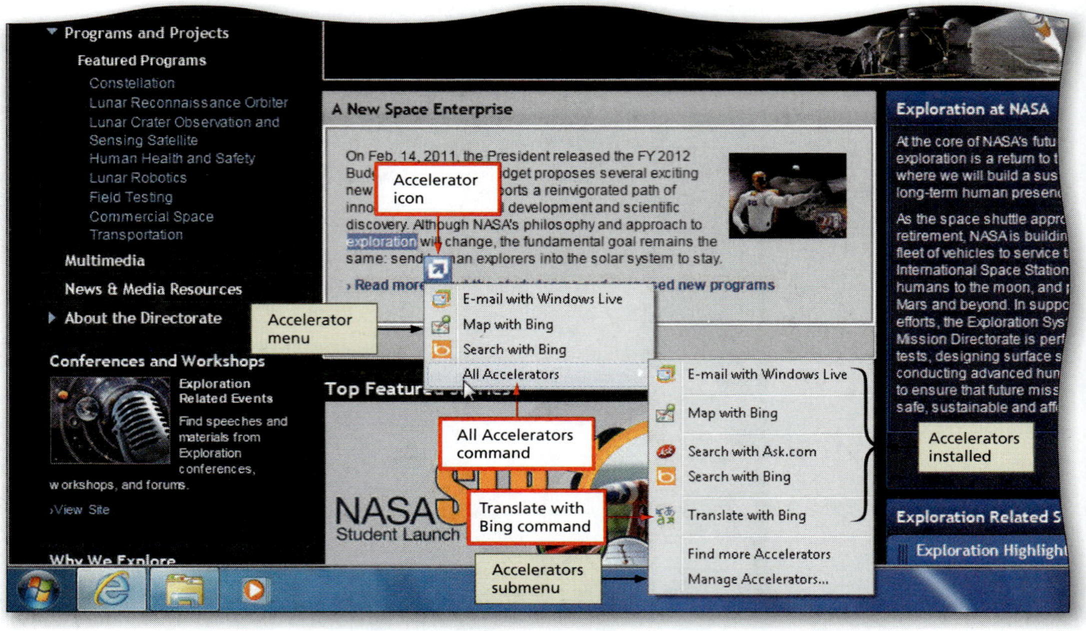

Figure 2–85

To Translate a Word Using a New Accelerator

The following steps use the Bing Translator Accelerator to translate a selected word to another language.

1

- With the text selected and the All Accelerators submenu displayed, point to the Translate with Bing command to display a preview of the current translation.

2

- Click the Translate with Bing command to display the Bing Translator in a new tab (Figure 2–86).

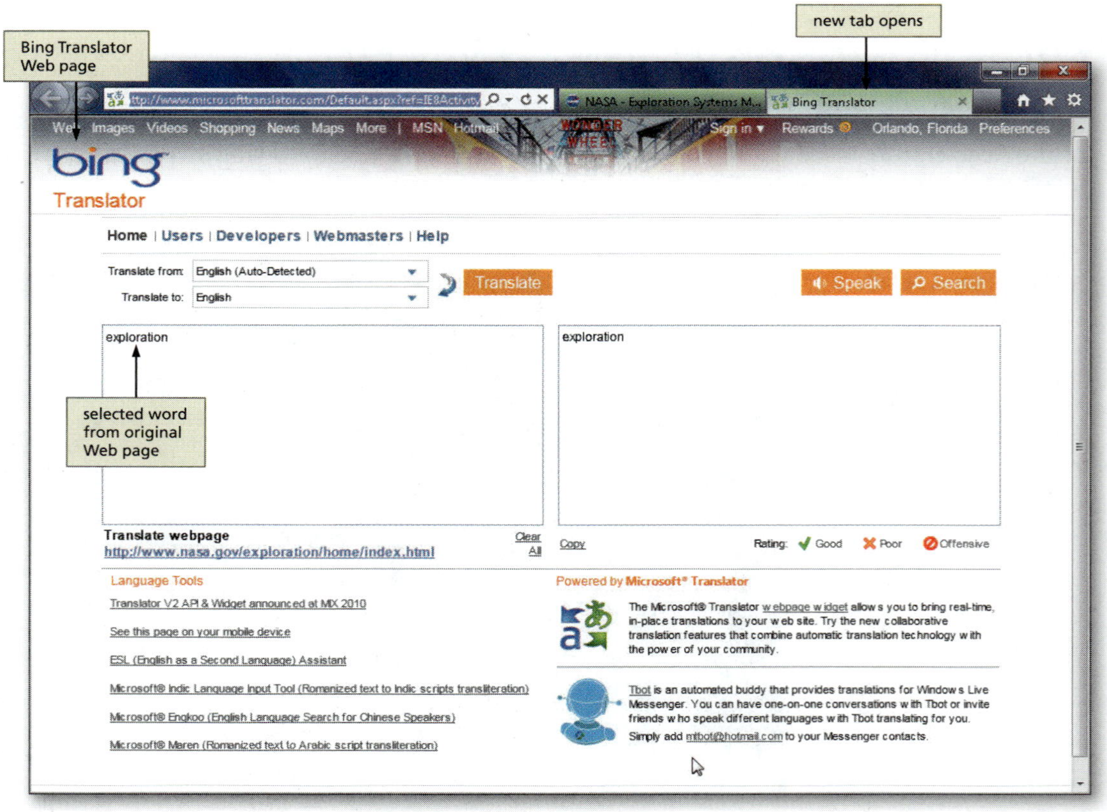

Figure 2–86

3
- Click the Translate to drop-down arrow, and then click Spanish (Figure 2–87).

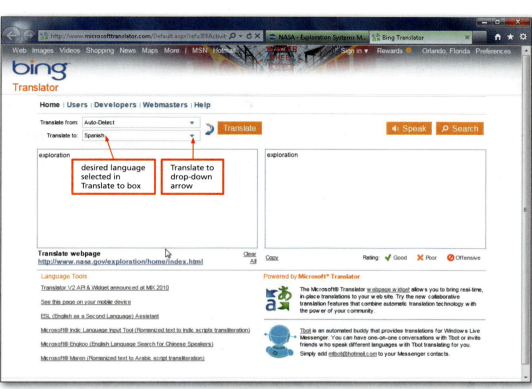

Figure 2–87

4
- Click the Translate button to translate the selected text to the desired language (Figure 2–88).

5
- Once you have finished viewing the translation, click the Close Tab button on the Bing Translator tab to close the tab.

Figure 2–88

To Remove an Accelerator

If your list of Accelerators becomes too long, if you add an Accelerator by mistake, or if you feel that you no longer will use a particular Accelerator, you can remove it from your computer. The following steps remove the Translate with Bing Accelerator from your computer.

1

- Click the Tools button to display the Tools menu.

- Click the Manage add-ons command to display the Manage Add-ons dialog box.

- Click the Accelerators add-on type to display a list of Accelerators that can be removed (Figure 2–89).

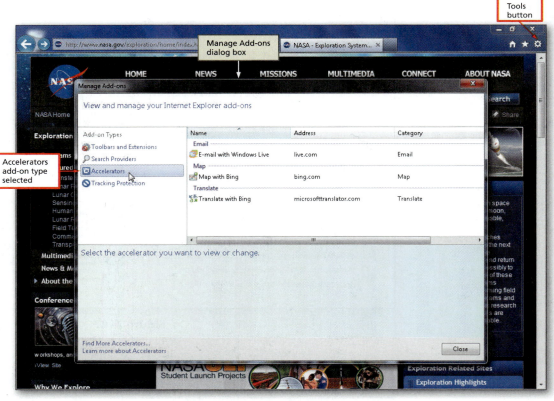

Figure 2–89

2

- Click the Translate with Bing Accelerator to select it (Figure 2–90).

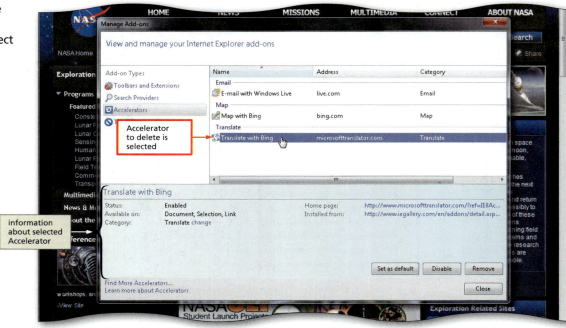

Figure 2–90

3

- Click the Remove button to display the Manage Add-ons dialog box confirming that you want to remove the Accelerator (Figure 2–91).

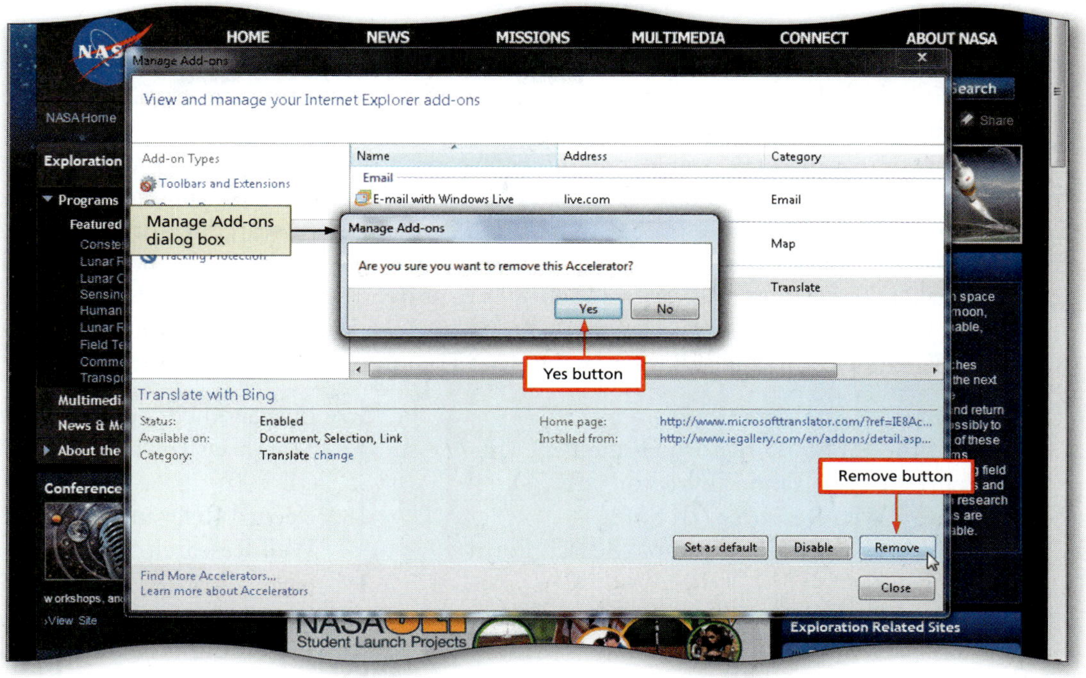

Q&A

Should I disable the Accelerator instead of removing it completely?

If your list of Accelerators is becoming too large to manage, but you feel that you might need an Accelerator again in the future, it might be easier to disable it instead of remove it. If at a later date you want to add it back to your list of Accelerators, you can enable it more quickly than you can add it to your computer again.

Figure 2–91

4

- Click the Yes button to remove the Accelerator (Figure 2–92).

- Click the Close button to close the Manage Add-ons dialog box.

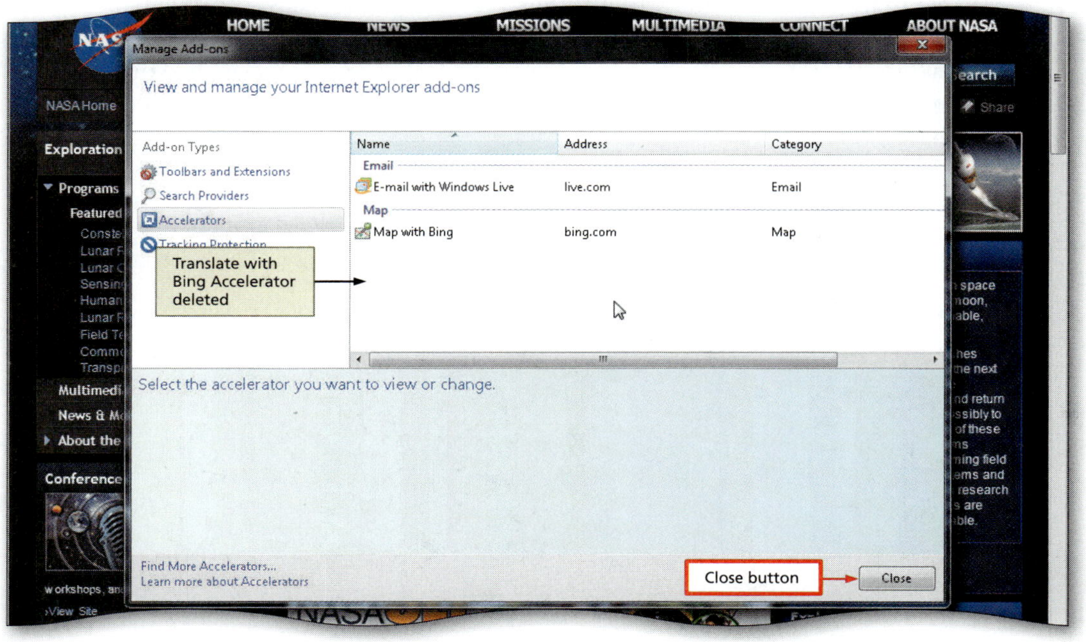

Figure 2–92

Other Ways

1. Select text on Web page, click Accelerator icon, point to All Accelerators, click Manage Accelerators

Chapter Summary

In this chapter, you have learned about the 13 general types of Web pages and the three general types of search tools. You learned how to evaluate a Web page as a potential source for research. You learned how to search the Internet using the Yahoo! Directory. You learned the techniques for using the Google search engine to enter keywords and use advanced search techniques. You learned how to use multiple tabs, including how to switch between tabs and how to tear off a tab. You learned how to search from the Address bar and how to add new search engines to the Address bar. You learned how to record relevant information about a potential source for future reference and how to write a citation for a Web resource. You used advanced search features in Google to explore your search topic using the Wonder Wheel feature and to view your search results in chronological order using the Timeline feature. You also saw how to use various Web sites to search the Internet for an address, a map, a definition, and an image. You learned how to use Accelerators to translate text, as well as how to add and remove Accelerators. The items listed below include all the new Internet Explorer skills you have learned in this chapter.

1. Start Internet Explorer (IE 76)
2. Display the Yahoo! Directory Home Page (IE 77)
3. Search Using the Yahoo! Directory (IE 78)
4. Evaluate a Web Resource (IE 80)
5. Search Using the Google Simple Search Form (IE 82)
6. Open a Link in a New Tab and Create a Tab Group (IE 84)
7. Switch Between Tabs (IE 85)
8. Show Tabs on a Separate Row (IE 86)
9. Show Tabs Next to the Address Bar (IE 87)
10. Tear Off a Tab (IE 87)
11. Switch Between Web Pages Using the Windows Taskbar (IE 88)
12. Drag a Tab from One Window to Another Window (IE 90)
13. Close a Tab (IE 91)
14. Customize the Address Bar by Adding a Search Engine (IE 92)
15. Search for Web Pages Using the Ask.com Search Engine (IE 96)
16. Display the Google Advanced Search Form (IE 99)
17. Search Using the Google Advanced Search Form (IE 100)
18. Record Relevant Information in WordPad About a Web Research Source (IE 102)
19. Save a WordPad Document (IE 105)
20. Locate Events Using Google Timeline (IE 106)
21. Search the Web for an Address (IE 109)
22. Search the Web for a Map of a Place or Landmark (IE 111)
23. Search the Web for a Definition of a Word (IE 112)
24. Search the Web for an Image (IE 114)
25. Search the Web Using an Accelerator (IE 118)
26. Add a New Accelerator (IE 120)
27. View the Accelerators Installed on Your Computer (IE 123)
28. Translate a Word Using a New Accelerator (IE 124)
29. Remove an Accelerator (IE 126)

Learn It Online

Test your knowledge of chapter content and key terms.

Instructions: To complete the following exercises, please visit **www.CengageBrain.com**. At the CengageBrain.com Web page, enter the book title **Windows Internet Explorer 9 Introductory** or the ISBN **0-538-48239-7** and click the Find button. On the product page for your book, click the Access Now button below the Study Tools heading. On the Book Companion Site Web page, click the drop-down menu, select Chapter 2, and then click the link for your desired exercise.

Chapter Reinforcement TF, MC, and SA

A series of true/false, multiple-choice, and short-answer questions that test your knowledge of the chapter content.

Flash Cards

An interactive learning environment where you identify chapter key terms associated with displayed definitions.

Practice Test

A series of multiple-choice questions that test your knowledge of chapter content and key terms.

Who Wants To Be a Computer Genius?

An interactive game that challenges your knowledge of chapter content in the style of the television quiz show.

Wheel of Terms

An interactive game that challenges your knowledge of chapter key terms in the style of the television show *Wheel of Fortune*.

Crossword Puzzle Challenge

A crossword puzzle that challenges your knowledge of key terms presented in the chapter.

Apply Your Knowledge

Reinforce the skills and apply the concepts you learned in this chapter.

Searching the Web for Art Exhibits Using the Yahoo! Directory

Instructions: To practice using the Yahoo! Directory, you will search for an art exhibit. You will need to print a Web page containing an image to complete this assignment.

Perform the following tasks:
1. Click the Address bar, type **dir.yahoo.com**, and then press the ENTER key to display the Yahoo! Directory.
2. Click the Arts & Humanities link to display the Arts & Humanities category.
3. Click the Museums, Galleries, and Centers link to display the Museums, Galleries, and Centers subcategory.
4. Click the Exhibits link to display the Exhibits subcategory.
5. Click the Universities@ link to display the Universities subcategory.

Continued >

Apply Your Knowledge *continued*

6. Click the American Art from the Howard University Collection link to display the Art@Howard Web page (Figure 2–93).

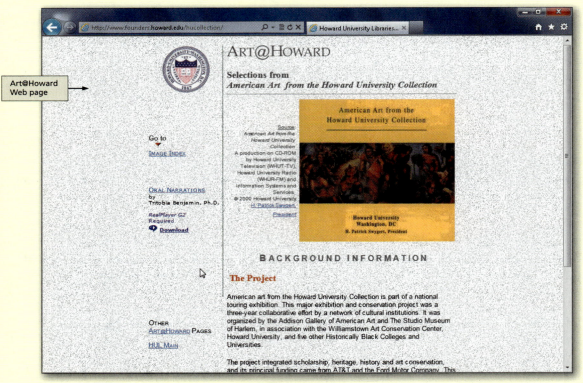

Figure 2–93

7. Print the page, write your name and a brief description of the contents on the printed page, and submit it to your instructor.

Extend Your Knowledge

Extend the skills you learned in this chapter and experiment with new skills. You might need to use Help to complete the assignment.

Searching the Web for Various Information Using Specific Keywords

Instructions: You will explore various search engines to find answers to the following questions. Submit the printed Web pages to complete the assignment.

Perform the following tasks:

1. Navigate to the Google Web page (google.com). Using specific keywords, locate sources of information about yoga and answer the following questions:

   a. List the Web addresses of three Web sites that discuss yoga.

   b. What are three styles of yoga?

   c. What are the benefits of yoga?

2. Print the Web page(s) containing the answers to these questions. Write the specific keywords you used in your Google search on the printout.

3. Using the Yahoo! search engine (yahoo.com), locate the home page of a private college in Cherokee County, South Carolina. Answer the following questions:

  a. What is the college name?

  b. In what city is the college located?

  c. What team name does the Athletic Department use?

4. Print the home page of the college. Write the specific keywords you used in your search on the printout.

5. Using the Bing search engine (bing.com) (Figure 2–94), use specific keywords to locate information about water parks in Canada and answer the following questions:

Figure 2–94

  a. What is the name of a water park in Canada?

  b. What are at least two rides or attractions at the park?

  c. Where is the park located?

6. Print the Web page(s) containing the answers to these questions. Write the specific keywords you used in your search on the printout.

7. Using the Excite search engine (excite.com), use specific keywords to locate information about the periodic table of elements and answer the following questions:

  a. What is the symbol for Bohrium?

  b. Which element is associated with the symbol Ge?

  c. What is the atomic weight of Aluminum?

8. Print the Web page containing the periodic table. Write the specific keywords you used in your search on the printout.

9. Submit the printed Web pages to your instructor.

In the Lab

Use Internet Explorer to navigate the World Wide Web by using the guidelines, concepts, and skills presented in this chapter. Labs are listed in order of increasing difficulty.

Lab 1: Searching the Web Using the Google Directory

Instructions: Use the Google Directory to find Web pages that contain information on antiques, games, and recreational activities. To complete this assignment, you will need to print the first page of each Web site you visit that supplies the requested information.

Perform the following tasks:

1. Display the Google Directory Web page (dir.google.com).
2. Starting with the Arts category and only using the Google Directory:
   a. Locate a Web page that contains information on antique Nikon cameras (Figure 2–95). Print the Web page. On each printout, write the categories and subcategories you clicked to arrive at the Web page you printed.

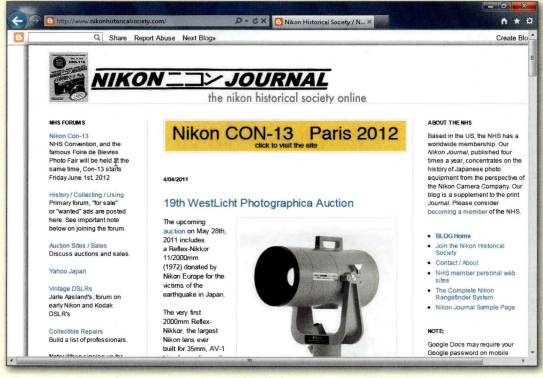

Figure 2–95

   b. Locate a Web page that contains information about antique bicycles, and print the Web page.
   c. Locate a Web page that contains information about antique phonographs, and print the Web page.
3. Using the Google Directory and the Games category:
   a. Locate a Web page that contains the rules for the Crazy Eights card game. Print the Web page.
   b. Locate a different Web page that contains the rules for the Canasta card game, and print the Web page.
   c. Locate a third Web page that contains rules for the Gin Rummy card game, and print the Web page.

4. Using the Google Directory and the Recreation category:

   a. Locate a Web page that contains images related to Paintball. Print the Web page.

   b. Locate a Web page that contains images of greyhounds, and print the Web page.

   c. Locate a Web page that contains information about jai-alai, and print the Web page.

5. Submit all printed Web pages to your instructor.

In the Lab

Lab 2: Searching the Web Using the Google Timeline

Instructions: Use the Google Timeline to search for Web pages about extreme sports during different time periods. You will need to record the Web address of each Web page and develop a short report on each topic using WordPad.

Perform the following tasks:

1. Click the Address bar, type `google.com`, and then press the ENTER key to display the Google home page. The home page contains the Google simple search form.

2. Use the Search text box and the Search button in the Google simple search form to search for the text, extreme sports.

3. If necessary, click the 'More search tools' link. Click the Timeline link to display the Google Timeline for the search results (Figure 2–96).

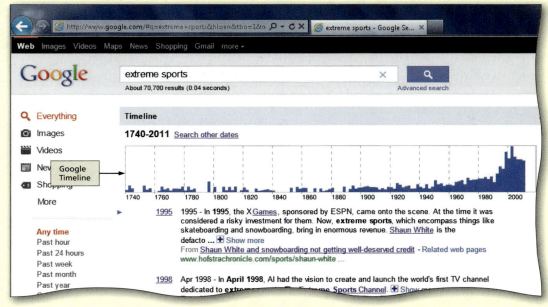

Figure 2–96

4. Click the appropriate time periods to display a Web page, published in 1995, related to an extreme sport of your choice. Next, type the appropriate search text and use the Timeline to locate a Web page that was published between 2000 and 2010 about the same extreme sport.

5. Using WordPad, copy information about your chosen extreme sport from the Web pages into a WordPad document and develop a short report about each time period. Add the Web addresses of the Web sites you used and your name to the end of the report.

6. Submit the WordPad document to your instructor.

In the Lab

Lab 3: Searching the Web Using Google and Keywords

Instructions: Use Google to find Web pages relating to several topics, to locate factual information, and to narrow searches by adding search terms. To complete this assignment, print the first page of each Web page you visit.

Perform the following tasks:

Part 1: Use Google for Simple Keyword Searches

1. Navigate to the Google home page.

2. Find a Web page containing inspirational quotations about children. Print the Web page.

3. Find the Web page containing the address, phone number, and e-mail address of your representative in the U.S. House of Representatives. Print the Web page.

4. Find the official Web site of Thurman Munson, and print the Web page.

5. Find the current temperature in Leavenworth, Kansas. Print the Web page and circle the temperature.

6. Using the keywords, movie database, find who directed the movie *Rio*. Print the Web page and write the director's name on the printed Web page.

7. Locate a Web address and address of a company or school that offers skydiving lessons, and print the Web page.

Part 2: Use the Google Advanced Search

1. Click Advanced search on the Google home page to display the Google Advanced Search form (Figure 2–97).

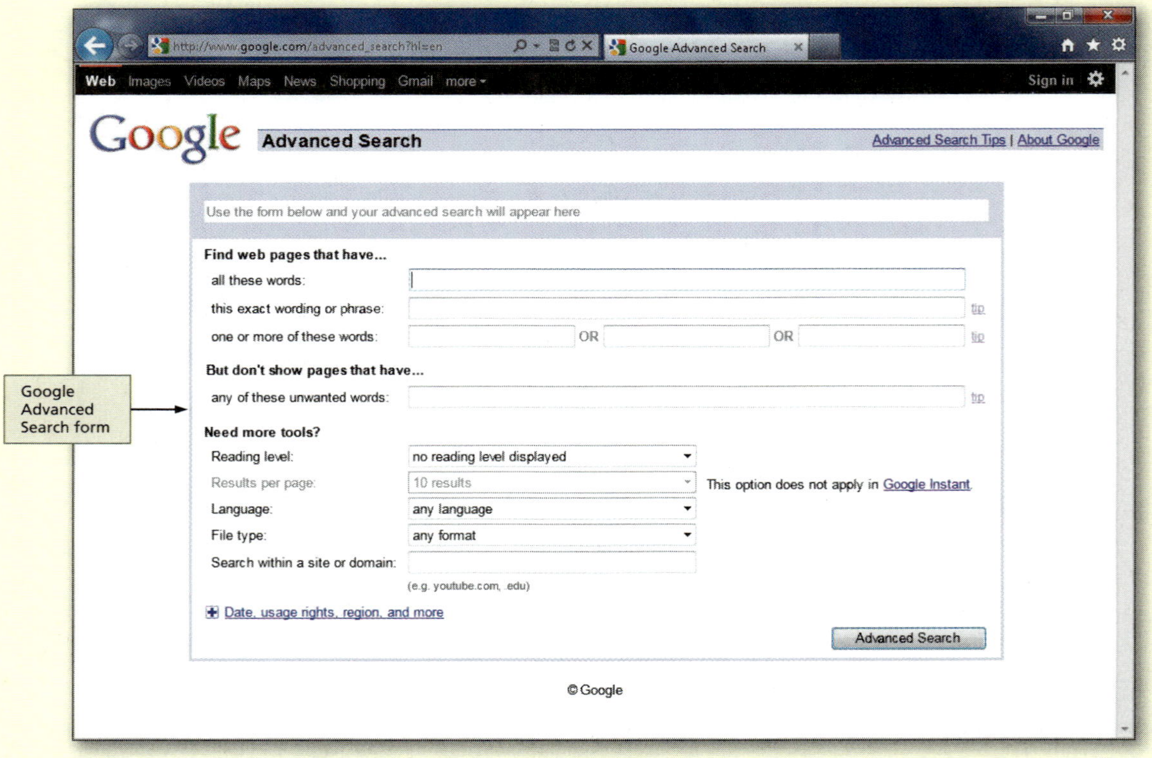

Figure 2–97

2. Find the number of Web pages that contain the keyword, airplane. Print the Web page and circle the number of search results that were returned.

3. Find the number of Web pages that contain the keywords, airplane and Boeing. Print the Web page and circle the number of search results that were returned.

4. Find the number of Web pages that contain the keywords, airplane, Boeing, and engines. Print the Web page and circle the number of search results that were returned.

5. Find the number of Web pages that contain the exact phrase, Canada geographic map. Print the Web page and circle the number of search results that were returned.

6. Find the number of Web pages that contain the exact phrase, geographic map, and the keyword, Mexico. Print the Web page and circle the number of search results that were returned.

7. Find the number of Web pages that contain the exact phrase, geographic map, the keyword, Mexico, and are written in the Spanish language. (*Hint:* Select the Spanish option in the Language box on the Google Advanced Search page.) Print the Web page and circle the number of search results that were returned.

8. Submit all printed Web pages to your instructor.

In the Lab

Lab 4: Using the Web for Research

Instructions: Use the Address bar to research and prepare a short report about one of the topics listed below. Remember to include a citation for each Web site you used in your report.

Perform the following tasks:
1. Perform a search using the Address bar for any one of the following topics: a Civil War battle, the life of a current political figure, an extreme weather event, milestones in aviation, an extraterrestrial sighting, or genetic engineering. Figure 2–98 on the next page shows a Web page about Hurricane Andrew, an extreme weather event that occurred in 1992.

Continued >

STUDENT ASSIGNMENTS

In the Lab *continued*

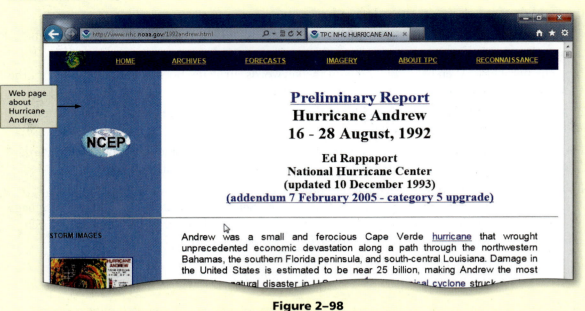

Figure 2–98

2. Find two informative Web pages about the topic you selected. Using WordPad, copy a relevant image from the Web pages into a WordPad document and write a short report summarizing what you learned. Be sure that the images you copy into your WordPad document are not protected by copyright.

3. Using the MLA documentation style (or the style requested by your instructor), create citations for the Web sites you referenced in the report.

4. Submit the WordPad document to your instructor.

In the Lab

Lab 5: Searching the Web for Specific Content

Instructions: You would like to become more familiar with search engines and be able to search for images, addresses, and maps. You will need to print the first page of each Web site you visit to complete this assignment.

Perform the following tasks:

Part 1: Search for Images Using Google

1. Using Google, search for the following and print a Web page for each:

a. A Web page containing an image of a red ear slider

b. A Web page containing an image of Simon Cowell or Jay Leno

c. A Web page containing an image of the northern lights (aurora borealis)

Part 2: Search for a Business Address

1. Navigate to the Superpages home page (superpages.com).

2. Use WordPad to create a list of business names, addresses, and telephone numbers for each of the following businesses: Progress Energy (Raleigh, North Carolina), Microsoft Corporation (Redmond, Washington), Calypso Bay Waterpark (Palm Beach, Florida), and Recreational Equipment, Inc. (Sumner, Washington).

Part 3: Search for a Map

1. Navigate to the Google Maps home page (maps.google.com).

2. Find and print a map for each of the following places or landmarks: Eiffel Tower (France), Gateway Arch (Missouri), and White House (District of Columbia).

3. Circle the place or landmark on the map and write your name on each map.

Part 4: Search for a Photo

1. Navigate to the Corbis home page (corbis.com) (Figure 2–99).

Figure 2–99

2. Find and print an image of the Brooklyn Bridge.

3. Find and print an image of the Sears Tower.

4. Find and print an image of the Statue of Liberty.

5. Submit all the printed Web pages and the WordPad document to your instructor.

In the Lab

Lab 6: Searching for Information Using Accelerators

Instructions: You currently are shopping for a new laptop, and would like to find the location of a store near your house that sells laptops, as well as perform additional research about the laptops you are considering purchasing.

Perform the following tasks:

Part 1: Locate the Web address for Best Buy

1. Navigate to a search engine of your choice.

2. Perform a search for Best Buy, navigate to the Best Buy home page, and then print the Web page.

Continued >

In the Lab *continued*

Part 2: Locate the Store Closest to You
1. Locate and navigate to the Web page that allows you to search for a store's location.
2. Search for the Best Buy located closest to your address.
3. Select the address and use the Map with Bing Accelerator to open a Web page displaying the location of the store and print the Web page.

Part 3: Research Laptops
1. Navigate to the page on the Best Buy Web site that displays HP laptops.
2. Locate a term in the laptop descriptions with which you are unfamiliar. Select the term and use an Accelerator to locate the definition and print the Web page.

Part 4: Search for the Dell Web Site Using Accelerators
1. Locate and select the word, Dell, on the Best Buy Web page.
2. Use the Search with Bing Accelerator to search for the Dell Web site and print the Web page containing the search results.
3. Submit all the printed Web pages to your instructor.

Cases and Places

Apply your creative thinking and problem-solving skills to design and implement a solution.

1: Designing Your Ideal Search Engine

Academic

Web search engines use different techniques for searching Web resources. If you were designing a search engine, what would you have the engine look for when determining whether a Web page successfully matches the keywords? Visit the Help page of a few search engines to get an idea of what criteria they use, and then write a list containing the criteria you would have your search engine use to determine whether a Web page is a successful match for keywords. Include an explanation for each item, such as the relative importance assigned, and then submit the list and explanations.

2: Searching the Web for Concert Tour Locations and Dates

Personal

Many musicians and musical groups have their own home pages on the Web. Using the search engine of your choice, find out when and where Carrie Underwood will be performing next. Find and print her home page. Next, find out when and where your favorite performer, band, or musical group will be playing next. Find and print their home page. Do these pages qualify as informational Web pages? Write your answer and the reasons supporting your position and submit the report to your instructor.

3: Locating and Comparing Search Engines

Professional

Identify at least five search engines, and prepare a report that compares and contrasts these search engines. Your report should discuss the different types of searches that each search engine is capable of performing. For example, the Google search engine can search for Web sites, images, news articles, maps, and more. You also should discuss how each search engine might be used in a professional environment, as well as the relevance of the search results returned by each search engine.

3 | Internet Communication

Objectives

You will have mastered the material in this project when you can:

- Open, read, print, reply to, and delete e-mail messages
- Open a file attachment
- Compose and format an e-mail message
- Attach a file to an e-mail message
- Send an e-mail message
- Add and delete a contact
- Locate and subscribe to an RSS feed
- Add a Web Slice to the Favorites bar

- View the contents of a Web Slice
- Sign up for an online social network and connect with others
- Identify other communication methods available on the Internet
- Start and sign in to Windows Live Messenger
- Add and remove a Windows Live Messenger contact
- Send an instant message

3 | Internet Communication

Introduction

In Chapters 1 and 2, you used Internet Explorer to navigate and search for information on the World Wide Web. In addition to searching for information, you also can use the Internet to communicate with others. Web services available from Microsoft that are designed for Internet communication include Windows Live Mail, which allows you to send and receive electronic mail and to read and post messages to a newsgroup; Windows Live Messenger, which allows you to communicate with other Windows Live Messenger members by sending and receiving instant messages; and Internet Explorer, which allows you to subscribe to RSS feeds and Web Slices, as well as to visit various Web sites to participate in other methods of communication, such as blogs, chat rooms, bulletin boards and forums, groups, and online social networks. In this chapter, you will use Windows Live Mail, Internet Explorer, and Windows Live Messenger to explore methods of Internet communication (Figure 3–1).

Overview

As you read this chapter, you will learn how to communicate over the Internet and use Windows Live Mail, Internet Explorer, and Windows Live Messenger by performing these general tasks:

- Send and receive e-mail messages
- Locate and view RSS feeds and Web Slices
- Learn about online social networks
- Send and receive instant messages

Plan Ahead

Internet Communication Guidelines

To communicate effectively, observe the following guidelines when communicating via the Internet, whether using e-mail, instant messaging, social networking Web sites, or other methods:

1. **Determine the information you need.** The Internet provides access to a wealth of information, whether it is current news, a note from a friend stating whether she can join you for dinner Friday, or an instant message from a colleague who is asking a question for a customer at his desk. The type of information and the speed at which you need it will help you choose the most effective method of communication.

2. **Consider who is most likely to have the information you need.** Some applications, such as e-mail or instant messaging, allow you to communicate easily with friends and family, while others, such as groups, provide you with access to people you might not know. If the information you are seeking is not available from those who are close to you, you will need to use a communication method that enables you to reach a broader audience.

(continued)

(a) **E-mail**

(b) **Contacts**

(c) **RSS**

(d) **Online Social Network**

(e) **Instant Messaging**

Figure 3–1

Plan Ahead

(continued)

3. **Communicate with people you trust.** The Internet enables anyone to communicate with you. In fact, it is possible to receive a large amount of unsolicited communication as well as harmful e-mail attachments. Communicate with people you trust or through exchanges that you initiate, and be cautious when communicating with strangers.

4. **Do not open unsolicited file attachments.** If you receive a file via an e-mail message or an instant message, do not open it unless you are expecting it from someone you know and trust. Some viruses that travel via file attachments are able to appear as if they originated from someone you know and trust, so it is especially important for you to be careful. If you receive a file that you suspect to be infected with a virus, contact the sender of the file immediately.

5. **Determine whether your communication should be formal or informal.** If you are communicating with a potential employer or a colleague at work, you should use proper spelling, grammar, and etiquette. If you are communicating with friends and family, you can be less formal, and you might not bother checking for spelling and grammatical errors.

6. **Gather e-mail and instant messaging addresses.** Before you can send e-mail or instant messages to your friends, family, and colleagues, you will need to obtain their e-mail addresses or instant messaging user names. Without this information, you will be unable to communicate with them.

Electronic Mail (E-mail)

Electronic mail (**e-mail**) has become an important means of exchanging messages and files between business associates and friends. Businesspeople find that using e-mail messages to send files electronically saves both time and money. Parents with students away at college or people with relatives who are scattered across the country find that exchanging e-mail messages is an inexpensive and easy way to stay in touch with family members. In fact, exchanging e-mail messages is one of the more widely used features of the Internet.

E-mail is so popular nowadays that many people have multiple e-mail accounts. For instance, you might have an e-mail account for your job and an e-mail account for personal use. It is important to recognize that if your employer supplies you with an e-mail account, all messages sent to and from that account are the property of, and accessible by, your employer. If you plan to send personal e-mail messages, it is recommended that you do not use the e-mail account provided by your employer. Some people also find it useful to have multiple personal e-mail accounts. They might give one e-mail address to their friends and family, and use another e-mail address when signing up for mailing lists, filling out registration forms, or entering a sweepstakes. This way, personal e-mail messages can be kept separate from bulk or junk e-mail messages.

E-mail messages can be accessed by using an e-mail program that is installed on your computer, such as Microsoft Outlook, Windows Live Mail, or Mozilla Thunderbird, or by using a Web-based e-mail service. A **Web-based e-mail service** allows you to send and receive e-mail messages by logging in to a Web site, instead of installing an e-mail program on your computer. By using a Web-based e-mail service, you are able to check your e-mail messages on any computer that has an Internet connection and a Web browser. Free Web-based e-mail services include Windows Live Hotmail (mail.live.com), Gmail (www.gmail.com), Yahoo! Mail (www.yahoo.com), and AOL Mail (mail.aol.com). These companies are able to provide free Web-based e-mail services by placing advertisements on their Web sites or directly in the e-mail messages sent through their service. Although all e-mail services offer the same basic functionality, such as sending and receiving e-mail messages and storing contact information, some features, such as the amount of storage space each service offers, might differ. Before choosing a Web-based e-mail service, compare the different options to determine which one might work best for you. Appendix B discusses how to sign up for a Windows Live Hotmail account.

If you work for an employer who provides you with an e-mail account, you most likely access your e-mail account by using an e-mail program installed on your computer. Some companies also provide Web-based access to their e-mail systems, enabling employees to send and receive e-mail messages from a location other than the office. It is common for the Web-based interface to resemble the interface of the e-mail program you use in the office to access your e-mail account. Although the interfaces and functionality might be similar between Web-based e-mail services and e-mail programs installed on your computer, some differences do exist. For example, if you are accessing your e-mail account by using an e-mail program installed on your computer, the e-mail messages will be transferred to and stored on your computer before you can read them. If you are accessing your e-mail account using a Web-based e-mail service, the e-mail messages are stored remotely on the e-mail server.

Part of Windows Live Essentials, a free downloadable collection of programs available from Microsoft, **Windows Live Mail** is an e-mail program that allows you to receive and store incoming e-mail messages, compose and send e-mail messages, store and retrieve contacts, manage your calendar, and read and post messages to Internet newsgroups. Although the steps in this chapter are for Windows Live Mail, other e-mail programs, whether they are installed on your computer or are Web-based, offer very similar functionality.

To Start Windows Live Mail

The following steps, which illustrate how to start Windows Live Mail, assume that you have Windows Live Mail installed on your computer and an e-mail account configured. For more information about installing Windows Live Mail or configuring an e-mail account, contact your instructor.

1

- Display the Start menu.

- Click All Programs on the Start menu to display the All Programs list.

- If necessary, scroll to display the Windows Live Mail command (Figure 3–2).

Figure 3–2

2

- Click Windows Live Mail to start Windows Live Mail 2011.

- If necessary, maximize the Inbox – Windows Live Mail window (Figure 3–3).

Q&A Why did Windows Live Mail ask me to configure an e-mail account?

If Windows Live Mail has not been configured to interact with an e-mail account, it will prompt you to set up an e-mail account the first time you start the program. Contact your instructor or Internet access provider for specific instructions regarding setting up your e-mail account.

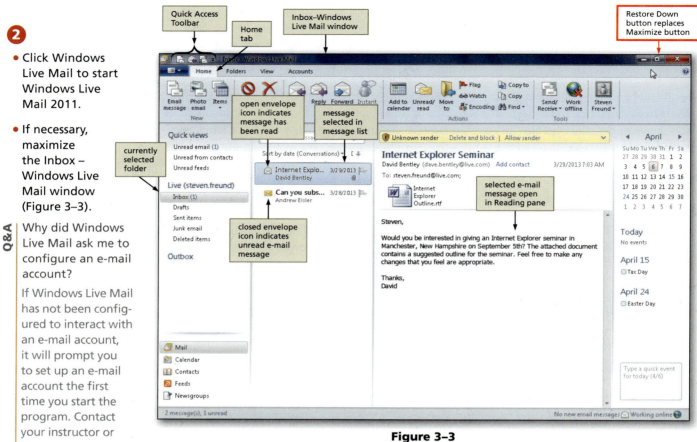

Figure 3–3

Q&A Why did Windows Live Mail ask me to log in?

Depending upon your computer's configuration, your login information (e-mail address and password) might not be saved. If these are not saved, you will be prompted to supply the information. Once you enter your e-mail address and password, click the Sign in button to continue.

Q&A Why does my screen look different from Figure 3–3?

Because you are accessing your own e-mail account, Windows Live Mail will display different e-mail messages in the message list and possibly a different folder structure. However, you still can follow the steps presented in this chapter by using the e-mail messages displayed in your message list.

Other Ways

1. Press CTRL+ESC, type **Mail**, click Windows Live Mail

BTW
Quick Access Toolbar
You can customize the buttons that appear on the Quick Access Toolbar. To add or remove buttons from the Quick Access Toolbar, click the Customize Quick Access Toolbar button, and then click the name of the button to add or remove.

The Windows Live Mail Window

The Inbox - Windows Live Mail window shown in Figure 3–3 contains a number of elements. The title bar contains the folder name (Inbox) and the application name (Windows Live Mail). The title bar also displays the Quick Access Toolbar, which contains frequently used commands. By default, three buttons appear on the Quick Access Toolbar (New, Reply, and Update all). The Ribbon displays below the title bar, and contains access to most of the features you will use while working with Windows Live Mail. The Ribbon contains five tabs (Windows Live Mail, Home, Folders, View, and Accounts). By default, the Home tab is displayed. The commands in the Home, Folders, View, and Accounts tabs are organized into groups. For instance, the Home tab contains five groups (New, Delete,

Respond, Actions, and Tools). Clicking the Windows Live Mail tab displays the Windows Live Mail menu, which contains commands for creating new items, saving items, printing items, importing and exporting e-mail messages, accessing Windows Live Mail options, displaying information about Windows Live Mail, and quitting Windows Live Mail.

The Inbox - Windows Live Mail window is divided into four sections. A listing of all accounts and folders appears along the left column of the Windows Live Mail window. The message list contains a listing of all e-mail messages in the selected folder. The Reading pane displays the contents of the e-mail message currently selected in the message list, and the Calendar pane displays a calendar for the current month as well as a list of upcoming events.

By default, a Windows Live Mail e-mail account contains five folders (Inbox, Drafts, Sent items, Junk email, and Deleted items). If you are using Windows Live Mail with an e-mail account from a different Web-based e-mail service provider, those folders might differ. The Inbox folder, shown in Figure 3–4 on the next page, is the destination for incoming messages. The Drafts folder retains copies of messages that you are not yet ready to send. The Sent items folder retains copies of messages that you have sent. The Junk email folder contains e-mail messages that have been flagged as junk. Windows Live Mail contains a feature that can automatically detect junk e-mail messages, otherwise known as unsolicited commercial e-mail messages, or **spam**. Although Windows Live Mail can identify most junk e-mail messages, it cannot detect them all. Similarly, Windows Live Mail might incorrectly flag an incoming message as a junk e-mail message. For this reason, it is important that you check your Junk email folder regularly to ensure that no legitimate messages have been filed there. The Deleted items folder contains messages that you have deleted. As a safety precaution, you can retrieve deleted messages from the Deleted items folder if you later decide you want to keep them. Deleting messages from the Deleted items folder removes the messages permanently. In addition to the five folders that display by default for your e-mail account, Windows Live Mail also contains an Outbox folder. The Outbox folder temporarily holds messages you send until Windows Live Mail is able to connect to the mail server and process the messages.

In addition to containing e-mail messages, the folders in Windows Live Mail can also contain faxes and files created in other Windows applications. A blue number in parentheses following a folder name indicates the number of messages in the folder that are unopened. Other folders might appear on your computer in addition to the folders shown in Figure 3–4.

The contents of the Inbox folder automatically appear in the message list when you start Windows Live Mail. The message list contains icons that provide information about the e-mail message, the subject and sender of the e-mail message, the date and/or time the e-mail message was received, and whether the e-mail message contains an attachment. Collectively, this information is referred to as the **message heading**.

Icons used in the message list include open and closed envelope icons, which indicate whether an e-mail has been opened or not; an exclamation point icon, which indicates that the e-mail message has been marked high priority by the sender, suggesting that it should be read immediately; and a paper clip icon, which indicates that the e-mail message contains an attachment. Other icons indicate whether the recipient performed an action, such as replying to or forwarding the message or that the sender digitally signed or encrypted the message. A red flag icon in the message list indicates that you have chosen to mark the e-mail message with a flag to highlight an important message that you want to revisit at a later time.

In Figure 3–4, the first e-mail message in the message list, from David Bentley, contains a paper clip icon, an open envelope icon, and a message heading that appears in normal type. The open envelope icon and normal message heading indicate that the e-mail message has been read (opened) and the paper clip indicates that the message has an attachment.

BTW

Mail Folders
You can create additional folders in your e-mail account. To do so, right-click the name of your e-mail account (Live, in this case), click New folder, type the folder name in the Create Folder dialog box, and then click the OK button. Similarly, you can delete a folder by right-clicking the folder name, clicking Delete, and then clicking the Yes button to confirm the deletion.

BTW

Message List
The message list displays e-mail messages in reverse chronological order. E-mail messages you received most recently will appear at the top of the message list, while older e-mail messages will appear at the bottom of the message list.

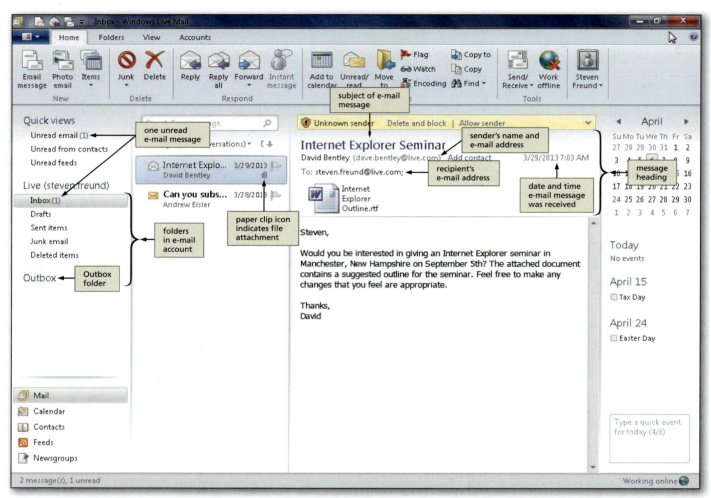

Figure 3–4

BTW

Digital Signatures
A digital signature, also referred to as an electronic signature, provides a way for the sender of the e-mail message to verify his or her identity.

BTW

Reading E-mail Messages
Many people minimize the Inbox - Windows Live Mail window when working in other applications. When they receive a new e-mail message, an envelope icon is displayed on the Windows Live Mail button on the Windows taskbar and a notification sound is played.

The Reading pane displays the e-mail message from David Bentley. The message heading is displayed at the top of the Reading pane and contains the subject of the e-mail message, the sender's name and e-mail address, and the recipient's e-mail address. The text of the e-mail message appears below the message heading. Double-clicking the message heading in the message list opens the e-mail message in a separate window.

The second e-mail message, from Andrew Eisler, contains a closed envelope icon and a message heading that appears in bold type. The icon and message heading indicate that the e-mail message has not been read. Because you will be accessing Windows Live Mail with a different e-mail account, other e-mail messages will display on your computer in place of these messages.

To Open (Read) an E-mail Message

The following steps display an e-mail message in the Reading pane and then open the message in a new window. Displaying or opening an unread e-mail message decreases by one the number that appears next to the Inbox folder.

1

- Click the message heading of the message from Andrew Eisler to display the message in the Reading pane (Figure 3–5).

Q&A

What should I do if I do not see the message from Andrew Eisler in the message list?

If you do not see the message from Andrew Eisler, click any message in your message list.

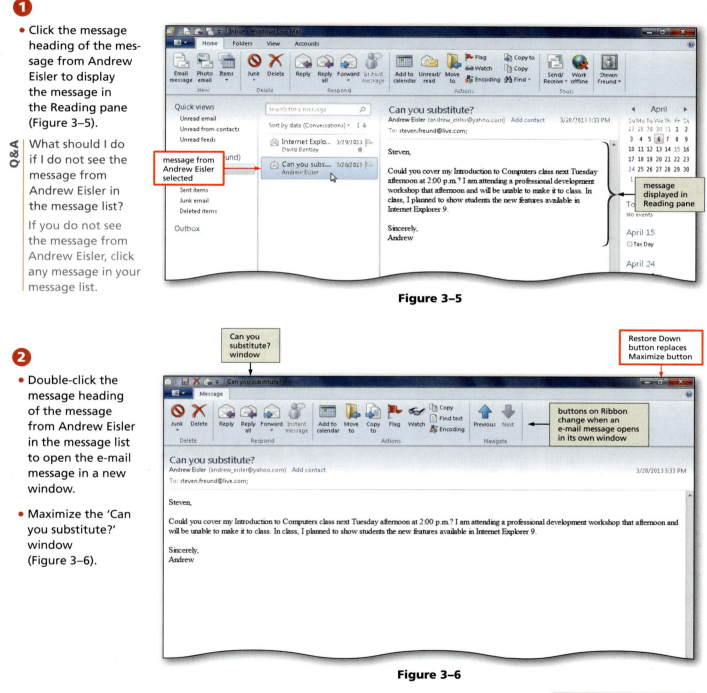

Figure 3–5

2

- Double-click the message heading of the message from Andrew Eisler in the message list to open the e-mail message in a new window.

- Maximize the 'Can you substitute?' window (Figure 3–6).

Figure 3–6

Other Ways

1. Right-click message heading with closed envelope icon, click Open on shortcut menu

2. Select message heading, press CTRL+O

To Print an Open E-mail Message

You can print the contents of an e-mail message before or after opening the message. The following steps print an opened e-mail message.

1

• Click the Windows Live Mail tab on the Ribbon to display the Windows Live Mail menu (Figure 3–7).

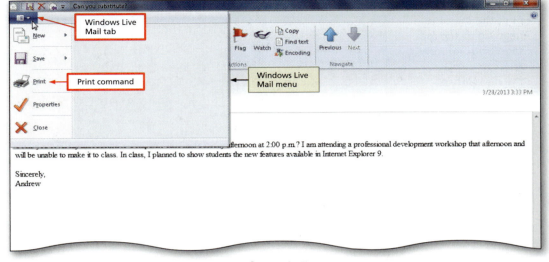

Figure 3–7

2

• Click the Print command on the Windows Live Mail menu to display the Print dialog box (Figure 3–8).

3

• Click the Print button in the Print dialog box.

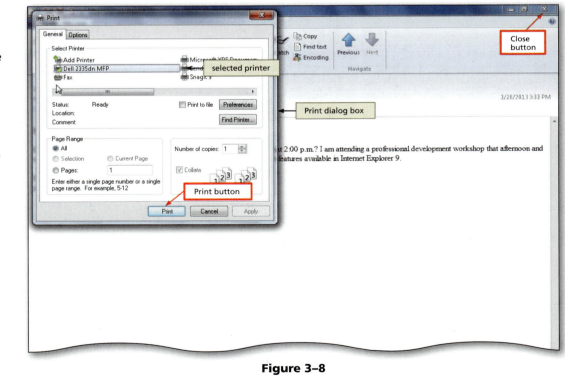

Figure 3–8

Other Ways

1. Press ALT+F, press P, press ENTER
2. Press CTRL+P, press ENTER

To Close an E-mail Message

When you have finished reading an e-mail message, you can close the window containing the message.

1

- Click the Close button on the title bar to close the window containing the e-mail message (Figure 3–9).

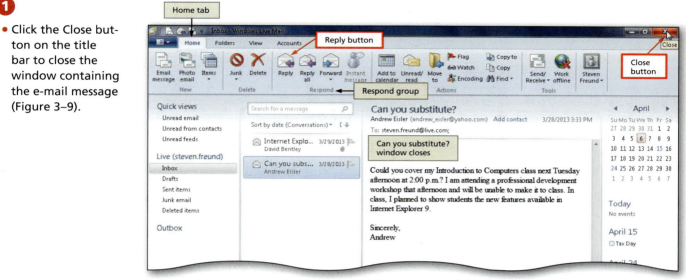

Figure 3–9

Other Ways

1. On Windows Live Mail menu, click Close
2. Press ALT+F4

Replying to an E-mail Message

Using the Reply button, located on the Quick Access Toolbar and the Ribbon (Home tab | Respond group), is an easy way to compose and send a reply to an e-mail message. The Reply button opens a new message and prefills the To text box with the e-mail address of the sender and the Subject text box with the subject line of the original message preceded by Re: (regarding). The tabs and buttons on the Ribbon change when you are composing an e-mail message instead of reading an e-mail message. Figure 3–10 shows the commands available on the Ribbon when you are replying to or composing an e-mail message.

BTW

Replying to an E-mail Message
Sometimes e-mail message replies are complicated to read or hard to understand when the original e-mail message appears following the reply message. To remove the original message from all e-mail replies, click the Windows Live Mail tab, point to Options, click Mail, click the Send tab, click to deselect the 'Include message in reply' check box, and then click the OK button.

Figure 3–10

To Reply to an E-mail Message

The following steps compose and send an e-mail reply to a sender, in this case, Andrew Eisler, using the Reply button.

1

- Click the Reply button on the Ribbon (Home tab | Respond group) to display the Re: Can you substitute? window.

- If necessary, maximize the Re: Can you substi- tute? window (Figure 3–11).

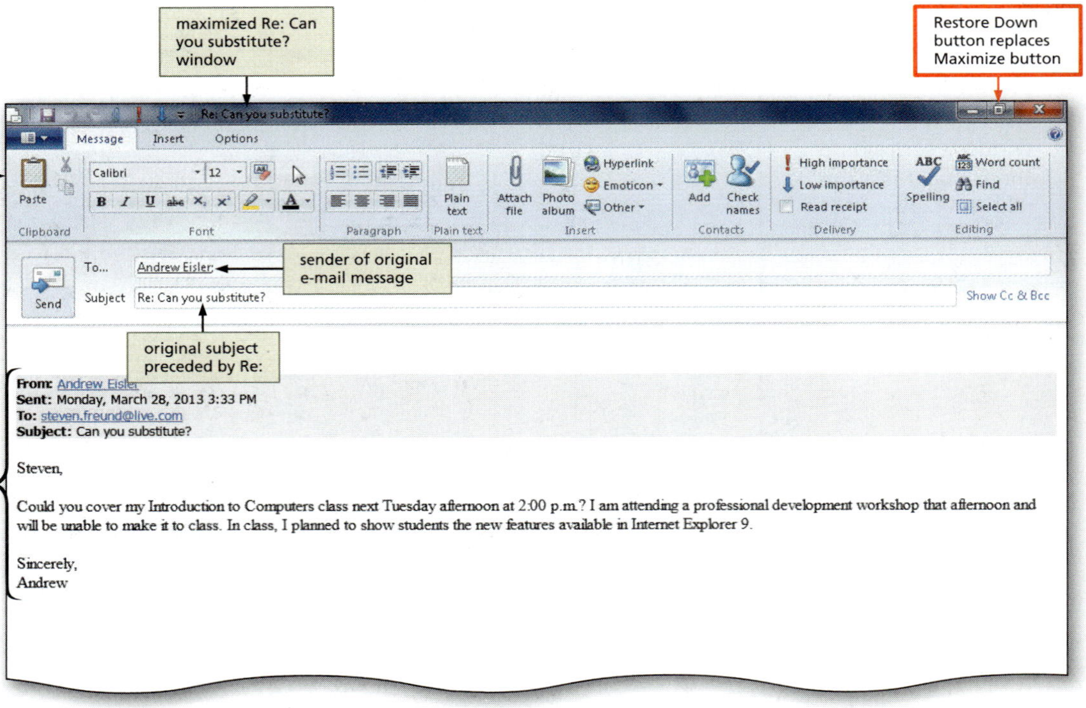

Q&A

If I am replying to a message that was sent to multiple recipients, will each recipient see my reply?

No. Your reply will be sent only to the sender of the original message. If you want all recipi- ents to see your reply, you should click the Reply all button (Home tab | Respond group) instead of the Reply button.

Figure 3–11

2

- Type I will be happy to teach your class. Please let me know what I will have to cover. (Figure 3–12).

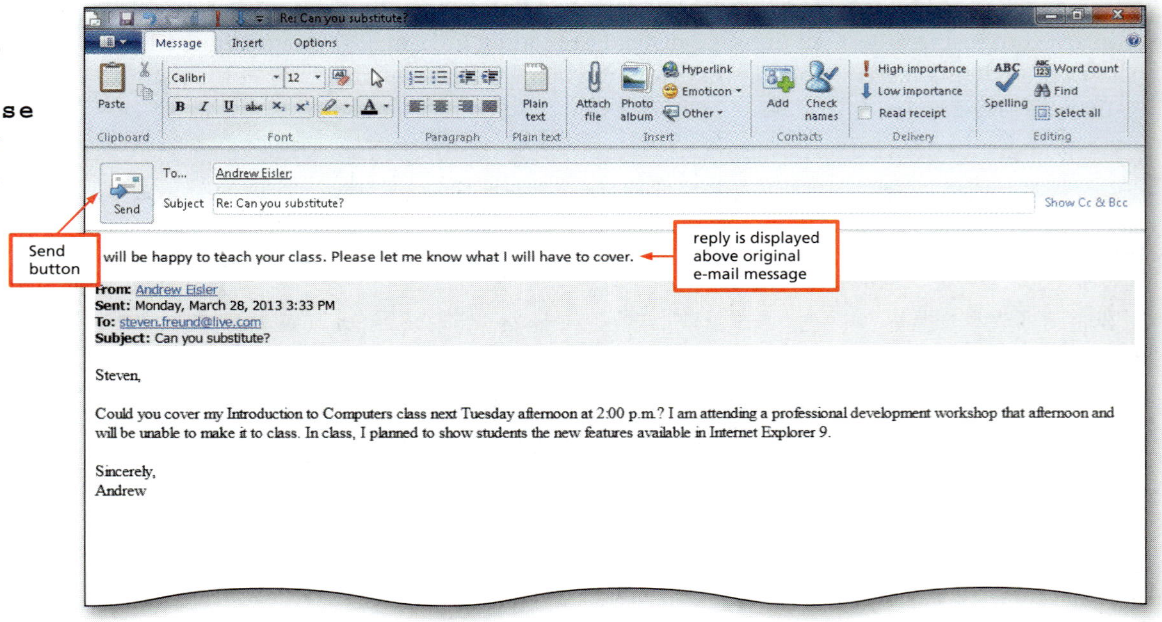

Figure 3–12

3

- Click the Send button to send the message (Figure 3–13).

Q&A

How can I be sure that the intended recipient will receive my e-mail message?

The best way to verify that the recipient has received your e-mail message is to ask him or her for a response. If an e-mail address is incorrect, you will receive an automated e-mail message stating that your message was unable to be delivered. If this happens, confirm the e-mail address of your recipient and try to send the e-mail message again.

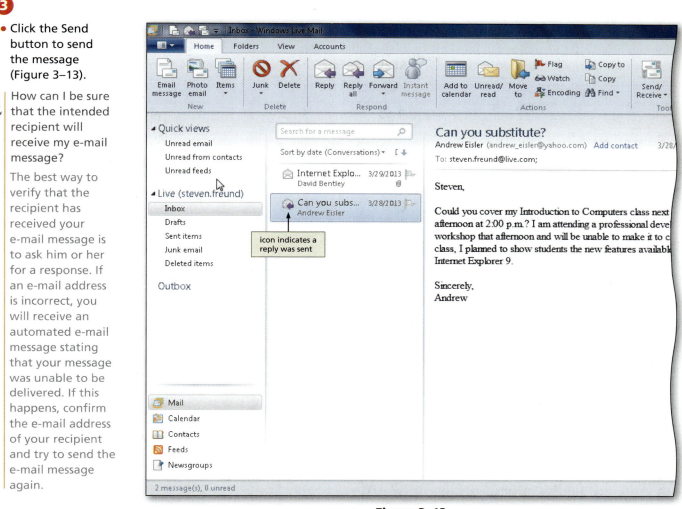

Figure 3–13

Other Ways

1. On Quick Access Toolbar, click Reply
2. Press ALT+H, Press R, Press R
3. Press CTRL+R

To Delete an E-mail Message

After reading and replying to an e-mail message, you want to delete the original e-mail message from the message list. Deleting a message moves it from the Inbox folder to the Deleted items folder. As you delete messages from the Inbox, the number of messages in the Deleted items folder increases. If you do not delete unwanted messages or move them from the Inbox to folders, as the number of messages in the Inbox folder increases, it will become more difficult to locate and read new and unread messages; this also wastes disk space. The following step deletes the e-mail message from Andrew Eisler.

1

- If necessary, click the message from Andrew Eisler in the message list to select it.

- Click the Delete button on the Ribbon (Home tab | Delete group) to delete the e-mail message from Andrew Eisler (Figure 3–14).

Q&A

What should I do if I accidentally delete an e-mail message?

Deleted messages remain on your computer until you delete them from the Deleted items folder. If you accidentally delete an e-mail message, click the Deleted items folder and then drag the message to the Inbox folder. To delete an e-mail message permanently, click the Deleted items folder and then delete the message from that folder.

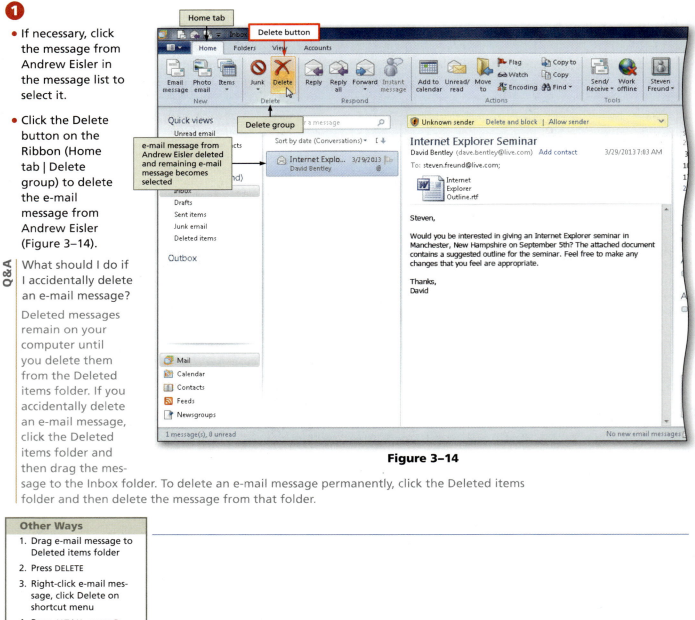

Figure 3–14

Other Ways

1. Drag e-mail message to Deleted items folder
2. Press DELETE
3. Right-click e-mail message, click Delete on shortcut menu
4. Press ALT+H, press D
5. Press CTRL+D

To Open a File Attachment

The remaining message in the message list, from David Bentley, contains a file attachment, as indicated by the paper clip icon displayed in the message heading. The following steps open the file attachment.

1

- Double-click the message from David Bentley in the message list.

- If necessary, maximize the Internet Explorer Seminar window (Figure 3–15).

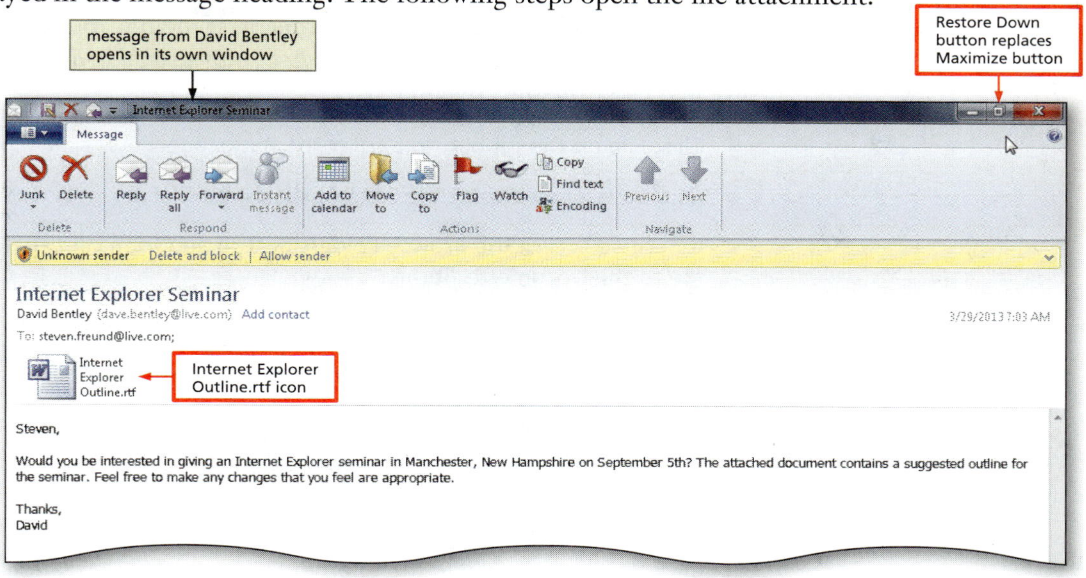

Q&A Is it okay to open a file attachment if I do not know who has sent it to me?

You should never open a file attachment sent from an unknown source. It usually is best to only open file attachments when you are expecting them from a trusted source.

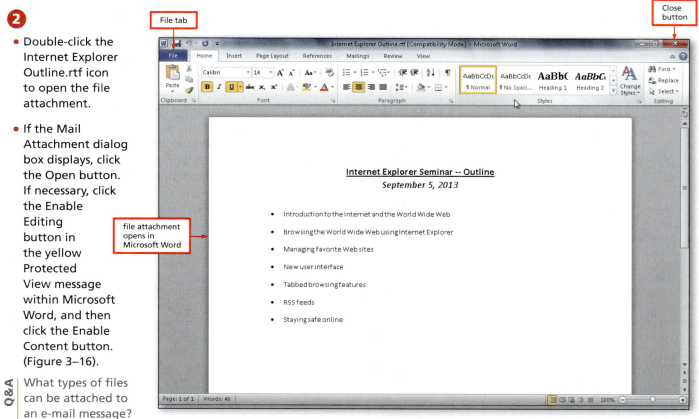

message from David Bentley opens in its own window

Restore Down button replaces Maximize button

Internet Explorer Outline.rtf icon

Figure 3–15

2

- Double-click the Internet Explorer Outline.rtf icon to open the file attachment.

- If the Mail Attachment dialog box displays, click the Open button. If necessary, click the Enable Editing button in the yellow Protected View message within Microsoft Word, and then click the Enable Content button. (Figure 3–16).

Q&A What types of files can be attached to an e-mail message?

File attachments can include documents, spreadsheets, presentations, and pictures.

File tab

Close button

file attachment opens in Microsoft Word

Figure 3–16

To Save and Close a File Attachment

After viewing the attachment, you decide to save it to your computer to read at a later time. The following steps, which assume Microsoft Word 2010 is installed on your computer, save and close the file attachment. If the file attachment opens in a program other than Microsoft Word 2010, contact your instructor for instructions about how to save and close the file attachment.

1 Click File on the Ribbon to display the Backstage view.

2 Click Save As to display the Save As dialog box.

3 If necessary, click the Browse Folders button and then click the Documents link to save the file to the Documents library.

4 Click the Save button.

Q&A
If I make changes to a file attachment before saving it, will the file attached to the original e-mail message also change?

No. If you open the e-mail message containing the attachment again, you will not see any of your changes. However, if you open the file that was saved to your computer, your changes will appear.

5 Click the Close button in the Internet Explorer Outline.rtf – Microsoft Word window.

6 Click the Close button in the Internet Explorer Seminar window.

Composing a New E-mail Message

In addition to opening and reading, replying to, and deleting e-mail messages, you also need to compose and send new e-mail messages. When composing an e-mail message, you enter a brief one-line subject that identifies the purpose or contents of the message in the subject line, and then type your text in the message area. You must know the e-mail address of the recipient before you can send it.

You also can format e-mail messages to enhance their appearance. **Formatting** is the process of altering how a document looks by modifying the style, size, or color of its text or by changing its background. For example, if you want to add a heading to your e-mail message, you might choose to center the text, increase the font size, and change the color of the heading text. In addition, some users choose to format their name in the closing of the e-mail message using a font that resembles cursive handwriting. It is important to note that in a business environment, it is inappropriate to apply excessive formatting to e-mail messages. In most cases, work-related e-mail messages use the default background and text colors (black text on a white background). If you are sending a personal or informal e-mail message, formatting it with various fonts, font sizes, and colors might be more appropriate.

BTW

Formatting E-mail Messages
Windows Live Mail, like many other e-mail programs, allows you to change the appearance of e-mail messages by using different fonts and formatting, changing the background graphic, attaching files, and adding links to Web pages.

To Compose a New E-mail Message with Formatting

The following steps compose an e-mail message to one of the authors (Steven Freund) of this book.

1

- Click the Email message button on the Ribbon (Home tab | New group) to display the New Message window.

- If necessary, maximize the New Message window (Figure 3–17).

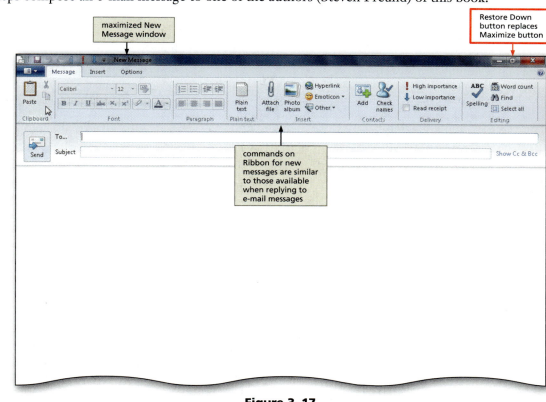

maximized New Message window

Restore Down button replaces Maximize button

commands on Ribbon for new messages are similar to those available when replying to e-mail messages

Figure 3–17

2

- Type **steven. freund@live. com** in the To text box.

- Click the Subject text box.

- Type **Internet Explorer Seminar** in the Subject text box (Figure 3–18).

 Q&A

How should I decide what to write as the subject of an e-mail message?

You should briefly describe the contents of the e-mail message in the subject line. It is not good practice to leave the subject line blank, as some spam filters might mark your e-mail message as spam and it will not reach the intended recipient.

e-mail address entered in To text box

subject entered in Subject text box

Figure 3–18

3

- Press the TAB key to move the insertion point into the message area of the Internet Explorer Seminar window.

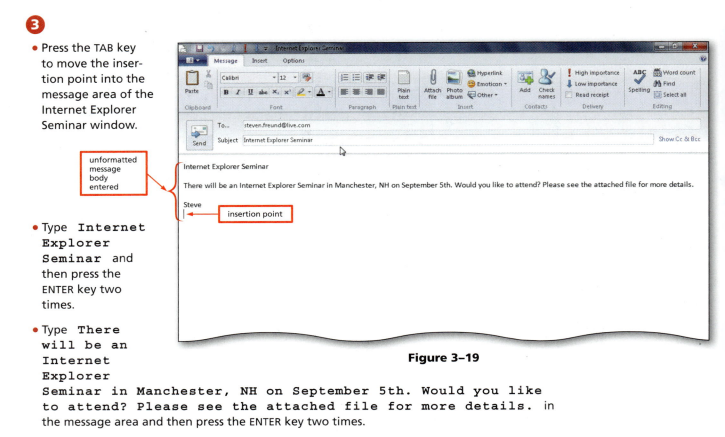

Figure 3–19

- Type **Internet Explorer Seminar** and then press the ENTER key two times.

- Type **There will be an Internet Explorer Seminar in Manchester, NH on September 5th. Would you like to attend? Please see the attached file for more details.** in the message area and then press the ENTER key two times.

- Type your name and then press the ENTER key (Figure 3–19).

Formatting an E-mail Message

The Font and Paragraph groups on the Message tab in the Internet Explorer Seminar window contain various options to format your e-mail message (Figure 3–20). For example, the buttons in the Font group allow you to change the font, font size, font style, highlight color, and font color. The buttons in the Paragraph group allow you to format items in your e-mail message as a list, change the alignment, and increase or decrease the indent.

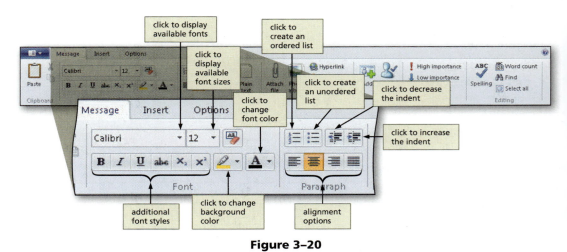

Figure 3–20

To Format an E-mail Message

The following steps center the text, Internet Explorer Seminar, and format it using the 36-point font size.

1

- Select the phrase, Internet Explorer Seminar, in the first line of the e-mail message by pointing to any word and then triple-clicking to select the entire phrase (Figure 3–21).

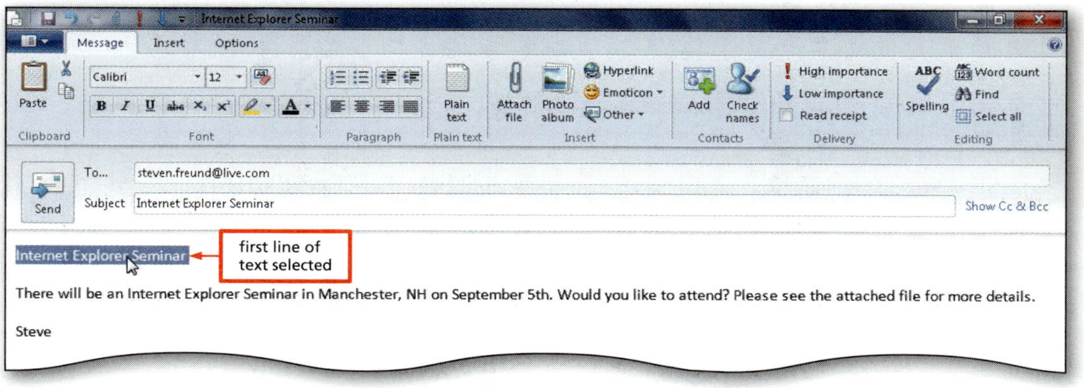

Q&A I have never heard of triple-clicking. What does it mean to triple-click?

Similar to how double-clicking refers to clicking the mouse twice in rapid succession, triple-clicking refers to clicking the mouse three times in rapid succession. Double-clicking a word will select it; triple-clicking a word will select the entire line.

Figure 3–21

2

- Click the Center text button on the Ribbon (Message tab | Paragraph group) to center the selected phrase, Internet Explorer Seminar, in the message (Figure 3–22).

Figure 3–22

3

- Click the Font size box arrow (Message tab | Font group) to display a list of available font sizes (Figure 3–23).

Q&A How is font size measured?

Font size is measured in **points**. One inch contains 72 points. Thus, a font size of 36 points is approximately one-half inch in height when printed.

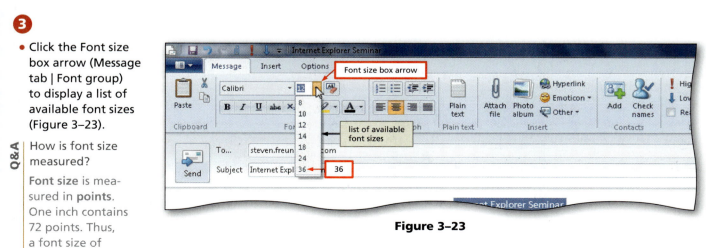

Figure 3–23

4

- Click 36 in the Font size list to change the font size of the phrase, Internet Explorer Seminar, to 36 points.

- Click the high-lighted text to deselect the text (Figure 3–24).

Q&A

Will the recipient of this e-mail message be able to view the formatting?

Many e-mail pro-grams are capable of displaying e-mail messages formatted with various fonts, styles, and backgrounds. If this e-mail message is read with an e-mail program that does not support this formatting, the text of the e-mail message will be formatted as plain text.

Figure 3–24

To Attach a File to an E-mail Message

It is sometimes necessary to supplement your e-mail message by attaching a file. People attach files to e-mail messages for different reasons: Friends and family share pictures, students submit assignments to their instructors, and professionals send documents to colleagues. The following steps attach a file to an e-mail message.

1

- Click the Attach file button (Message tab | Insert group) to display the Open dialog box (Figure 3–25).

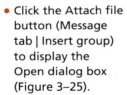

Figure 3–25

2

- Click the Internet Explorer Outline file in the Open dialog box to select it (Figure 3–26). If the Internet Explorer Outline file does not display, navigate to the folder containing the file.

Q&A What types of files can I attach to my e-mail messages?

You can attach just about any type of file to an e-mail message, but you should make sure that the files are not too large in size. Large files can take the recipient a long time to download or can cause the recipient's e-mail program to reject the message.

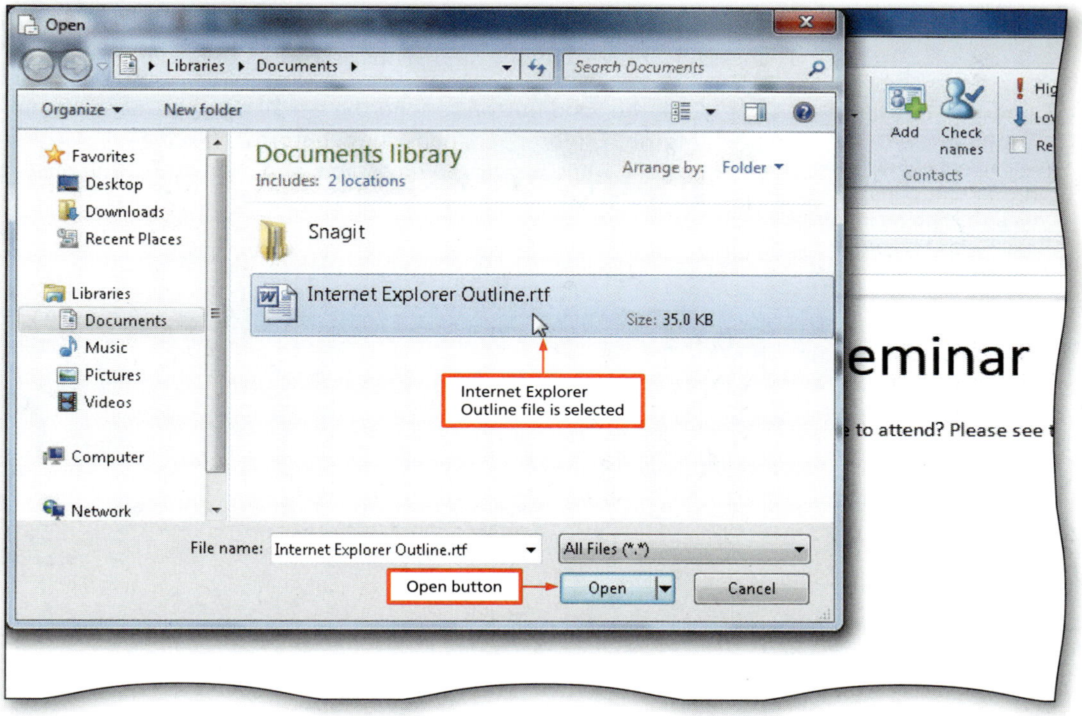

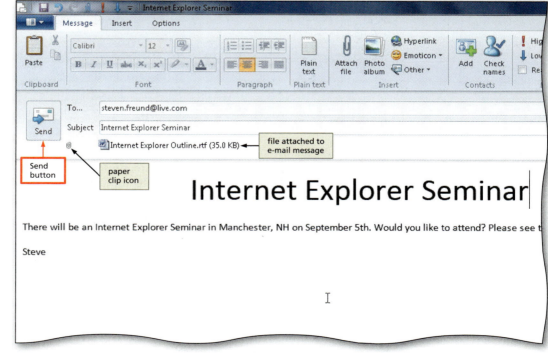

Figure 3–26

3

- Click the Open button to attach the Internet Explorer Outline file to the e-mail message (Figure 3–27).

Q&A How do I know that my file has been attached?

After you click the Open button, the name and size of the file, along with the file icon, should appear in the Internet Explorer Seminar window below the Subject text box. If the file does not appear, repeat the previous steps to try again.

Figure 3–27

To Send an E-mail Message

After composing and formatting an e-mail message, you are ready to send the message. The following step sends an e-mail message.

1 Click the Send button to send the e-mail message. Sending the e-mail message closes the Internet Explorer Seminar window, stores the e-mail message in the Outbox folder temporarily while it sends the message, and then moves the message to the Sent items folder (Figure 3–28).

BTW

Abbreviations in E-mail Messages
The use of abbreviations has become popular when composing informal e-mail messages. Examples include: ASAP for As Soon As Possible, CU for See You, HTH for Hope This Helps, NRN for No Reply Necessary, PLS for Please, and THX for Thanks.

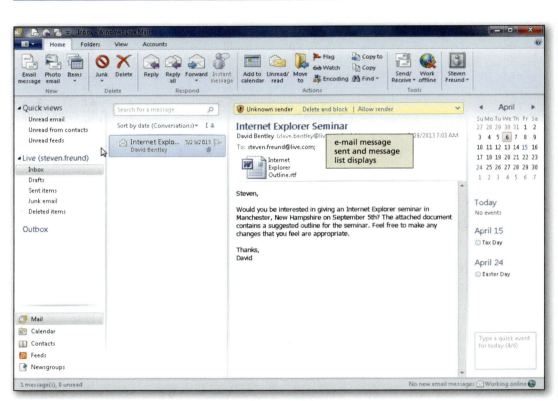

Figure 3–28

Contacts

The Contacts feature in Windows Live Mail allows you to store information about your family, friends, colleagues, and others. Contact information includes e-mail addresses; home and work addresses; telephone, mobile phone, and fax numbers; digital IDs; notes; Web addresses; and personal information such as birthdays or anniversaries. The information stored about each person is referred to as a **contact**.

When you add a contact in Windows Live Mail, the Add a Contact dialog box contains a series of categories. Each category allows you to store different types of information about the contact. If you are entering information for a business contact, you can enter business-related information using the Work category, such as the company's name and business address (street address, city, state/province, ZIP/postal code, and country/region), and business information such as the company name, job title, pager number, and work Web site. Using the Personal category, you can enter personal information about your contact, such as his or her significant other's name, their personal Web site address, and birthday and anniversary dates. The IM category stores instant messaging

BTW

Contacts
Switching to Windows Live Mail does not mean leaving your old contact information behind. You can import your personal address books from numerous popular e-mail programs, including Microsoft Outlook, Outlook Express, Eudora, Netscape Mail, Mozilla Thunderbird, and any other program that exports text files with comma-separated values (CSV).

addresses for popular instant messaging programs, including Windows Live Messenger, while the Notes category allows you to enter notes about the contact. The IDs category allows you to view the digital IDs for a selected e-mail address. Using a **digital ID** allows you to encrypt messages sent over the Internet and to prove your identity in an electronic transaction on the Internet in a manner similar to showing your driver's license when you cash a check.

Additionally, you can use the Contacts feature to create categories in which to organize groups of friends, relatives, or business associates, making it easy to send a single e-mail message to a group of contacts, without having to type each person's e-mail address individually.

To Add a Contact

Before you can use the Contacts feature in Windows Live Mail to send an e-mail message, you first need to add the recipient's contact information. The following steps add the contact information (first name, last name, e-mail address, home telephone, and business telephone) for Miriam Winick.

1

- Click the Contacts button in the Inbox - Windows Live Mail window to display your contacts (Figure 3–29).

Q&A

Why are there contacts in my list? I do not remember adding any.

As you send and receive e-mail messages, Windows Live Mail might add these people to your Contacts list.

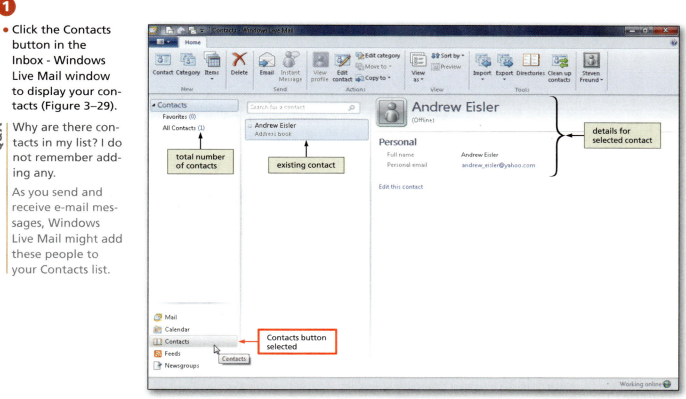

Figure 3–29

2

- Click the Contact button (Home tab | New group) to display the Add a Contact dialog box (Figure 3–30).

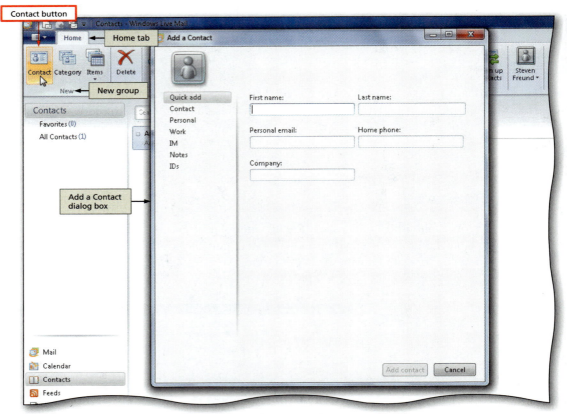

Figure 3–30

3

- Type **Miriam** in the First name text box.

- Click the Last name text box and then type **Winick** in the text box.

- Click the Personal email text box and then type **miriam_ winick@ hotmail.com** in the text box (Figure 3–31).

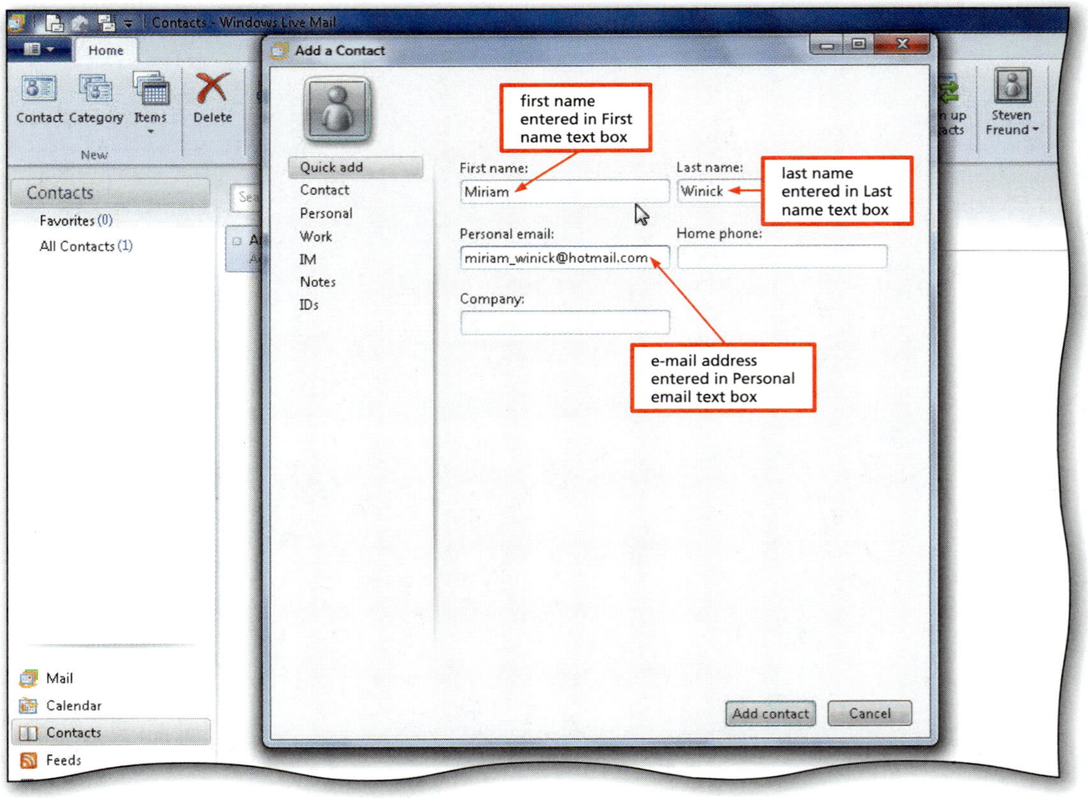

Figure 3–31

4

- Click the Personal button in the left pane of the Add a Contact dialog box.

- Type **17325 Winding Lane** in the Street address text box.

- Click the City text box and then type **Brea** as the name of the city.

- Click the State/province text box and then type **CA** as the name of the state.

- Click the ZIP/postal code text box and then type **92821** as the ZIP code.

- Click the Home phone text box and then type **(714) 555-3292** as the telephone number (Figure 3–32).

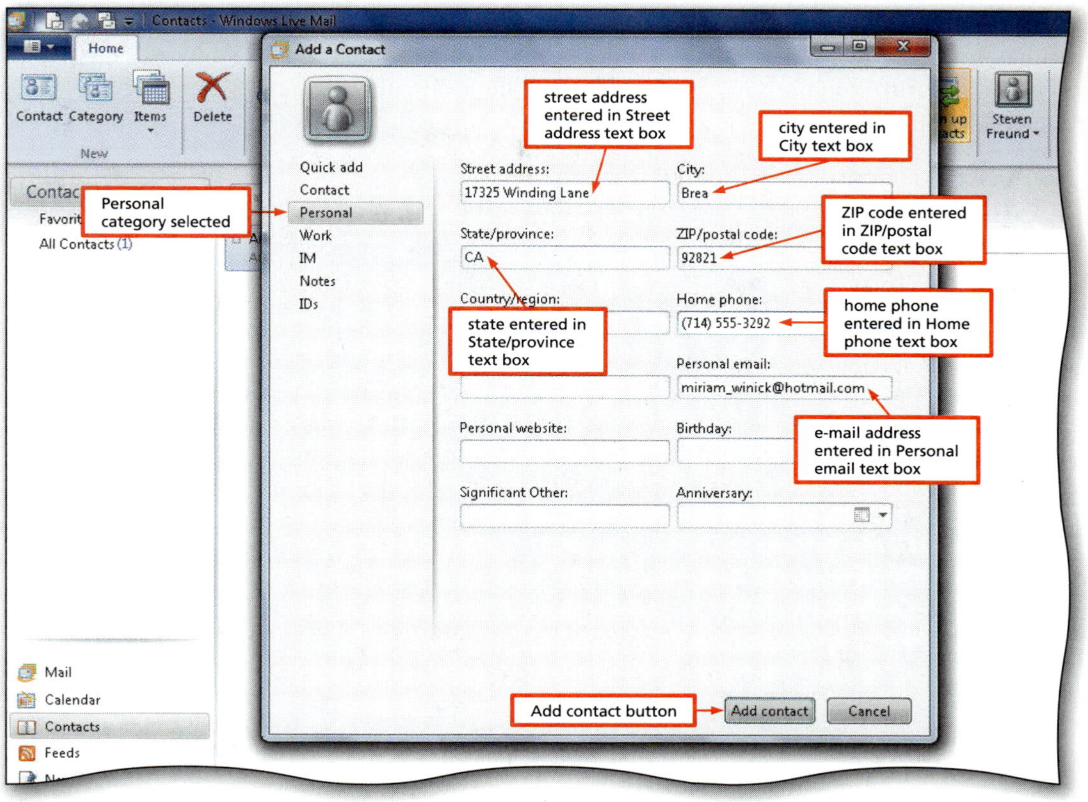

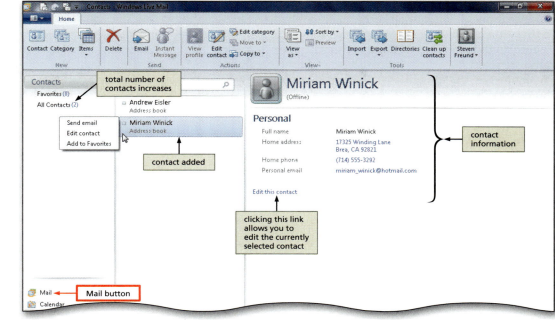

Figure 3–32

5

- Click the Add contact button in the Add a Contact dialog box to close the dialog box and add the contact.

- If necessary, click the Miriam Winick contact to view the contact information (Figure 3–33).

Figure 3–33

To Compose a New E-mail Message Using a Contact

To send an e-mail message, you must know the e-mail address of the recipient. Previously, you addressed an e-mail message by typing the e-mail address in the To text box in the New Message window. Now you can use the Contacts feature to enter an e-mail address. The following steps compose an e-mail message to Miriam Winick using the e-mail address in her contact information.

1

- Click the Mail button to display the message list.

- Click the Email message button (Home tab | New group) to display the New Message window.

- If necessary, maximize the New Message window (Figure 3–34).

maximized New Message window

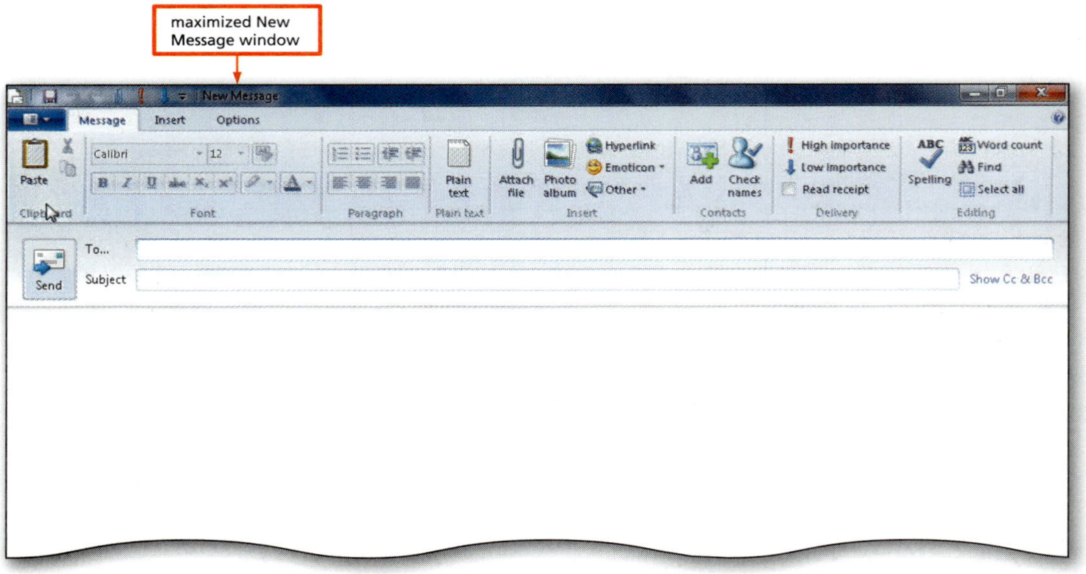

Figure 3–34

2

- Click the To button in the New Message window to display the Send an Email dialog box.

- If necessary, click the Miriam Winick entry in the list box to select it (Figure 3–35).

Q&A

What is the difference between the Cc and Bcc fields?

Recipients whose e-mail addresses are entered in the Cc or Bcc field will receive a copy of the e-mail message. The names and e-mail addresses of recipients listed in the Cc field will be visible to all recipients, whereas those listed in the Bcc field will be hidden from all recipients.

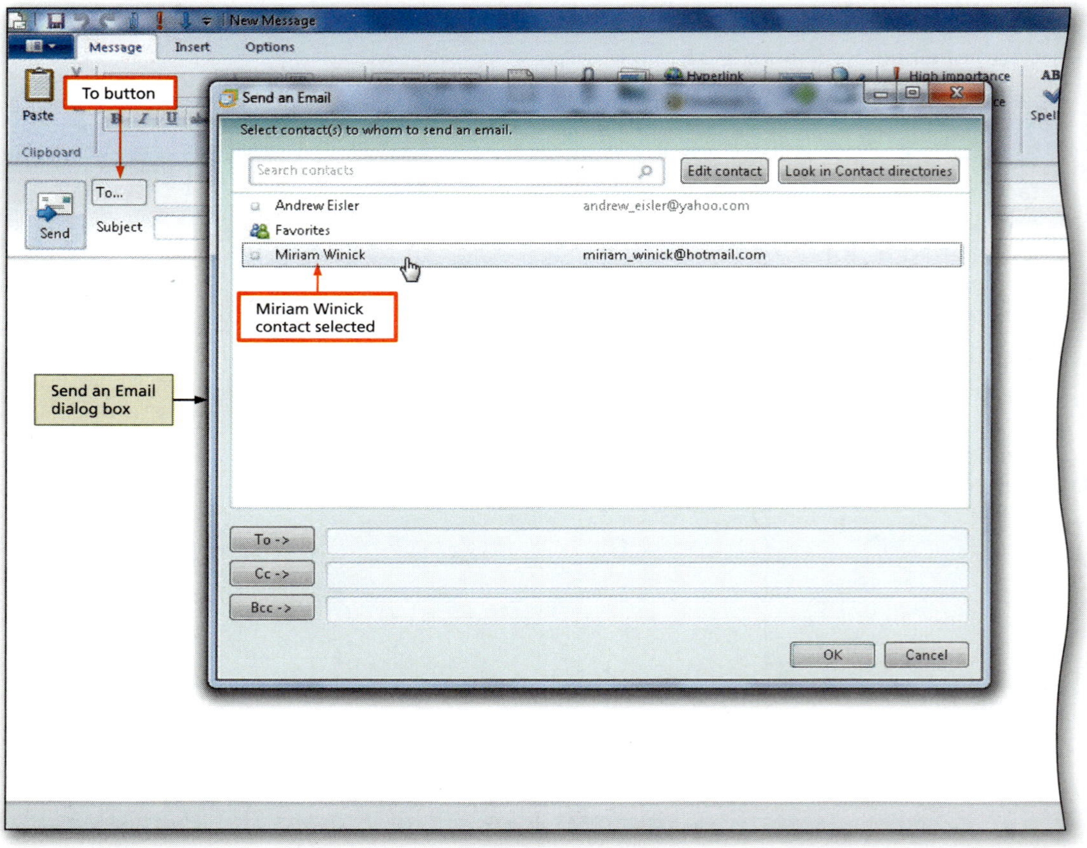

To button

Miriam Winick contact selected

Send an Email dialog box

Figure 3–35

3

- Click the To button in the Send an Email dialog box to add Miriam Winick as the recipient of the message (Figure 3–36).

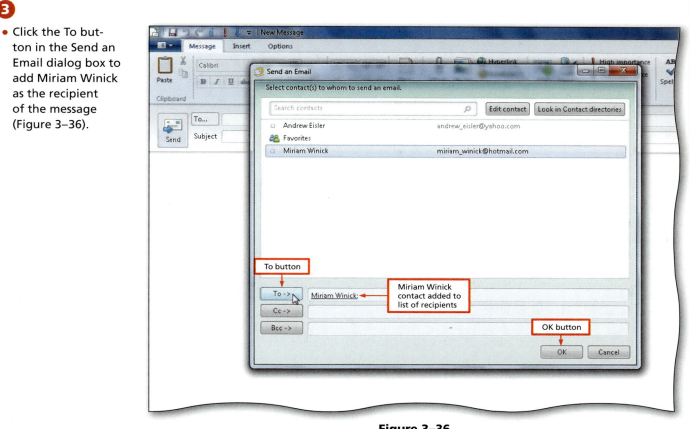

Figure 3–36

4

- Click the OK button to close the Send an Email dialog box and add Miriam Winick's name to the To text box in the New Message window.

- Click the Subject text box and then type **Contacts Folder** in the text box (Figure 3–37).

5

- Press the TAB key to move the insertion point to the message area.

- Type **Great News!** and then press the ENTER key two times.

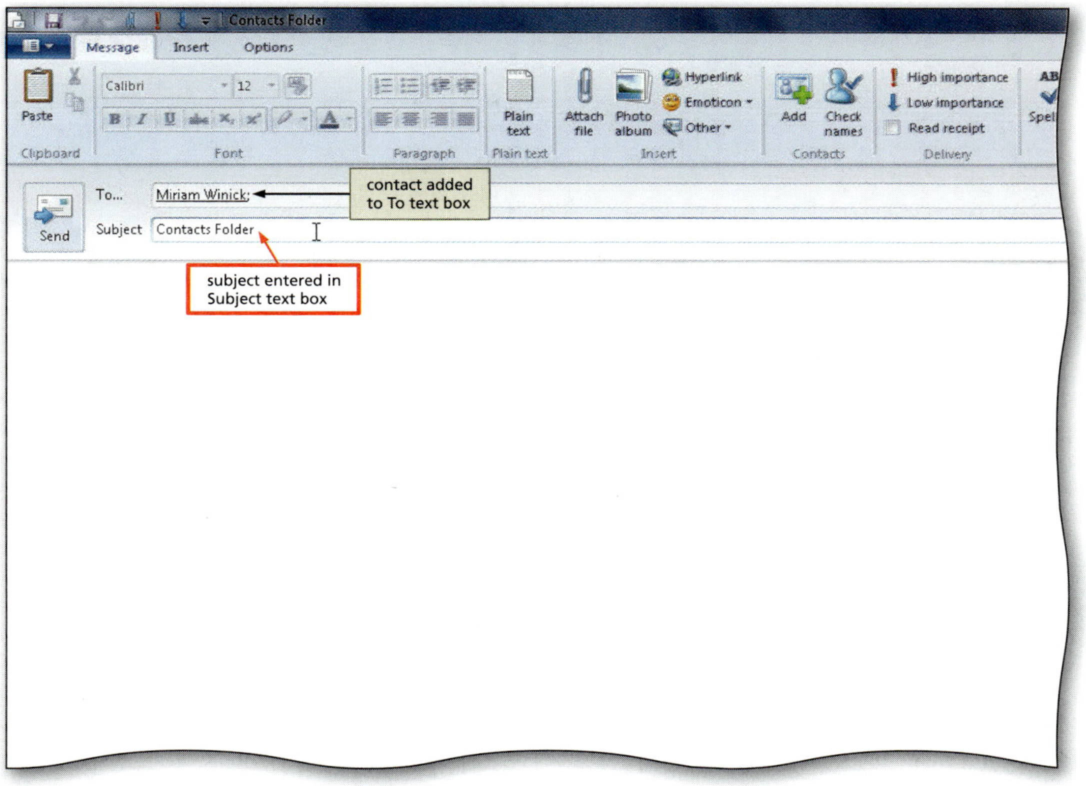

Figure 3–37

- Type I have learned how to enter an e-mail address using the Contacts feature. and then press the ENTER key twice.

- Type your name and then press the ENTER key.

- Select the words, Great News!, in the message area, click the Center text button (Message tab | Paragraph group) to center the text, click the Font size box arrow (Message tab | Font group), and then click 36 in the Font size list to increase the font size to 36 points.

- Click the selected text to deselect it (Figure 3–38).

Figure 3–38

To Send an E-mail Message

The following step sends the e-mail message.

1 Click the Send button to send the message (Figure 3–39).

Figure 3–39

To Delete a Contact

Occasionally, you will want to remove a contact from your list of contacts. The following steps delete the Miriam Winick contact from Windows Live Mail.

1

- Click the Contacts button to display the Contacts window.

- Click the Miriam Winick entry in the Contacts list (Figure 3–40).

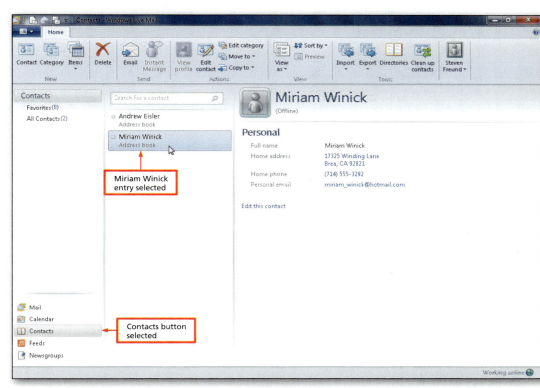

Figure 3–40

2

- Click the Delete button (Home tab) to display the Windows Live Mail dialog box (Figure 3–41).

Q&A

What does the text in the dialog box mean?

Various other Windows Live programs access the contacts you create using Windows Live Mail. When you delete a contact in Windows Live Mail, the contact no longer will be available for use by Windows Live programs.

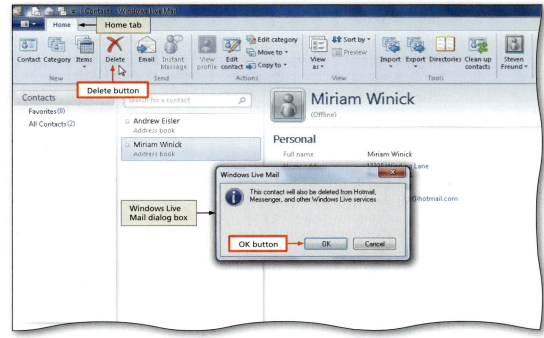

Figure 3–41

3

- Click the OK button to delete the Miriam Winick contact (Figure 3–42).

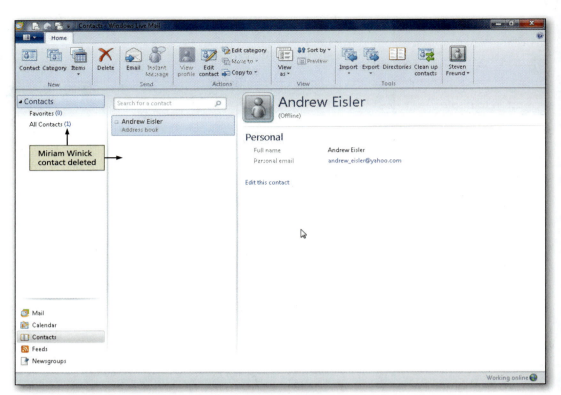

Miriam Winick contact deleted

Figure 3–42

Other Ways

1. Click contact, press DELETE, click OK
2. Right-click contact, click Delete Contact on short-cut menu, click OK

Web Feeds

Internet Explorer provides access to two types of Web feeds: RSS feeds and Web Slices. A **Web feed**, or news feed, is a format for providing frequently updated content. Web feeds enable users to have content from Web pages pushed to them without having to provide their e-mail address or navigate to the Web page. For example, by using Web feeds you can access recent news stories from the MSNBC Web site without first having to navigate to msnbc.com, or keep track of an auction on eBay without visiting the eBay Web site.

RSS

One of the Web feed technologies on the Internet is **RSS**, which stands for Really Simple Syndication. The RSS format allows Web page authors to easily distribute, or syndicate, Web content, which you can then access using a feed reader or aggregator. If you frequently visit Web sites that offer RSS feeds, you can quickly review the feed content of those Web sites in one simple list in your browser by subscribing to their RSS feeds, without having to first navigate to each individual site. If you subscribe to an RSS feed using Internet Explorer, you will be able to access the feed in the Favorites Center. RSS feeds are found on news Web sites, discussion boards, blogs, and other Web sites that frequently update their content.

To Subscribe to an RSS Feed

Before you can view the contents of an RSS feed, you must subscribe to it. The following steps subscribe to an RSS feed on the msnbc.com Web site.

1

- Start Internet Explorer.

- Type **msnbc.com** in the Address bar and then press the ENTER key to display the msnbc.com Web page.

- Click the Tech & science link to display the 'Technology & science on msnbc.com' Web page (Figure 3–43).

Figure 3–43

2

- Right-click the title bar to display a shortcut menu.

- Click Command bar to display the Command bar.

- Click the 'View feeds on this page' button arrow to display a list of available RSS feeds (Figure 3–44).

Figure 3–44

3

● Click the MSNBC – Technology Science command on the menu to display the msnbc.com: Technology & Science RSS feed (Figure 3–45).

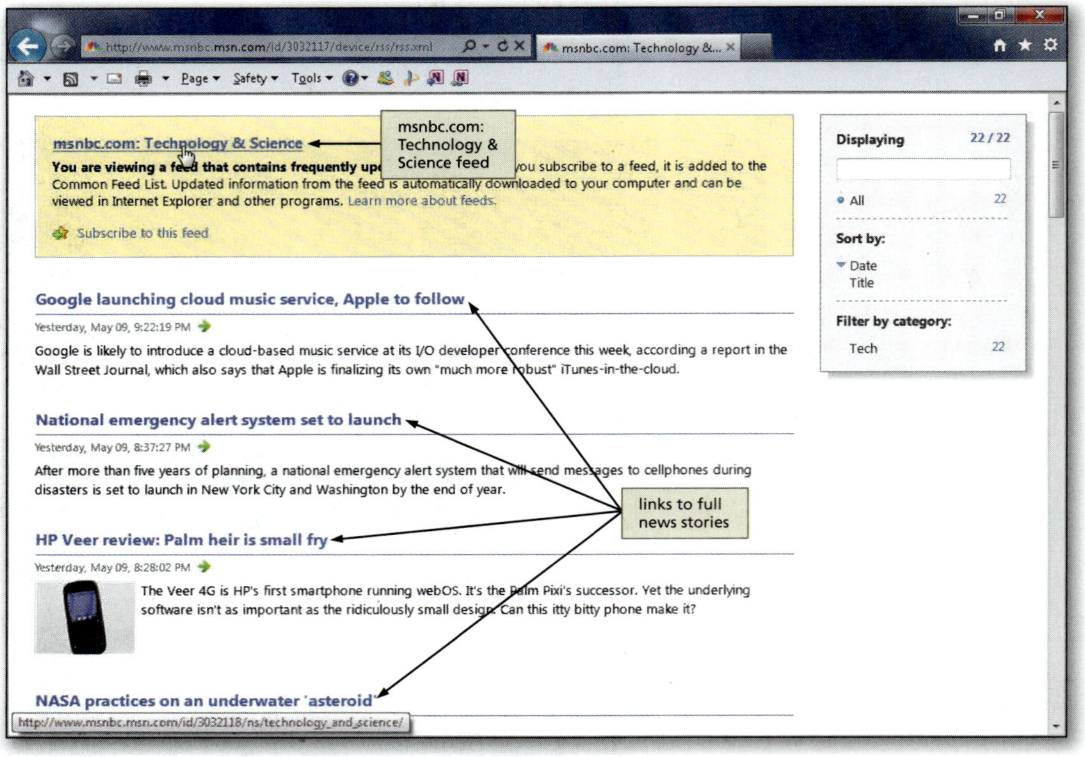

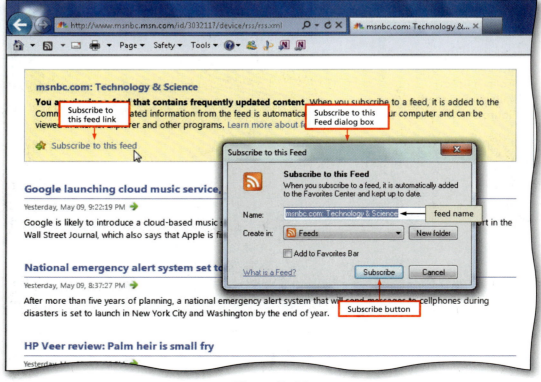

Figure 3–45

4

● Click the 'Subscribe to this feed' link to display the Subscribe to this Feed dialog box (Figure 3–46).

Figure 3–46

5

- Click the Subscribe button in the Subscribe to this Feed dialog box to subscribe to the RSS feed (Figure 3–47).

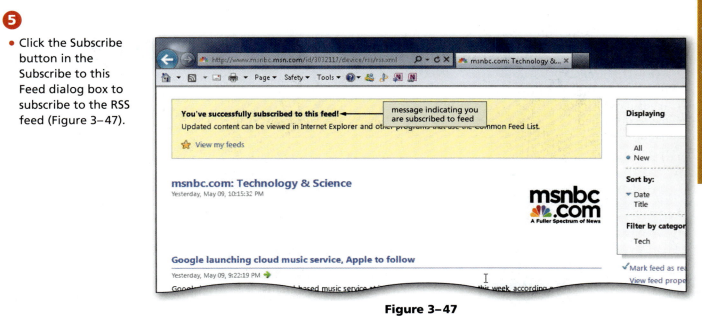

Figure 3–47

To View Your RSS Feeds in the Favorites Center

After you subscribe to an RSS feed, you are able to view the feed in the Favorites Center. The following steps display your subscribed feeds in the Favorites Center.

1

- Click the Home button to display your home page.

- Click the 'View favorites, feeds, and history' button to display the Favorites Center (Figure 3–48).

Q&A

Can I also click the Home button on the Command bar to display the home page?

Yes. If the Command bar is displayed, clicking the Home button will display your home page.

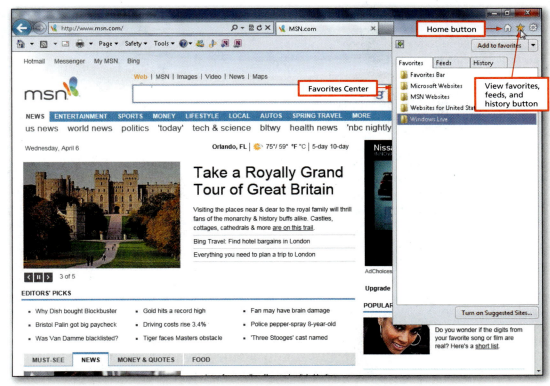

Figure 3–48

2

- Click the Feeds tab in the Favorites Center to display the list of RSS feeds to which you have subscribed (Figure 3–49).

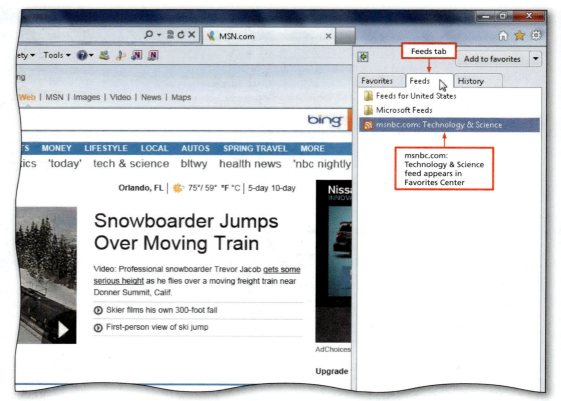

Figure 3–49

3

- Click the msnbc.com: Technology & Science feed to display the RSS feed. If necessary, click the Close the Favorites Center button to close the Favorites Center (Figure 3–50).

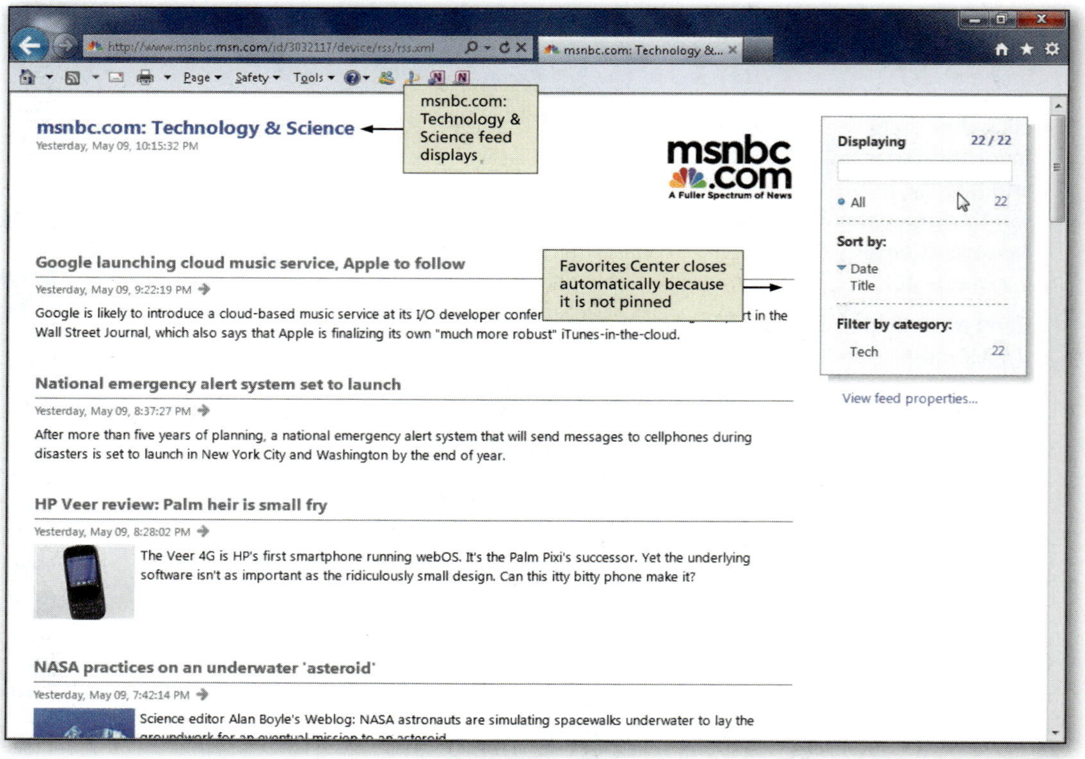

Figure 3–50

To Modify Feed Properties

As previously mentioned, because RSS feeds disseminate frequently updated information, Internet Explorer automatically downloads updated RSS content every day. If you want Internet Explorer to download the RSS feeds more frequently so that you are sure that you are viewing the most up-to-date information, you can modify the feed properties. The following steps modify the properties for the msnbc.com: Technology & Science RSS feed so that the feed will update every four hours.

1

- Click the 'View feed properties' link to display the Feed Properties dialog box (Figure 3–51).

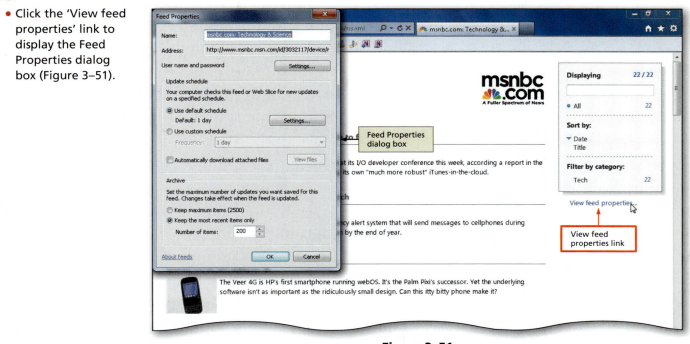

Figure 3–51

2

- Click the 'Use custom schedule' option button in the Update schedule area of the Feed Properties dialog box (Figure 3–52).

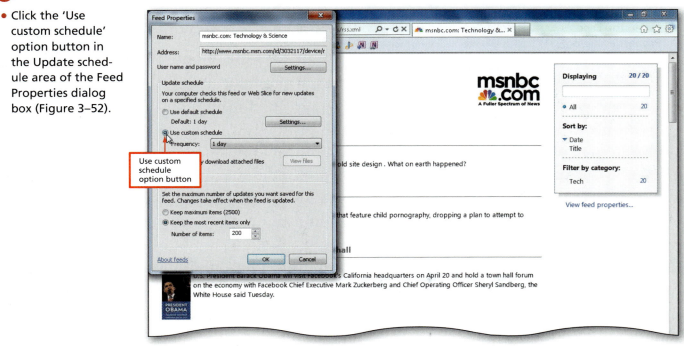

Figure 3–52

3

- Click the Frequency box arrow to display the Frequency list (Figure 3–53).

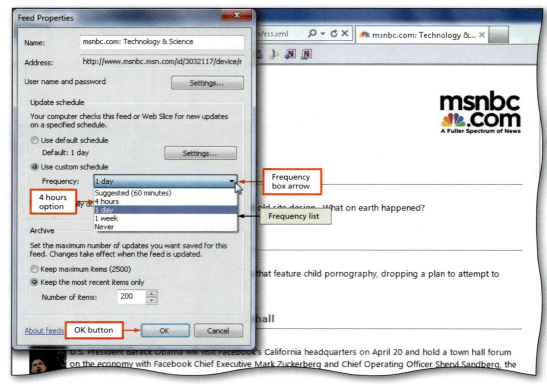

Figure 3–53

4

- Click the 4 hours option in the Frequency list (Figure 3–54).

- Click the OK button in the Feed Properties dialog box to save your changes and to close the Feed Properties dialog box.

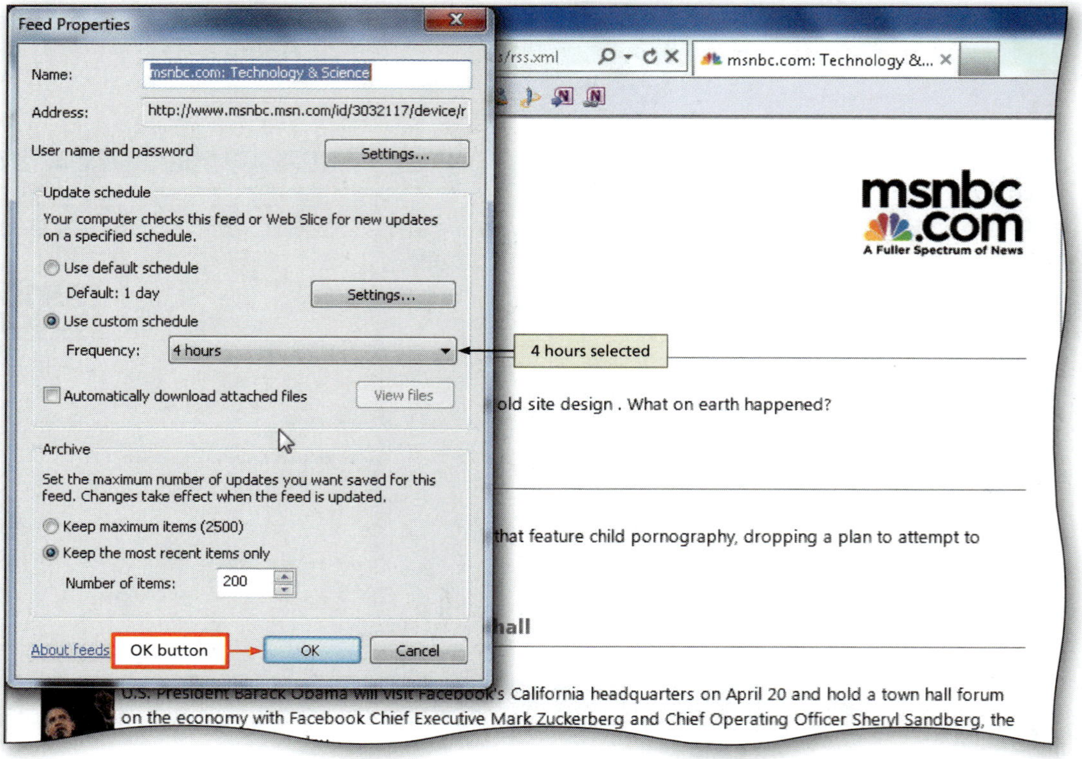

Figure 3–54

Web Slices

In addition to supporting RSS feeds, Internet Explorer also supports Web Slices. Using a subscription model similar to RSS feeds, a **Web Slice** enables users to view a portion of a Web page to which they have subscribed, and receive notifications when the content in the Web Slice has been updated. For example, you can use a Web Slice to monitor the current weather forecast. The Web Slice might include information such as the current temperature, high and low temperature for the day, wind speed and direction, humidity, and a link to the Web page associated with that Web Slice.

When a Web Slice is available on a particular Web page, the Add Web Slices button will display on the Command bar (Figure 3–55a). You also might notice that the Add Web Slices button will appear when your mouse hovers over a Web Slice on a Web page (Figure 3–55b). The Add Web Slices button displays in the same location as the 'View feeds on this page' button, but with a slightly different appearance. When you click the Add Web Slices button arrow, a list of Web Slices and RSS feeds available on the Web page will display.

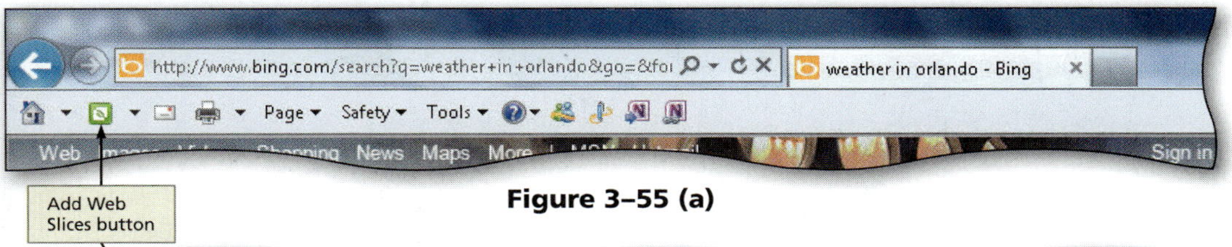

Add Web Slices button

Figure 3–55 (a)

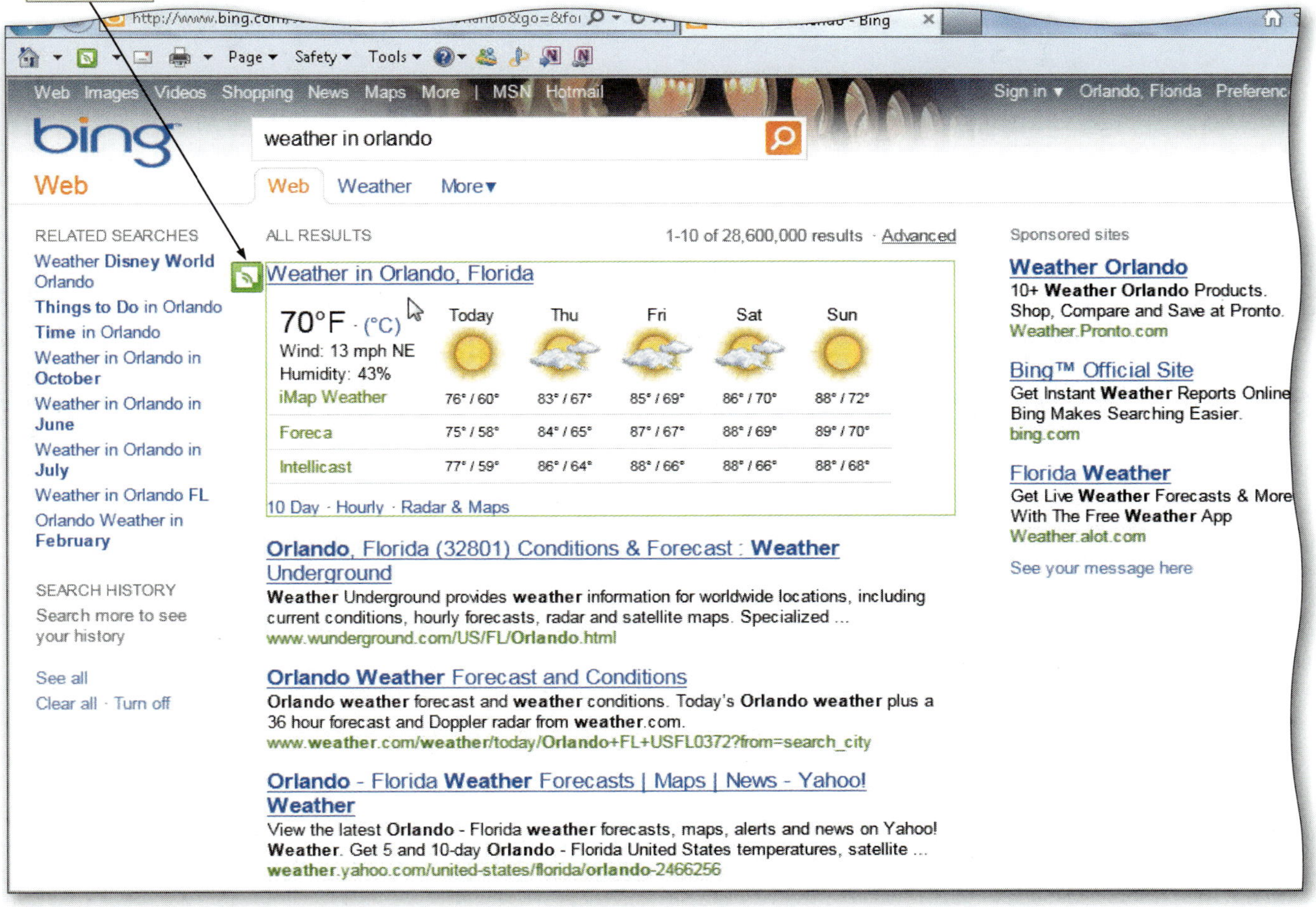

Figure 3–55 (b)

To Add a Web Slice

When you add a Web Slice, Internet Explorer adds a button associated with that Web Slice to your Favorites bar. When the content in the Web Slice is updated, the button on the Favorites bar changes color, to notify you of the new content. The following steps add a Web Slice to the Favorites bar.

 1 Navigate to a Web page containing a Web Slice.

2 Click the Add Web Slices button arrow to display a list of Web Slices available on the Web page.

3 Click the Web Slice to which you would like to subscribe (Figure 3–56).

Figure 3–56

4 In the Internet Explorer confirmation dialog box, click the Add to Favorites bar button to subscribe to the Web Slice and display an associated button on the Favorites bar.

To View a Web Slice

Once you have subscribed to a Web Slice, you can view it at any time by clicking the corresponding button on the Favorites bar. If you hover your mouse pointer over the button, Internet Explorer will display the name and Web address of the Web Slice, as well as when it was last updated. The following steps display the Web Slice.

1 Click the button on the Favorites bar that corresponds to the Web Slice you want to view (Figure 3–57).

2 To close the Web Slice, click the button on the Favorites bar again.

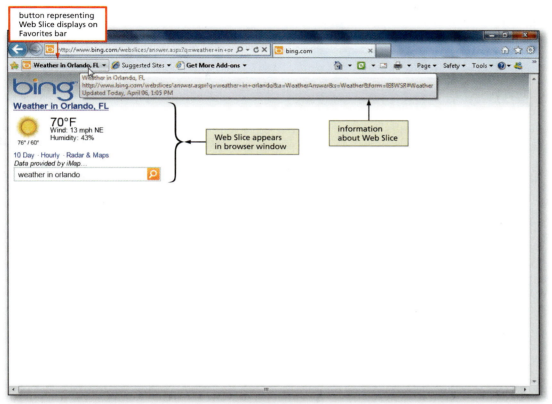

Figure 3–57

To Delete a Web Slice

If your Favorites bar becomes too crowded, or you decide that you are not interested in a particular Web Slice any longer, you can delete it. For example, if you subscribed to a Web Slice to monitor the weather in a vacation destination, you might want to delete the Web Slice and remove it from the Favorites bar at the conclusion of the vacation. When you delete a Web Slice, the corresponding button on the Favorites bar is removed. The following steps delete a Web Slice from the Favorites bar.

1 Right-click the Web Slice button on the Favorites bar.

2 Click the Delete command on the shortcut menu to display the Delete Shortcut dialog box.

3 Click the Yes button in the Delete Shortcut dialog box to delete the Web Slice.

To Hide the Favorites Bar and Command Bar

Now that you have finished using the Favorites bar and Command bar, the following steps hide these two toolbars.

1 Right-click the Favorites bar to display a shortcut menu, and then click Favorites bar to hide the Favorites bar.

2 Right-click the Command bar to display a shortcut menu, and then click Command bar to hide the Command bar.

Online Social Networks

The popularity of online social networks has exploded during the past several years. As mentioned in Chapter 2, an online social network is a Web site that encourages members in its online community to share their interests, ideas, stories, photos, music, and videos with other registered users. Individuals choose to join online social networks for personal or work-related reasons. For example, you might join an online social network such as Facebook to keep in touch with, or get in touch with, friends from school or work. You also might join an online social network such as LinkedIn to connect with colleagues, meet others in their industry, or provide recommendations for or request recommendations from coworkers. Although some of the more popular online social networks allow almost anyone to register and focus their content on the general population, some online social networks target a specific audience. For instance, there are online social networks that focus on topics such as hospitality, movies, music, investing, or books.

Because almost anyone can sign up for an online social network, it is especially important for parents to monitor their children's activities. It is recommended that children should not post their age, address, or even the name of their school. In fact, it is not advisable for anyone to post personally identifiable information for public viewing. Furthermore, because some online social networks allow subscribers to post and customize their page, called a **profile**, you should carefully evaluate what a potential friend or connection has posted on their public profile before interacting with them. For example, it is possible for someone to post a link to a Web site containing a computer virus that automatically downloads when the page is visited. For this reason, no matter how interesting a link might appear, it is always advisable to err on the side of caution before clicking the link.

Joining a social network involves registering and providing your e-mail address, confirming your e-mail address, and then building your network of friends, colleagues, and acquaintances. For example, LinkedIn (Figure 3–58) is an online social network that enables you to connect with business associates, people who work in your industry, and others who share your professional interests. Signing up for a LinkedIn account is free, and only requires that you have a valid e-mail address. During the sign-up process, LinkedIn will prompt you for information about yourself, your employment, and your educational background. Before you are able to access your LinkedIn account, you will need to confirm the e-mail address you specified while signing up for the account. This confirmation process requires that you log in to your e-mail account and click a link in the confirmation e-mail message.

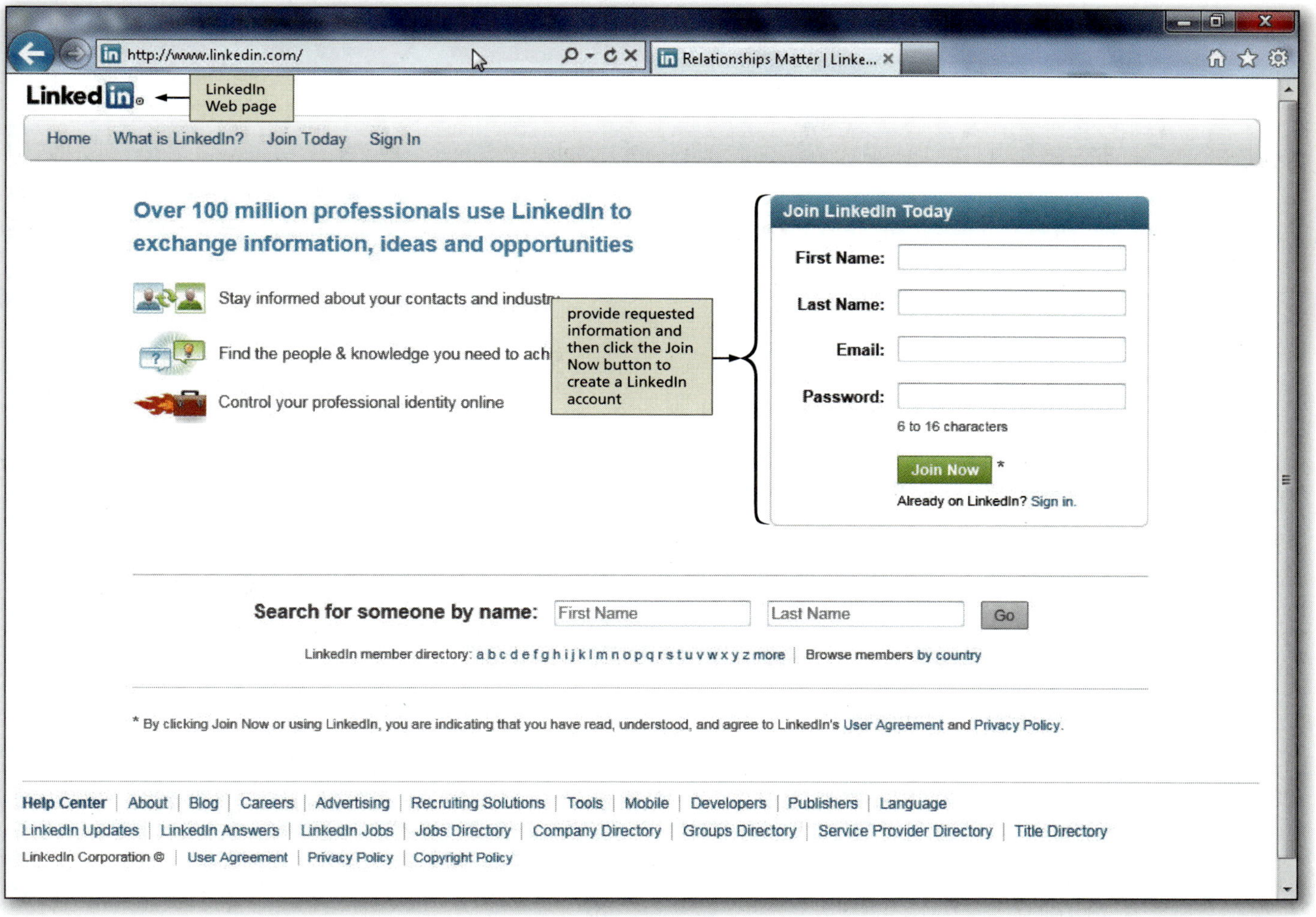

http://www.linkedin.com/   Relationships Matter | Linke... ✕

Linked in ⬅ LinkedIn Web page

Home What is LinkedIn? Join Today Sign In

Over 100 million professionals use LinkedIn to exchange information, ideas and opportunities

Stay informed about your contacts and industr...

Find the people & knowledge you need to ach...

Control your professional identity online

provide requested information and then click the Join Now button to create a LinkedIn account

Join LinkedIn Today

First Name:

Last Name:

Email:

Password:

6 to 16 characters

 Join Now *

Already on LinkedIn? Sign in.

Search for someone by name: First Name   Last Name   Go

LinkedIn member directory: a b c d e f g h i j k l m n o p q r s t u v w x y z more | Browse members by country

* By clicking Join Now or using LinkedIn, you are indicating that you have read, understood, and agree to LinkedIn's User Agreement and Privacy Policy.

Help Center | About | Blog | Careers | Advertising | Recruiting Solutions | Tools | Mobile | Developers | Publishers | Language
LinkedIn Updates | LinkedIn Answers | LinkedIn Jobs | Jobs Directory | Company Directory | Groups Directory | Service Provider Directory | Title Directory
LinkedIn Corporation © | User Agreement | Privacy Policy | Copyright Policy

Figure 3–58

After completing the sign-up process, you are ready to begin building your LinkedIn network (Figure 3–59 on the next page). You can use LinkedIn to build a **network** consisting of people you know and with whom you work. Each person you add to your network is referred to as a **connection**. When you add a connection to your network, you gain the ability to view their connections. You can build your network by searching the LinkedIn Web site for people you know who might have a LinkedIn account, by allowing LinkedIn to search the contacts in your e-mail account and identify other LinkedIn members, or by sending e-mail messages to invite colleagues to become part of your LinkedIn network. After you have built your network, LinkedIn will e-mail you periodically to inform you of updates to connections in your network, including changes in employment or new connections.

Figure 3–59

LinkedIn also analyzes your network for common connections and then suggests people with whom you might share a connection. For example, if you have 25 connections in common with another LinkedIn member, you most likely will see them as a suggested connection.

When you send a request to add a connection to your network, that person has to accept the invitation before you will be able to view their full profile. Full profiles can include information such as job title(s), location, employment history, recommendations, number of connections, links to Web sites, and education (Figure 3–60).

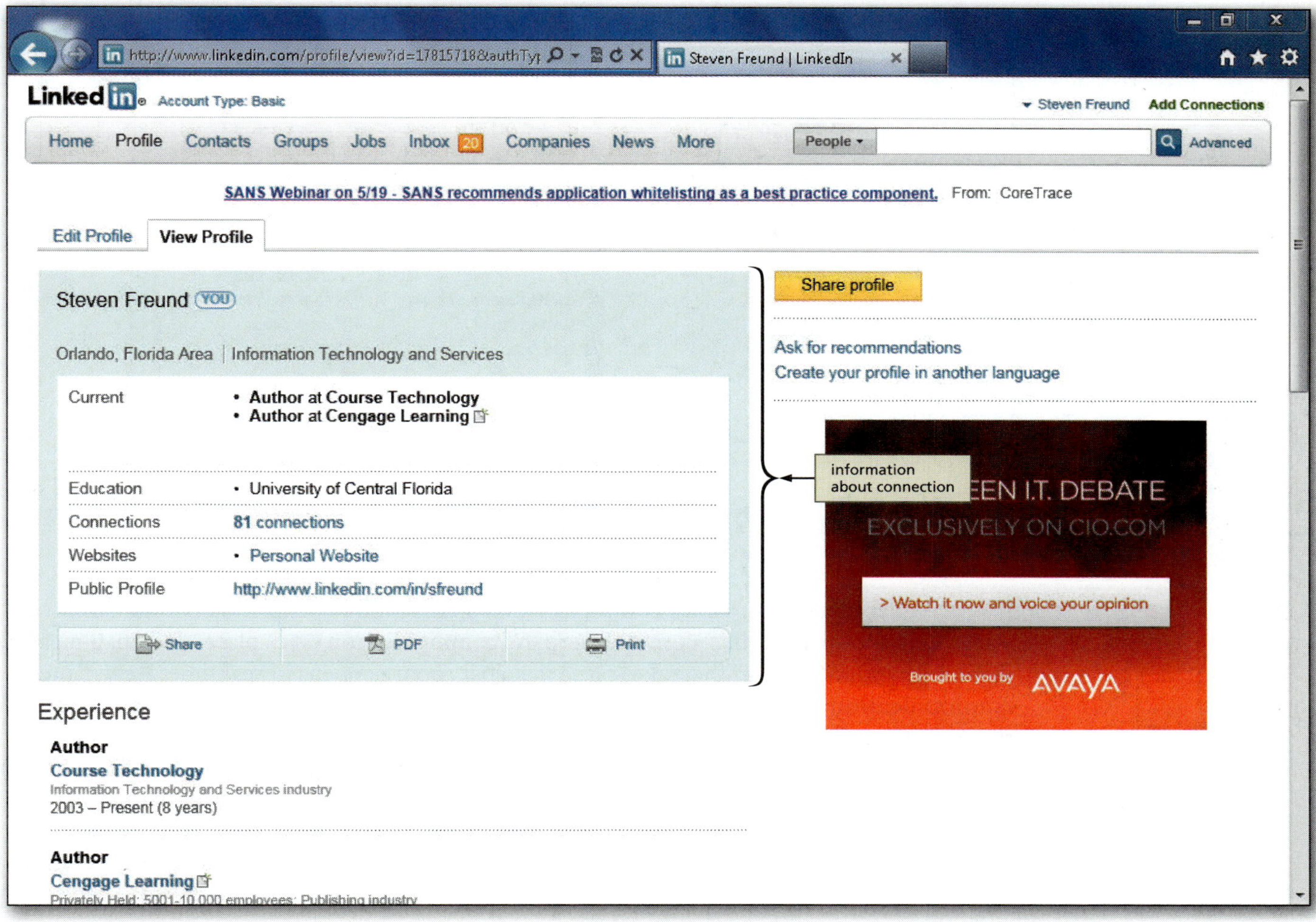

Figure 3–60

When you have finished using LinkedIn, you should sign out. Signing out from LinkedIn ensures that others who use your computer are not able to access your profile.

Communicating via Web Sites

This chapter has so far discussed how to communicate over the Internet by using e-mail programs, subscribing to RSS feeds and Web Slices, and joining online social networks. In addition, several other types of Web sites facilitate communication between individuals over the Internet, including wikis, blogs, groups, chat rooms, and newsgroups.

Some Web sites, such as Google and Yahoo!, allow their visitors to communicate with others via groups. A **group** is a Web application (also called a Web app) that enables people to form an online community for discussion around specific topics, such as space exploration, Internet Explorer 9, or your favorite video game. Typically, all e-mail messages and replies are sent to all members of the group and are also available from the group's password-protected Web page. You also can upload files, create a shared calendar, store group member information, and create Web pages inside your group. If you are unable to find a group that matches your interests, you can create a new group. Figure 3–61 on the next page shows the Google Groups home page.

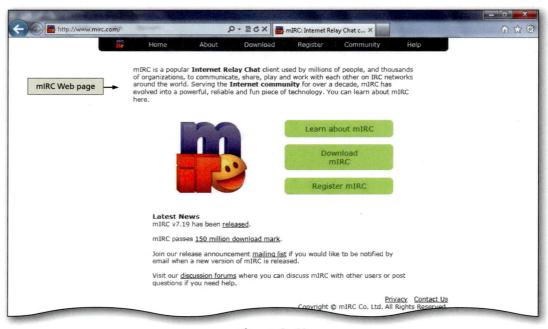

Figure 3–61

Similar to a group, a **chat room** is a Web app that allows people to communicate with each other. However, unlike a group where the communication takes place via e-mail messages, the communication that takes place in a chat room happens in real time. **Real-time communication** means that users participating in the communication must be online at the same time. For example, a telephone conversation is one type of communication that takes place in real time. If one person was not on the phone, it would be impossible for the phone conversation to take place. On the other hand, an e-mail conversation does not take place in real time because you are able to send someone an e-mail message regardless of whether they are online. When you enter a chat room, messages that you send are viewable by everyone else who is in the same chat room. Some chat rooms are available via Web sites, and others are accessible only by first downloading a special program to your computer that allows you to enter and participate in chat rooms. Figure 3–62 shows a Web site that allows you to download a popular chat program called mIRC.

Figure 3–62

Another way by which people on the Internet can communicate is via a mailing list. A **mailing list** allows you to send the same e-mail message to multiple recipients at the same time. For example, many colleges and universities allow instructors to communicate with their students outside of class by using a mailing list. At the beginning of the semester, students subscribe to the mailing list with their e-mail address. When the instructor needs to disseminate information to the students, he or she sends a message to the mailing list, which is forwarded to everyone who has subscribed. In addition to schools using mailing lists, many companies also offer mailing lists to periodically update their customers about their products or services. If you no longer want to receive e-mail messages from a mailing list, you have to unsubscribe from it. Mailing lists offer different methods of unsubscribing, typically including instructions for unsubscribing at the bottom of each e-mail message sent to the list. If you are unable to find instructions for unsubscribing, contact the mailing list administrator. Figure 3–63 shows a Web page that contains a subscription form for mailing lists that distribute information from the Centers for Disease Control and Prevention.

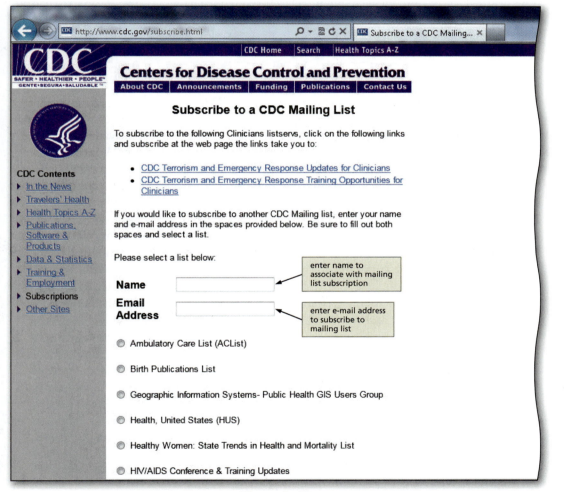

Figure 3–63

Finally, people can communicate via the Internet by reading and placing messages on a newsgroup. A **newsgroup** is an online discussion group devoted to a particular topic and consisting of a collection of messages that can include pictures, movies, and audio, posted by many people around the world. A special computer, called a **news server**, contains related groups of newsgroups.

To participate in a newsgroup, you must use a program called a **newsreader**. The newsreader enables you to access a newsgroup to read existing messages, or **articles**, and to add a new message, called **posting**. A newsreader also keeps track of which articles you have and have not read. Although there are stand-alone newsreader programs that you can download from the Internet, many e-mail programs, including Windows Live Mail, include functionality for reading newsgroups.

Newsgroup members often post articles in reply to previous postings — either to answer questions or to comment on material in the original posting. These replies often prompt the author of the original article, or other interested members, to post additional articles. This process resembles a conversation, one which can be short-lived or go on indefinitely, depending on the nature of the topic and the interest of the participants. The original article and all subsequent related replies are called a **thread**, or a **threaded discussion**.

BTW

Local Newsgroups
Some colleges and universities maintain local newsgroups to disseminate information about school events and answer technical questions asked by students. To locate your local newsgroup, search for the school's name in the list of newsgroup names.

Windows Live Messenger and Instant Messaging

Another communication tool is **instant messaging (IM)**. An instant messaging application allows two people who are online at the same time to exchange messages in real time. **Windows Live Messenger**, an instant messaging application, is available for free as part of Windows Live Essentials, which can be downloaded from the Microsoft.com Web site. The advantage of using Windows Live Messenger instead of an e-mail program is that once sent, your instant message appears immediately on the recipient's computer, and they can reply immediately, provided they also are signed in to Windows Live Messenger.

Windows Live Messenger users can perform a variety of functions, including performing real-time communication with a single friend or a group of friends, placing a telephone call from the computer using the microphone and headset, sending files to another computer, sending instant messages to a mobile device, adding friends to their contact lists, reading their friends' social network updates, and inviting a friend to an online meeting or to play an Internet game.

You sign in to Windows Live Messenger using your Windows Live ID. This section assumes that you already have Windows Live Messenger installed and have created a Windows Live ID. A **Windows Live ID** is a secure way for you to sign in to multiple Microsoft Web sites. If you need a Windows Live ID, see your instructor for assistance.

Before you can communicate via instant messaging, your friend or contact also must have a Windows Live ID and the Windows Live Messenger software installed on his or her computer. If you have a Windows Live Hotmail account, you already have a Windows Live ID because your Windows Live Hotmail sign-in name and password are your Windows Live user name and password.

To Start Windows Live Messenger and Sign In

Before using Windows Live Messenger, you must start Windows Live Messenger and sign in using your Windows Live ID and password. The following steps start and sign you in to Windows Live Messenger.

1

- Display the Start menu.

- Display the All Programs list.

- Click Windows Live Messenger to start Windows Live Messenger (Figure 3–64).

Q&A What else displays in the Windows Live Messenger window?

In addition to the contact list, Windows Live Messenger displays social networking updates or news.

Figure 3–64

2

- Type your Windows Live ID into the first text box in the Windows Live Messenger window.

- Type your Windows Live password into the Password text box.

- Click the Sign in button to sign in to Windows Live Messenger and to display your Windows Live Messenger account (Figure 3–65).

Q&A Where is my list of friends?

If you are logging in for the first time, Windows Live Messenger will present you with a series of steps to set up your account and add friends.

Figure 3–65

To Add a Contact to the Contact List

After starting Windows Live Messenger, you can add a contact to the contact list if you know their instant messaging address. A contact must have a Windows Live Hotmail account or a Windows Live ID and have the Windows Live Messenger software installed on his or her computer. If you want to add a contact who does not meet these requirements, you can send the friend an e-mail invitation, or a text message to their mobile device, that explains how to get a Windows Live ID and download the Windows Live Messenger software. The following steps add a contact to the contact list using the e-mail address of someone you know who has signed in to Windows Live Messenger.

1

• Click the add button in the Windows Live Messenger window to display the add menu (Figure 3–66).

Q&A

Why do I not see the add button?

Depending on whether you have signed in to Windows Live Messenger before and had people on your contact list, the add button might not display. Instead, you might see the 'Add a contact' link. Clicking this link will display a wizard that allows you to add a contact.

Figure 3–66

2

• Click the 'Add a friend' command to display the Windows Live Messenger dialog box.

• Type **dave. bentley@live. com** in the 'Enter your friend's email address' text box (Figure 3–67).

Figure 3–67

3

- Click the Next button.

- Because you do not want to add this person as a favorite, verify that a check mark does not appear in the 'Make this person a favorite' check box (Figure 3–68).

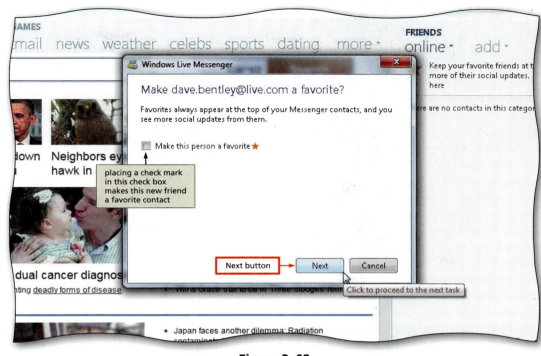

Figure 3–68

4

- Click the Next button.

- A Windows Live Messenger dialog box displays that provides the status of your friend request (Figure 3–69).

Q&A

What if the friend I am attempting to add does not have a Windows Live account?

If the friend you are attempting to add does not have a Windows Live account, an e-mail message will be sent to him or her with instructions about how to com-

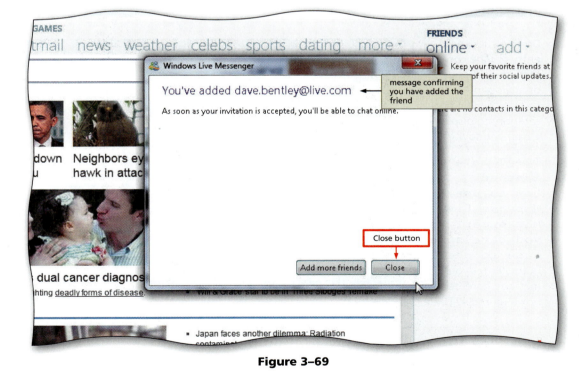

Figure 3–69

municate with you using Windows Live Messenger. If your friend does have a Windows Live account, an invitation will appear in their Windows Live Messenger window asking if he or she would like to become your friend, and once he or she accepts the invitation, you will see their contact information on your contact list.

5

- Click the Close button to close the Windows Live Messenger dialog box and return to your contact list (Figure 3–70).

Figure 3–70

To Send an Instant Message

To use Windows Live Messenger, the person with whom you want to communicate must be online. The Online category shown in Figure 3–70 displays that David Bentley is online. The following steps send an instant message to someone who you know is online.

1

- Double-click the entry for the contact you just added, or any online contact, in the Online category to display a chat window.

- Type **I have learned how to use Windows Live Messenger! Do you have some time to chat?** in the 'Enter your message here' text box (Figure 3–71).

Figure 3–71

2

• Press the ENTER key to send the instant message (Figure 3–72).

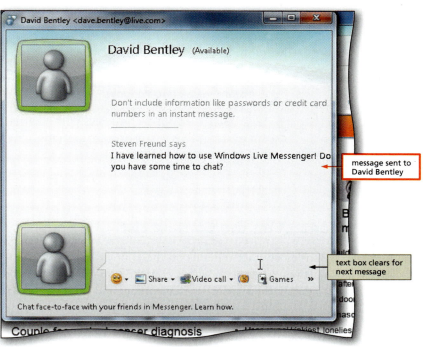

Figure 3–72

3

• Your chat contact sends a response (Figure 3–73).

Experiment

• Feel free to send additional messages to the David Bentley contact or the contact you are communicating with in Windows Live Messenger.

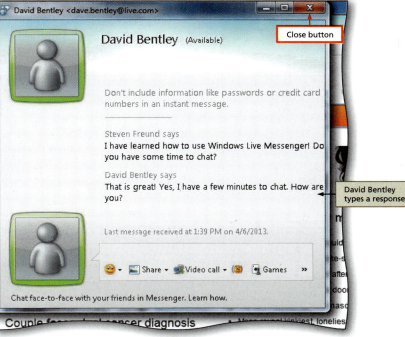

Figure 3–73

Other Ways

1. Right-click contact name, click Send IM on shortcut menu

To Close the Instant Messaging Window

When you have finished with your conversation, you should close the instant messaging window to end the conversation. The following step closes the instant messaging window.

1 Click the Close button in the David Bentley <dave.bentley@live.com> window to close the instant messaging window.

Q&A What happens if my contact sends me an instant message after I close the window?

If a contact sends you an instant message, a new window containing the message content will appear on your desktop.

To Delete a Contact on the Contact List

The David Bentley contact remains on the contact list below the Online heading in the Windows Live Messenger window. If you lose touch with a contact, you might want to delete that contact from your contact list. The following steps delete the David Bentley contact and remove the entry from the contact list.

1

• Right-click the David Bentley entry on the contact list to display the shortcut menu (Figure 3–74).

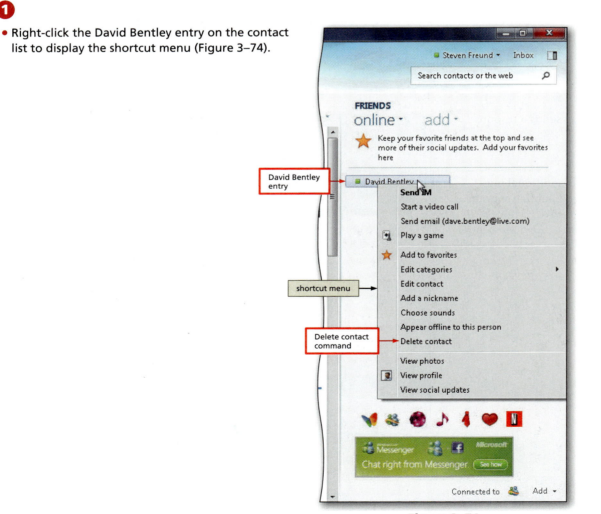

Figure 3–74

2

● Click Delete contact on the shortcut menu to display the Windows Live Messenger confirmation dialog box (Figure 3–75).

Windows Live Messenger dialog box

message confirming you want to delete contact

Windows Live Messenger

Delete David Bentley from your contact list?

You'll delete this person from your contact list and from your list of friends.

Delete button → Delete Cancel

Which star got shown the door 'Dancing'?

Figure 3–75

3

● Click the Delete button in the Windows Live Messenger dialog box to delete the David Bentley friend and remove the entry from your contact list (Figure 3–76).

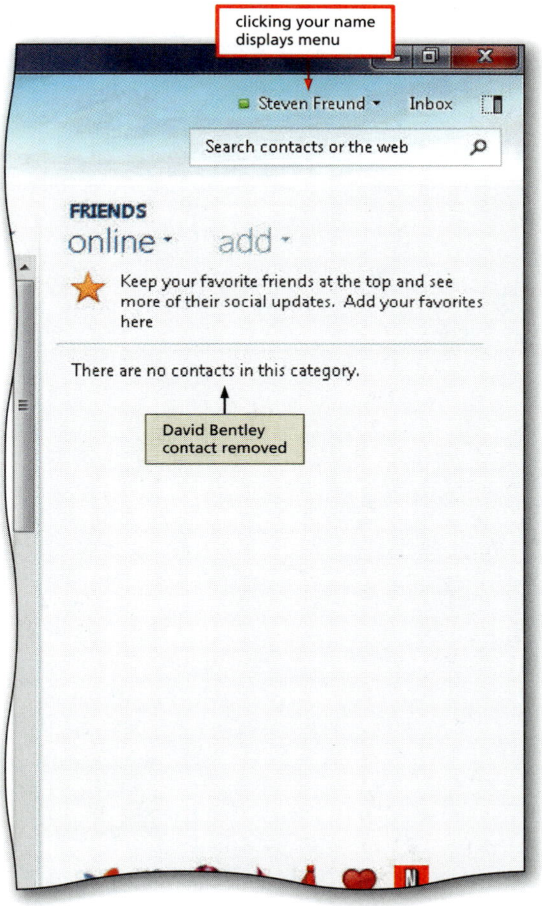

clicking your name displays menu

Steven Freund ▾ Inbox

Search contacts or the web

FRIENDS
online ▾ add ▾

Keep your favorite friends at the top and see more of their social updates. Add your favorites here

There are no contacts in this category.

David Bentley contact removed

Figure 3–76

To Close and Sign Out from Windows Live Messenger

When you have finished using Windows Live Messenger, you will need to close the Windows Live Messenger window and sign out from the Windows Live Messenger service.

1 Click your name in the upper-right corner of the Windows Live Messenger window to display a menu (Figure 3–77).

2 Click Exit Messenger to close Windows Live Messenger. If necessary, click the OK button, click 'No, do not save my messages on this computer (recommended for shared computers)', and then click the OK button.

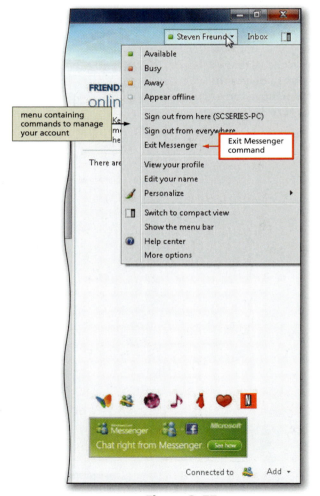

Figure 3–77

To Close Internet Explorer

The following steps close Internet Explorer.

1 If necessary, click the Internet Explorer button on the Windows taskbar to display the Internet Explorer window.

2 Click the Close button to close Internet Explorer.

To Close Windows Live Mail

The following steps close Windows Live Mail.

1 If necessary, click the Windows Live Mail button on the Windows taskbar to display the Contacts – Windows Live Mail window.

2 Click the Windows Live Mail tab to display the Windows Live Mail menu.

3 Click Exit to close Windows Live Mail.

Chapter Summary

In this chapter, you learned how to use Windows Live Mail to read, write, format, and send e-mail messages, to attach a file, and to view file attachments. You added and deleted contacts using the Contacts features in Windows Live Mail. You also used Internet Explorer to subscribe to RSS feeds and Web Slices. You learned about other Web applications, including online social networks, groups, mailing lists, chat rooms, and newsgroups. Finally, you used Windows Live Messenger to send an instant message. The items listed below include all the new skills you have learned in this chapter.

1. Start Windows Live Mail (IE 143)
2. Open (Read) an E-mail Message (IE 147)
3. Print an Open E-mail Message (IE 148)
4. Close an E-mail Message (IE 149)
5. Reply to an E-mail Message (IE 150)
6. Delete an E-mail Message (IE 152)
7. Open a File Attachment (IE 153)
8. Save and Close a File Attachment (IE 154)
9. Compose a New E-mail Message with Formatting (IE 155)
10. Format an E-mail Message (IE 157)
11. Attach a File to an E-mail Message (IE 158)
12. Send an E-mail Message (IE 160)
13. Add a Contact (IE 161)
14. Compose a New E-mail Message Using a Contact (IE 164)
15. Delete a Contact (IE 167)
16. Subscribe to an RSS Feed (IE 169)
17. View Your RSS Feeds in the Favorites Center (IE 171)
18. Modify Feed Properties (IE 173)
19. Start Windows Live Messenger and Sign In (IE 185)
20. Add a Contact to the Contact List (IE 186)
21. Send an Instant Message (IE 188)
22. Delete a Contact on the Contact List (IE 190)

STUDENT ASSIGNMENTS

Learn It Online

Test your knowledge of chapter content and key terms.

Instructions: To complete the following exercises, please visit **cengagebrain.com**. On the CengageBrain.com home page, enter the book title **Windows Internet Explorer 9 Introductory** or the ISBN **0-538-48239-7** and then click the Find button. On the product page for this book, click the Access Now button below the Study Tools heading. On the Book Companion Site Web page, click the drop-down menu, select Chapter 3, and then click the link for the desired exercise.

Chapter Reinforcement TF, MC, and SA
A series of true/false, multiple-choice, and short-answer questions that test your knowledge of the chapter content.

Flash Cards
An interactive learning environment where you identify chapter key terms associated with displayed definitions.

Practice Test
A series of multiple-choice questions that test your knowledge of chapter content and key terms.

Who Wants To Be a Computer Genius?
An interactive game that challenges your knowledge of chapter content in the style of the television quiz show.

Wheel of Terms
An interactive game that challenges your knowledge of chapter key terms in the style of the television show *Wheel of Fortune*.

Crossword Puzzle Challenge
A crossword puzzle that challenges your knowledge of key terms presented in the chapter.

Apply Your Knowledge

Reinforce the skills and apply the concepts you learned in this chapter.

Sending an E-mail Message to Your Instructor
Instructions: You want to send an e-mail message to the instructor of your course stating what you like best about his or her class. Use Windows Live Mail to send the e-mail.

Perform the following tasks:
1. Search for the home page for your college or university. Figure 3–78 shows the home page for Palm Beach State College.
2. Locate the e-mail address of your instructor.
3. Start Windows Live Mail.
4. Click the Email message button (Home tab | New group).
5. Using the e-mail address of the instructor you obtained in Step 2, compose a mail message to this instructor summarizing what you like best about the class.
6. Send the e-mail message to your instructor.

Figure 3–78

Extend Your Knowledge

Extend the skills you learned in this chapter and experiment with new skills. You might need to use Help to complete the assignment.

Joining a Yahoo! Group

Instructions: You are looking to find and communicate with other people who are interested in tent camping. Using Yahoo! Groups, you will locate a group dedicated to tent camping, join the group, read a posting, and post a message of your own.

Perform the following tasks:

1. Navigate to Yahoo! Groups (groups.yahoo.com) and search for a group for people interested in discussing tent camping.

2. Once you have located a group (Figure 3-79 on the next page), join the group. Because a Yahoo! account is required to join a group, you either can use an existing account or create a new one. For more information about creating a Yahoo! account, contact your instructor.

Continued >

STUDENT ASSIGNMENTS

Extend Your Knowledge *continued*

3. Once you have joined the group and confirmed your membership, view the list of messages, display a message of interest to you, and then print the message.

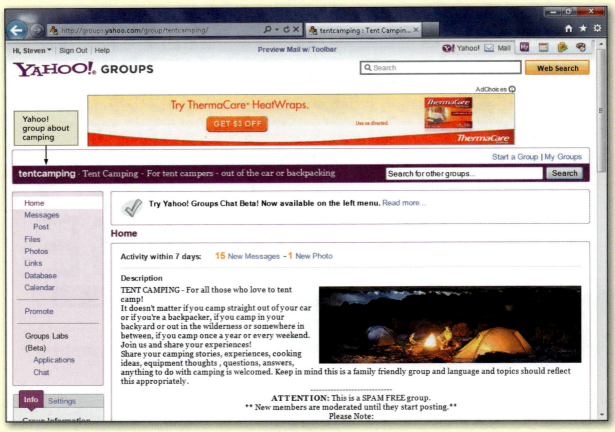

Figure 3–79

4. Compose and then post a message to the group that asks a question about tent camping. Before sending your message, print a copy of the Web page.

5. Once you have sent your message, sign out from Yahoo! Groups and submit your printouts to your instructor.

In the Lab

Use Internet Explorer and Windows Live Mail by employing the guidelines, concepts, and skills presented in this chapter. Labs are listed in order of increasing difficulty.

Lab 1: Adding Your Contacts to Windows Live Mail

Instructions: You decide to use the Contacts feature in Windows Live Mail to keep track of the names, e-mail addresses, home addresses, and home telephone numbers of your contacts.

Perform the following tasks:

1. In Windows Live Mail, click the Contacts button to display your contacts. If necessary, maximize the window (Figure 3–80).

2. Use the Contact button (Home tab | New group) to add the contacts listed in Table 3–1.

Table 3–1 Contact List

Name	E-mail Address	Address	Home Phone
Jim Burns	jburns@isp.com	8451 Colony Dr., Brea, CA 92821	(714) 555-2831
Joanna Hopkins	jhopkins@isp.com	3544 Clayton Rd., Placentia, CA 92871	(714) 555-1484
Judith Jacobs	jjacobs@isp.com	5689 State St., Fullerton, CA 92834	(714) 555-2318
Madelyn Norris	mnorris@isp.com	7812 Bennington Dr., Atwood, CA 92811	(714) 555-8622
Matt Stepman	mstepman@isp.com	257 W. Wilson St., Yorba Linda, CA 92885	(714) 555-2782
Thomas Timmons	ttimmons@isp.com	648 Flower Rd., Brea, CA 92821	(714) 555-6495

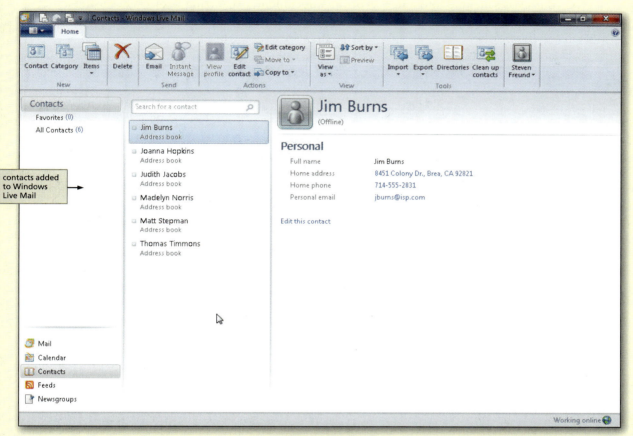

Figure 3–80

3. Print the information for each contact by clicking a contact name, clicking the Windows Live Mail tab, clicking the Print command on the Windows Live Mail menu, and then clicking the Print button in the Print dialog box. Write your name on each printed contact and submit your printouts to your instructor.

4. Delete each contact by selecting the contact name and then clicking the Delete button on the Home tab.

In the Lab

Lab 2: E-mailing Your Class Schedule as an Attachment

Instructions: Your instructor is changing her office hours and requests the class schedules of all of her students to help her determine her new office hour schedule. You will create a WordPad document containing your class schedule, and then send it as an attachment in an e-mail message to your instructor.

Perform the following tasks:

1. Type your class schedule into a new WordPad document, organizing your classes using a method of your choosing. A sample WordPad document containing a class schedule is illustrated in Figure 3–81.

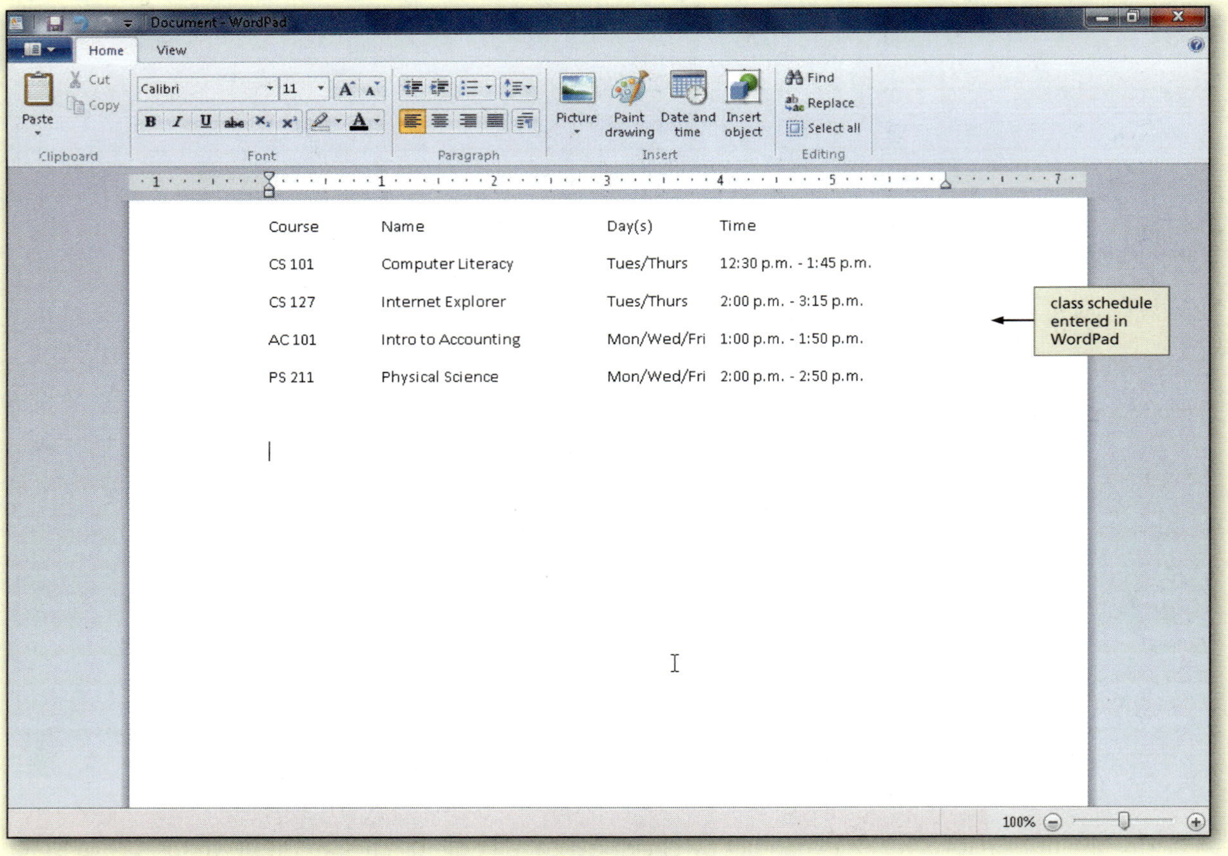
Document - WordPad
Home
View
Paste
Cut
Copy
Clipboard
Calibri
11
Font
Paragraph
Picture
Paint drawing
Date and time
Insert object
Insert
Find
Replace
Select all
Editing
Course Name Day(s) Time
CS 101 Computer Literacy Tues/Thurs 12:30 p.m. - 1:45 p.m.
CS 127 Internet Explorer Tues/Thurs 2:00 p.m. - 3:15 p.m.
AC 101 Intro to Accounting Mon/Wed/Fri 1:00 p.m. - 1:50 p.m.
PS 211 Physical Science Mon/Wed/Fri 2:00 p.m. - 2:50 p.m.
class schedule entered in WordPad
100%

Figure 3–81

2. Using your first and last name as the file name, save the WordPad document to your Documents library.
3. In Windows Live Mail, or the e-mail program of your choice, compose a new e-mail message to your instructor. Type your instructor's e-mail address into the To text box. Type **`My Class Schedule`** for the subject. For the body of the e-mail message, type **`I have created a document with WordPad that contains my class schedule. The file is attached to this e-mail message.`** Press the ENTER key twice, and then type your name.
4. Format your name using a font, font size, and color of your choosing.
5. Attach the WordPad file you created to the e-mail message.
6. Send the e-mail message.

In the Lab

Lab 3: Subscribing to RSS Feeds of News Web Sites

Instructions: To keep up with local and national news, you decide to subscribe to RSS feeds of three news Web sites. Two will cover national news and the third will cover local news for the Boston area. After subscribing to these feeds, display the feeds in Internet Explorer and print the first story for each feed.

Perform the following tasks:
Part 1: Subscribe to an RSS Feed on CNN.com
1. Navigate to the CNN.com Web site (www.cnn.com).
2. Subscribe to and display the RSS feed on the CNN.com Web site that contains recent stories.
3. Click the link for the first news story (Figure 3–82). The news story that displays on your computer will be different from the one in Figure 3–82.

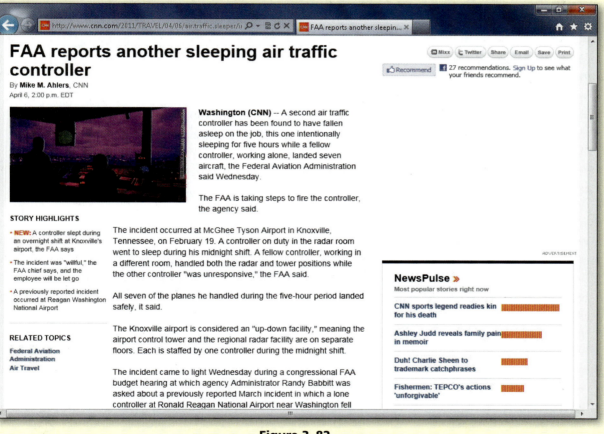

Figure 3–82

4. Print the Web page and write your name on it.

Part 2: Subscribe to the FOX News U.S. RSS Feed
1. Navigate to the FOXNews.com Web site (www.foxnews.com).
2. Subscribe to and display the FOX News RSS feed.
3. Click the link for the first news story.
4. Print the Web page and write your name on it.

Continued >

In the Lab *continued*

Part 3: Subscribe to the Boston.com / News RSS Feed
1. Navigate to the Boston.com News Web site (www.boston.com/news).
2. Subscribe to and display the Boston.com – Latest news RSS feed.
3. Click the link for the first news story.
4. Print the Web page and write your name on it.
5. Submit the printed Web pages to your instructor.

In the Lab

Lab 4: Using Windows Live Messenger

Instructions: You want to practice using instant messaging. First you will sign in to Windows Live Messenger, and then you will add a new person to your Windows Live Messenger contact list. After adding your contact, send instant messages to him or her and then sign out of Windows Live Messenger.

Perform the following tasks:
Part 1: Add a Friend to the Contact List
1. Identify a friend, family member, or classmate who has a Windows Live ID.
2. Add this person's Windows Live ID to your contact list in Windows Live Messenger.
3. If necessary, contact the individual so that they can accept your request to add them as a friend.

Part 2: Send an Instant Message
1. Double-click the icon of the friend you added in the contact list.
2. Type a message, press the ENTER key, wait for the response, and type your response.
3. Continue conversing in this manner until you have typed at least four messages. Figure 3–83 shows a sample conversation.

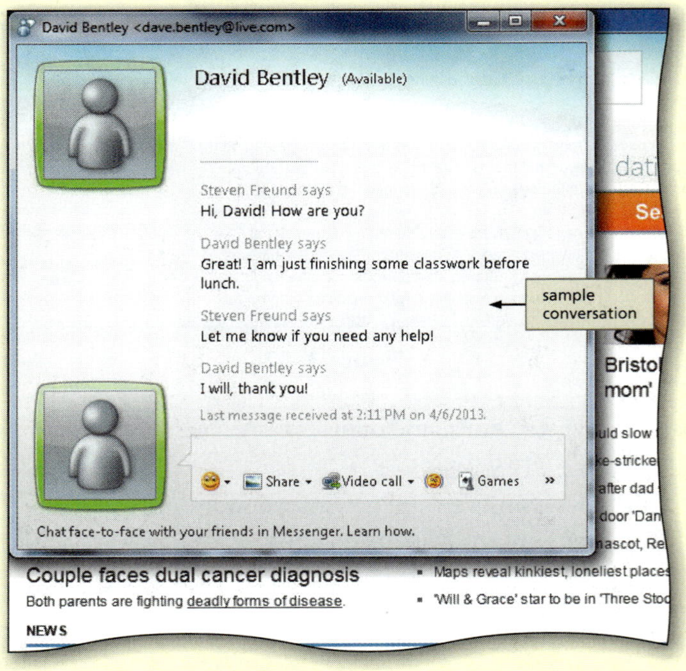

Figure 3–83

Part 3: Delete a Contact on the Contact List and Exit Windows Live Messenger

1. In the Windows Live Messenger window, right-click the contact you want to delete.

2. Click Delete contact on the shortcut menu.

3. Click the Delete button in the Windows Live Messenger dialog box.

4. Exit Windows Live Messenger.

Cases and Places

Apply your creative thinking and problem-solving skills to design and implement a solution.

1: Creating a Google Group

Academic

Groups are a popular way for people to communicate with each other about specific topics via the Internet. Create a Google Group about a topic of your choice (groups.google.com) and post messages to the group to initiate a conversation. Wait two days to see if anyone has signed up for your group. Find one other group that discusses a similar topic. How many people have joined that group? Consider ways you could attract more people to your group. Submit your answers to your instructor.

2: Researching Online Social Networks

Personal

The popularity of social networks has skyrocketed during the past several years. People of all ages, including children, parents, and grandparents, are now signing up for accounts on the most popular online social networks. Research three online social networks. Can anyone sign up for an account on these social networks? Do they cater to a specific audience? What steps has each social network taken to ensure the safety and privacy of its members? Of the three you researched, what is your preferred social network? Write a brief report containing your responses and submit it to your instructor.

3: Comparing Windows Live Mail and Microsoft Outlook 2010

Professional

Using computer magazines, advertising brochures, the Internet, or other resources, compile information about Windows Live Mail (Figure 3–84a) and Microsoft Outlook 2010 (Figure 3–84b). In a brief report, compare the two programs. Include the differences and similarities, how to obtain the software, the function and features of each program, and so forth. If possible, test Microsoft Outlook and add your personal comments.

Continued >

Cases and Places *continued*

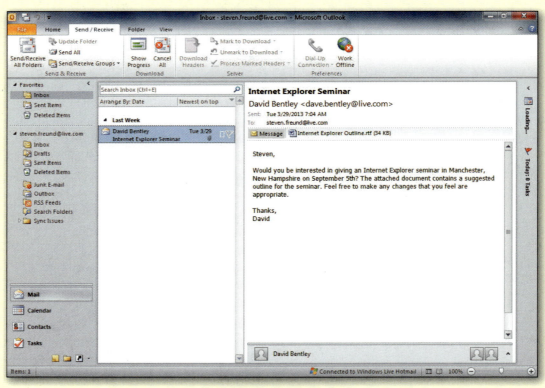

(a) Windows Live Mail

(b) Microsoft Outlook
Figure 3–84

Appendix A
Internet Explorer Options

Internet Options Dialog Box

When you use Internet Explorer to browse the World Wide Web, perform Internet research, and communicate using the Internet, default settings control your interactions. You can view and modify many of these settings by using the Internet Options dialog box shown in Figure A–1.

The Internet Options dialog box contains seven tabs (General, Security, Privacy, Content, Connections, Programs, and Advanced) that allow you to view and modify Internet Explorer's default settings. When you click a tab, its associated sheet displays with related settings. Using these settings, you can change which home page is displayed when you start Internet Explorer, delete cookies and temporary Internet files, specify a privacy setting when using the Internet, choose tabbed browsing options, assign a Web site to a security zone, control the Internet content that a user can access, set up an Internet connection, and select which programs will send and receive e-mail messages.

To display the Internet Options dialog box, click the Tools button and then click Internet options. The remainder of this appendix explains the contents of the seven sheets in the Internet Options dialog box.

Figure A–1

The General Sheet

The General sheet (Figure A–2) contains the Home page area, Browsing history area, Search area, Tabs area, and Appearance area. The Home page area allows you to change the Web address of the Web page that is displayed when you start Internet Explorer. Consider making your home page a Web page that you visit frequently. You also can designate multiple home pages by typing the Web address for each home page on a separate line in the text box. When you have multiple home pages, each page will open in its own tab when you start Internet Explorer. The text box in the Home page area contains the Web address for the current home page. The three buttons below the text box allow you to use the Web page or Web pages currently displayed in the Internet Explorer window as the home page (Use current), use the default home page (Use default), or not display a home page (Use blank).

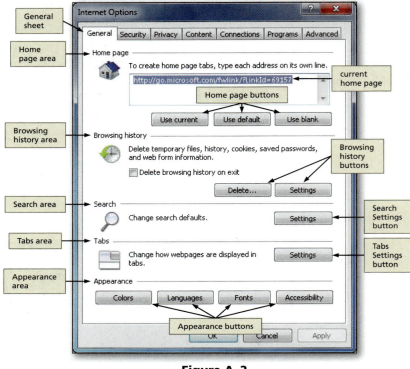

Figure A–2

The Browsing history area permits you to delete temporary files, your browsing history, cookies, saved passwords, and any information you might have entered on a Web page. A **cookie** is a file created by a Web site that captures information about your visit to that site, such as your preferences or shopping cart items. The Delete button in the Browsing history area allows you to delete some or all of the files that are associated with your browsing history.

When you display a Web page in the Internet Explorer window, one or more files called temporary Internet files are stored in a special folder on your computer. **Temporary Internet files** store information about and components of the Web page you are viewing. The next time you display that Web page, the page might appear more quickly because Internet Explorer retrieves the page from this folder instead of from the Internet. You can delete all files in this folder by clicking the Delete button to display the Delete Browsing History dialog box. First make sure that all check boxes contain a check mark and then click the Delete button in the Delete Browsing History dialog box. By clicking the Settings button in the Browsing history area, you can view a list of the temporary Internet files, set how often Internet Explorer checks for new versions of pages that you visit, change the amount of disk space reserved to store these files, and move the folder storing these temporary files to another location on your hard disk. The Settings button also allows you to control the number of days the Web pages in the History list are kept before they are deleted automatically.

The Search area on the General sheet allows you to add, modify, and remove search providers that are used when search keywords are entered in the Address bar.

You can view and modify the tabbed browsing settings through the Settings button in the Tabs area. You can enable and disable tabbed browsing, modify other tabbed browsing settings, and decide how Internet Explorer treats pop-ups and links from other programs.

You can use the four buttons in the Appearance area of the General sheet to change the default text, background, and link colors; specify which language to use when displaying Web pages; change the default fonts used to display a Web page; and change accessibility options.

The Security Sheet

The Security sheet shown in Figure A–3 allows you to specify how Internet Explorer handles content from various Web pages. If you visit a Web site for the first time, you might not completely trust the site's content. As discussed in Chapter 1, some Web sites might contain malicious code that can be automatically downloaded to your computer. To protect your computer, you might want to prevent any Web site from having the ability to download anything to your computer without your intervention. On the other hand, you might frequently visit a Web site that you trust. You can use the Security sheet to configure Internet Explorer so that you allow a trusted Web site to download to or install anything on your computer. The Enable Protected Mode check box, when it contains a check mark, prevents malicious programs from being installed on your computer from a Web page. This check box contains a check mark by default, and it is recommended that you do not disable this option.

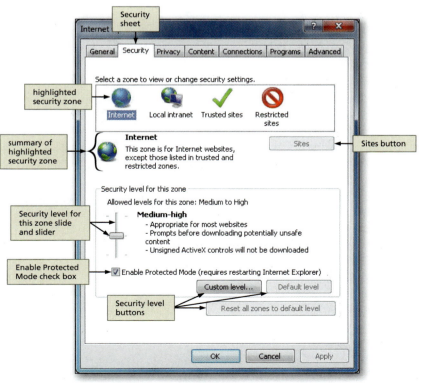

Figure A–3

Internet Explorer divides the Internet into four zones of content to which you can assign a security setting. Called **security zones** (Internet, Local intranet, Trusted sites, and Restricted sites), Internet Explorer allows you to assign a Web site to a zone with a suitable security level. The four security zones are described in the following list:

- **Internet**: This zone contains all Web sites that you have not placed in other zones. The default security level for this zone is Medium-high.
- **Local intranet**: This zone contains all Web sites that are on an organization's intranet, including sites specified on the Connections sheet in the Internet Options dialog box (shown in Figure A–6 on page APP 7), network paths, and local intranet sites. The default security level for this zone is Medium-low.
- **Trusted sites**: This zone contains Web sites that are trusted not to damage the computer or the data on the computer. The default security level for this zone is Medium. You must manually add a Web site to this zone by clicking the Trusted sites zone and then clicking the Sites button.
- **Restricted sites**: This zone contains Web sites that you do not trust because they could possibly damage the computer or the files on the computer. The default security level for this zone is High. You might put a site in this zone if you feel that the content on the site is malicious.

To assign a Web site to a security zone, click the appropriate icon in the security zone box, click the Sites button, and then follow the instructions to assign a security zone. Each time you attempt to open or download content from a Web site, Internet Explorer checks the security settings and responds appropriately.

The three buttons at the bottom of the Security sheet allow you to customize the settings for a security zone (Custom level) and set the security level or reset the security level to the default level for the security zone (Default level). You also can reset all zones to their default security zone (Reset all zones to default level).

To change the security level of the highlighted security zone, move the slider along the slide to display the different security levels. If the security level for the selected zone is at its default setting, the Default level button will be disabled.

The Privacy Sheet

The Privacy sheet shown in Figure A–4 contains the Settings area, Location area, Pop-up Blocker area, and InPrivate area. The Settings area displays the privacy setting (Medium) and allows you to change the privacy setting for the four security zones (Internet, Local intranet, Trusted sites, and Restricted sites) by moving the slider along the slide. When you select a privacy setting, a description of the setting appears on the Privacy sheet in the Internet Options dialog box. Whereas the Security sheet protects your computer from malicious Web sites you might visit, the Privacy sheet protects information about you from being revealed or transmitted, such as which Web sites you visit and your physical location.

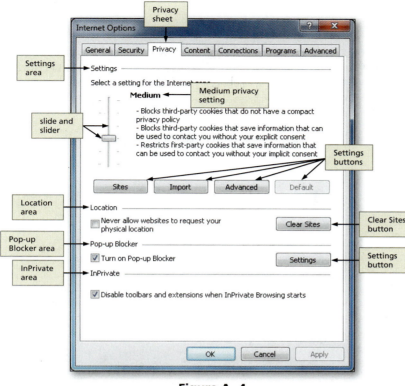

Figure A–4

The four buttons at the bottom of the Settings area allow you to customize privacy settings and override the default setting for cookies, small files that Web sites use to track Web browsing habits. Two types of cookies that could be downloaded to your computer are first-party cookies and third-party cookies. A **first-party cookie** is a cookie that either originates on or is sent to the Web site you currently are viewing. A **third-party cookie** is a cookie that either originates on or is sent to a Web site that is distinct from the one you are viewing.

The Location area allows you to specify whether Web sites are able to request your physical location. Web sites sometimes can use information from your Internet access provider (such as your IP address) to determine your physical location. If you do not want Web sites to identify your physical location, click to place a check mark in the 'Never allow websites to request your physical location' check box. The Clear Sites button allows you to clear the list of Web sites that currently are allowed to request your physical location.

The Pop-up Blocker area allows you to enable and disable the **pop-up blocker**, which prevents Web sites you visit from opening unwanted tabs or browser windows. The Settings button allows you to specify which Web sites are allowed to open the pop-up windows. You also can set whether you hear a sound or see the Notification bar when a pop-up is blocked.

The InPrivate area contains the 'Disable toolbars and extensions when InPrivate Browsing starts' check box. When this check box contains a check mark, all toolbars and extensions will be disabled during an InPrivate Browsing session. When browsing the Web during an InPrivate browsing session, no information about your session is stored. For example, the Web sites you visit will not remain in your History list, and cookies will not be retained on your computer.

The Content Sheet

The Content sheet shown in Figure A–5 contains five areas: Parental Controls area, Content Advisor area, Certificates area, AutoComplete area, and Feeds and Web Slices area. The Parental Controls area allows you to access Windows' parental controls, where you can choose which Web sites can be accessed by each user account on your computer. You also can collect information about computer usage and restrict computer usage.

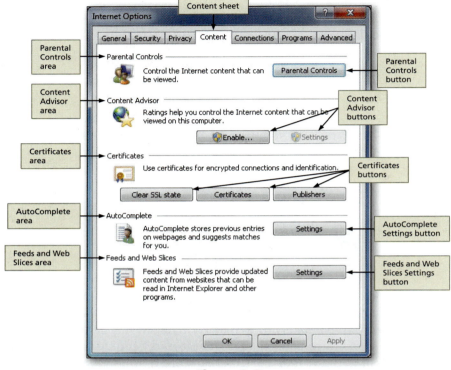

Figure A–5

The Content Advisor area permits you to control the types of content (content that creates fear, content showing the use of questionable substances, and so on) that a user can access on the Internet. After turning on Content Advisor, only the content meeting or exceeding the chosen criteria will be displayed. Initially, Content Advisor is set to the most conservative (least likely to offend) setting. The two buttons in the Content Advisor area allow you to turn on Content Advisor (Enable) and modify the Content Advisor ratings for Internet sites (Settings).

The Certificates area allows you to positively authenticate identity and provide security for browser communication. A **certificate** is a statement guaranteeing the identity of a person or the security of a Web site. The Clear SSL state button allows you to remove all client authentication certificates from the SSL cache. The **SSL cache** is a memory location that stores all certificates until you restart your computer. The Certificates button in the Certificates area allows you to manage your certificates, and the Publishers button displays a list of trusted software publishers whose software can safely be placed on the computer.

In the AutoComplete area, you can set whether Internet Explorer uses the AutoComplete feature to store personal information that you enter on forms or Web addresses you enter in the Address bar. For example, if you begin to type the Web address for a Web site you have previously visited, Internet Explorer will display matching Web addresses so that you do not have to type the complete Web address.

The Feeds and Web Slices area allows you to set feed or Web Slice properties, including how often to check feeds or Web Slices for updates, as well as other actions to perform when a feed or Web Slice is discovered on a Web page or when a feed is read. Feeds and Web Slices were discussed in additional detail in Chapter 3.

The Connections Sheet

The Connections sheet shown in Figure A–6 allows you to set up a new connection to the Internet, control dial-up and virtual private networking connections, and modify local area network (LAN) settings. The Setup button at the top of the sheet lets you create a new Internet connection. The Dial-up and Virtual Private Network settings area displays the current dial-up settings and allows you to add, remove, and modify connections. The Local Area Network (LAN) settings area permits you to edit the LAN settings if the computer is connected to a local area network.

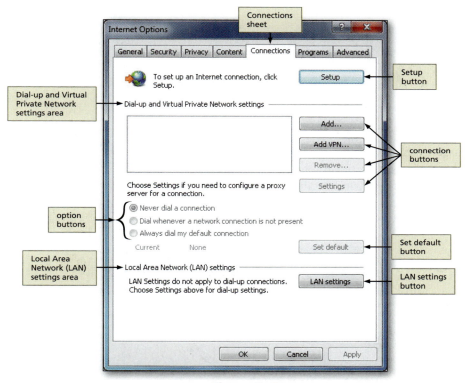

Figure A–6

The Programs Sheet

The Programs sheet shown in Figure A–7 on the next page allows you to select the default Web browser, manage browser add-ons, choose the default program that Internet Explorer uses to edit Web pages, and set the programs that Internet Explorer uses for other services. If Internet Explorer is not the default Web browser, click the Make default button to select it as the default Web browser. The Manage add-ons button allows you to enable and disable Internet Explorer add-ons that have been installed in addition to the Web browser. Internet Explorer add-ons could be installed with Internet Explorer, they might be installed when you are installing another program on your computer, or you can install them manually. The HTML editing area allows you to select the program you would like to use to edit Web pages from those installed on your computer. The Internet programs area allows you to set the programs that Windows uses by default for various other Internet services such as e-mail.

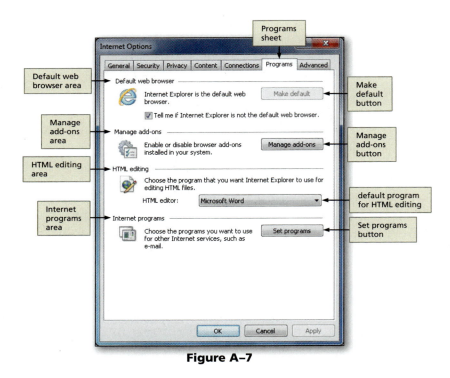

Figure A–7

The Advanced Sheet

The Advanced sheet (Figure A–8) contains a list of settings, organized into the following categories: Accelerated graphics, Accessibility, Browsing, HTTP 1.1 settings, International, Multimedia, and Security. A check mark indicates that the setting is selected. The 'Restore advanced settings' button returns all settings in the Settings list box to their original (default) settings, and the Reset button returns the browser to its original state.

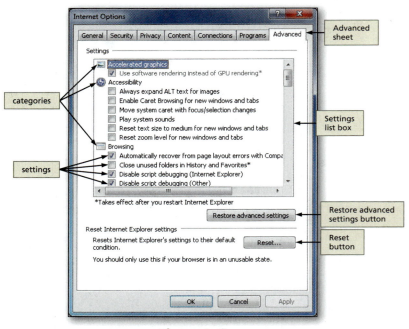

Figure A–8

Appendix B
Web-Based E-mail Accounts

Windows Live Mail

Chapter 3 assumes that you have an e-mail account set up in Windows Live Mail as you work through the steps. If you cannot set up an e-mail account in Windows Live Mail, you might consider signing up for a Web-based e-mail account. Many Web-based e-mail providers offer e-mail accounts for free, including Windows Live, Yahoo! Mail, and Gmail from Google. The following steps sign you up for a free Windows Live e-mail account.

1. Start Internet Explorer.
2. Navigate to the Windows Live Sign in page (**mail.live.com**) (Figure B–1).

Figure B–1

BTW

CAPTCHA
CAPTCHA, which stands for **C**ompletely **A**utomated **P**ublic **T**uring test to tell **C**omputers and **H**umans **A**part, requires you to read distorted text and correctly type the text into a text box. Because some automated computer programs, called bots, are designed to sign up for various online services (including Web-based e-mail accounts) in bulk, it is necessary to distinguish whether a computer or human is completing the form. Many bots are unable to interpret the distorted text, which prevents them from signing up for any online services that use CAPTCHA technology.

3. Click the Sign up button to begin the process of creating a new Windows Live ID and display the Create your Hotmail account Web page (Figure B–2).

Figure B–2

4. Create your Windows Live ID by entering your information into the appropriate fields. As you create your Windows Live ID, keep the following in mind:

   • Your Windows Live ID must be different from all other registered Windows Live IDs. After choosing a Windows Live ID, you can click the Check availability button to determine whether the ID you chose is available.

   • Select an e-mail domain. Windows Live offers two different domains, hotmail.com and live.com. It is possible that the ID you selected might not be available in hotmail.com, but is available in live.com.

- Choose a password that is easy for you to remember, but difficult for others to guess. A password that is difficult for others to guess might include uppercase and lowercase letters, numbers and special characters, and be at least eight characters in length.

- Note that in order to sign up for a Windows Live ID, you should have another e-mail address to use as a backup, in case you forget your password and must have it e-mailed to you.

5. Read the Microsoft service agreement and privacy statement.

6. Click the I accept button.

7. You can sign in to your Windows Live e-mail account at any time by navigating to the Windows Live Sign In page (`mail.live.com`), typing your Windows Live e-mail address in the Windows Live ID text box and your password in the Password text box, and then clicking the Sign in button.

Index

Quick Reference Summary

In Internet Explorer 9, you can accomplish a task in a number of ways. The following table provides a quick reference to common tasks presented in this textbook. The first column identifies the task. The subsequent columns list the different ways the task in the first column can be carried out.

Basic Navigation

Task	Page Number	Mouse	Keyboard Shortcut
Go back one page	IE 21	Back button	ALT+LEFT ARROW
Go forward one page	IE 22	Forward button	ALT+RIGHT ARROW
Stop transfer of current page	IE 19	Stop button	ESC
Refresh current page	IE 20	Refresh button	F5 or CTRL+F5
Go to your home page	IE 21	Home button	ALT+HOME
Print current page	IE 44	Tools button | Print menu | Print or File menu | Print | Print	CTRL+P
Scroll down	IE 17	Down scroll arrow	SPACEBAR or DOWN ARROW
Scroll up	IE 17	Up scroll arrow	SHIFT+SPACEBAR or UP ARROW
Display the menu bar	IE 13	View menu | Toolbars | Menu bar	ALT+V | T | M
Display the Favorites bar	IE 14	View menu | Toolbars | Favorites bar	ALT+V | T | F
Display the Command bar	IE 14	View menu | Toolbars | Command bar	ALT+V | T | C
Display the status bar	IE 12	View menu | Toolbars | Status bar	ALT+V | T | S
Find a word or phrase on a page	IE 13	Tools button | File menu | Find on this page or Edit menu | Find on this page	CTRL+F
Zoom in		Hold CTRL and move mouse wheel up	CTRL+PLUS SIGN (+)
Zoom out		Hold CTRL and move mouse wheel down	CTRL+MINUS SIGN (−)
Select zoom percentage		Tools button | Zoom menu | Select percentage or View menu | Zoom | Select percentage	
Select 100%		Tools button | Zoom menu | 100% or View menu | Zoom | 100%	CTRL+0
Close Internet Explorer	IE 48	Close button	ALT+F4

Address Bar Shortcuts

Task	Page Number	Mouse	Keyboard Shortcut
Select text in the Address bar	IE 13	Click Address bar	ALT+D
Add "http://www." and ".com" to Address bar entry			CTRL+ENTER
Open address in Address bar in new tab			ALT+ENTER (insertion point must be in Address bar)
View previously typed addresses	IE 22	Click Show Address bar Autocomplete button	F4

Window and Tab Shortcuts

Task	Page Number	Mouse	Keyboard Shortcut
Open link in new window		Right-click link | Open in new window	SHIFT+click
Open current Web page in a new window		File menu | New window	CTRL+N
Open a new tab	IE 13	New Tab button	CTRL+T
Close a tab	IE 91	Close Tab button	CTRL+W
Open link in new foreground tab	IE 84		CTRL+SHIFT+click
Open link in new background tab			CTRL+click
Switch to next tab	IE 85	Click tab	CTRL+TAB
Switch to previous tab	IE 85	Click tab	CTRL+SHIFT+TAB

Favorites Center Shortcuts

Task	Page Number	Mouse	Keyboard Shortcut
Open Favorites Center	IE 27	View favorites, feeds, and history button or View menu | Explorer bars | Favorites	CTRL+I
Open Favorites Center in pinned mode		View favorites, feeds, and history button | Pin the Favorites Center button or View menu | Explorer bars | Favorites | Pin the Favorites Center button	CTRL+SHIFT+I
Organize Favorites	IE 27	Favorites menu | Organize favorites	CTRL+B
Add current page to Favorites	IE 27	View favorites, feeds, and history button | Add to favorites button or Favorites menu | Add to favorites	CTRL+D
Add current page to Favorites bar		Click Add to Favorites bar button	
Open Feeds	IE 171	View favorites, feeds, and history button | Feeds tab or View menu | Explorer bars | Feeds	CTRL+G
Open Feeds in pinned mode		View favorites, feeds, and history button | Feeds tab | Pin the Favorites Center button or View menu | Explorer bars | Feeds | Pin the Favorites Center button	CTRL+SHIFT+G
Open History	IE 24	View favorites, feeds, and history button | History tab or View menu | Explorer bars | History	CTRL+H
Open History in pinned mode		View favorites, feeds, and history button | History tab | Pin the Favorites Center button or View menu | Explorer bars | History | Pin the Favorites Center button	CTRL+SHIFT+H